Paper Doll

Brian W. Peterson

To the families whose loved ones never came home.

To the small towns that were never the same after World War II.

To my father, James William Peterson, who was named for his grandfathers: Jens Christensen and William Peterson. Although I wrote this novel, my dad was the driving force behind it. He gathered information, attended multiple 489th Bomb Group reunions, and convinced me that I should let others know about our family's incredible yet heartrending story.

Thank you, Dad, for convincing me to write this and for being the man you are. I even understand you a little better after learning more about our family. You will always be my hero.

Foreword

While some aspects of the story which follows might seem unbelievable, this is a true story, with some creativity added where needed. For example, dialogue had to be invented in order to carry the story and time was compressed when exploring the relationship between my great-uncle Bud and his girlfriend, but I know what they talked about thanks to their letters. In fact, a great deal of dialogue was based on statements made in the more than 300 letters between the family members portrayed herein. The few situations which had to be created for the sake of flow remain consistent with what I knew or learned of the people involved. In cases where I had nothing to go on, such as Hulda's time working for a family near the Twin Cities, I extrapolated based on what little information I possessed and changed the family's name because I did not wish to associate a real person with potentially inaccurate descriptions.

All of the difficult-to-believe events happened. What I did create was of minor impact to further the story or expand upon what I knew of a person; however, to ensure I did not overshadow impactful, million-to-one-odds incidents such as the discovery of the Short Snorter and Hulda's dreams and premonitions, I did not "create" any significant events. If something is difficult to believe in this story, then it is true, whether the subject is premonitions, bears, or journeys through bitter cold.

Because of the wild and strange things which happened to or around the family, which I know are difficult enough to believe, I did not wish to confuse the reader or leave the reader wondering whether a particular event happened, thus my approach. At the back of this book, I address specific information for family members, but the information also will help readers to understand what became of the people who lived this story.

Like Diocletian stepping down as the Emperor of Rome in order to grow cabbage, sometimes truth is indeed stranger than fiction.

— BWP

"Though wars can bring adventures which stir the heart, the true nature of war is composed of innumerable personal tragedies, of grief, waste and sacrifice, wholly evil and not redeemed by glory."
— *Knut Lier-Hansen, World War II Norwegian resistance fighter*

Cast of Characters

Main Characters
Hulda Peterson; born 1894; wife of William, mother of Thelma, Carl, Elsie, Bud, and Conrad
Carl Peterson; born 1915; Hulda's eldest son
Eugene (Bud) Peterson; born 1922; Hulda's second son
Conrad Peterson; born 1924; Hulda's youngest child

Important Characters
Adolph "Uncle Hap" Gustafson; born 1898; Hulda's younger brother
Anne Peterson; born 1917; Carl's wife
Beverly; born 1939; Thelma's daughter
Carla; born 1940; Carl's eldest child
Chrissy Anderson; born 1924; Bud's girlfriend, from Williston, North Dakota
Delbert; born 1944; Thelma's son
Elsie Buzick; born 1918; Hulda's second daughter
Eugene Morris Peterson; born 1944; Carl's son
Grandma Johanna Thompson; born 1868 in Norway; Hulda's mother
Jake Buzick; born 1909; Elsie's husband
James; born 1943; Carl's eldest son
JoAnne; born 1938; Elsie's daughter
Judy; born 1941; Elsie's daughter
Ray Beckstrand; born 1914; Thelma's husband
Thelma Beckstrand; born 1913; Hulda's eldest child
Valrae (or Val); born 1938; Thelma's eldest child
William Peterson; (1883-1929); Hulda's deceased husband, father of all five of her children

Military
The Original Crew of Paper Doll, besides Bud:

Robert Gast, pilot, officer
Robert Savage, co-pilot, officer
Andy Goshtoian, Bombardier, officer
Gilman Sund, Navigator, officer
Donald Holbert, radio operator
George Scofield, gunner
Fred Stodtmeister, gunner
Lige McIntosh, engineer; gunner
Alfred Lane, gunner

Paper Doll Replacements:
Frank Fulks, pilot, officer
Robert Clendinning, navigator, officer

Ground Crew, Paper Doll:
Lionel Bousquet, Crew Chief
Neville Dortch, armorer

Chapter One

The baby-blue Ford Granada, its fuel tank full of unleaded gasoline, chugged westbound in the slow lane of Interstate 80. The elderly man at the wheel looked older than his sixty-one years. His strength and vigor had been left behind in prior decades. His wire-framed glasses slid down his nose at a slow, patient pace, only to be pushed up again at irregular intervals.

The former boxer, ship builder, lumberjack, and carpenter had shrunk from his peak of six-feet tall. Retired and inactive—other than his daily walks through his neighborhood—his sturdy frame had given way to atrophy. Carl August Peterson was still the same tough, intelligent, and street-smart man of days gone by, but his body could not keep up. A heart attack at forty-nine was but one health concern which limited his vitality.

Not prone to chatter, he brought the Ford up to speed with the light traffic.

"Well, would you look at this?" The amazement in Anna Marie Peterson's voice did not always signify incredulity in the same way it would to Carl. She was the quintessential grandmother: kind, caring, and sweet to her family. Of course, as her upbringing mandated, her toughness was close to that of her husband's, but with a veil of love and warmth covering her. On the occasions when the veil slipped off; however, she was not a woman to cross.

As he often did, Carl failed to respond to his wife's small outburst.

"Carl! This dollar has a bunch of names on it!"

1

Carl answered with a detached grunt. So, there were names on the dollar bill. Why should he care?

Anne, as she was known, studied the bill. The hunched shoulders over her plump figure, along with the intent glare of her blue eyes, gave the appearance of someone in the process of throwing her entire being into this dollar bill. "It's a silver certificate," she announced with certainty. "It's old, but it sure is in good shape." Her voice maintained an energy which stayed with her most of her life: a cadence without pause, full of highs and lows, like a song set to violin music, but with a slight accent betraying her northern Minnesota upbringing.

Carl did not flinch.

"Carl, this is odd. You should see this. It says, 'E.M. Peterson.'"

Carl lifted his foot off the accelerator. He looked at the bill, firmly grasped in Anne's fingers, then to his wife of thirty-seven years. His eyes narrowed and his glasses slid another couple millimeters farther down his nose. "How the hell can it have Bud's name on it?!" His gruff voice cut through the air of the passenger compartment and lingered for both to ponder.

"That man at the gas station gave me these bills as change when I paid for the gas." She tucked the now-unfolded remaining bills into her purse with all the alacrity she could muster so as to not inhibit the conversation.

"It says, 'Short Snorter E.M. Peterson,' followed by other names and ranks."

"Let me see that," Carl barked, his disbelief apparent; the glance had failed to quench his curiosity. His eyes darted between the back of the silver certificate and the road in front of him. "Well, I'll be damned. Those are some names from Paper

2

Doll, all right." He studied the names with more than a passing interest, but at the moment, only the tremendous coincidence intrigued him. "I'll be damned," he muttered.

He glanced at Anne as he handed her the bill. "Can you read all the names?"

"You mean 'E.M. Peterson' is really your brother? Doesn't that sound almost impossible?"

"I recognize a couple of the names. I hadn't heard them in years, but I remember some of 'em." He turned his head to change lanes as he passed a slow tractor-trailer. "And that date in Brazil has got to be about right."

Anne stared at the bill, flipped it over, then flipped it again. Her flustered demeanor frustrated Carl. "Read the other names," he ordered in a flat tone. "I couldn't read them all."

The excited passenger donned a pair of reading glasses and strained her eyes the best she could. "F.O. Andy Gosh— Goshtoian. C.O. Joe Parker. Sergeant W.H. Stod…" Her voice trailed off. With the background of the Great Seal of the United States—the bald eagle clutching arrows in one talon, an olive branch in the other, and a ribbon reading "e pluribus unum" in its mouth—the federal ink made the signatures difficult to read.

Her eyes returned to the edge of the paper, where "SHORT SNORTER E.M. PETERSON" was written in all capital letters on the white background. She read, "4-30-44 FORTALEZA, BRAZIL," written upside down along the bottom of the bill.

"I guess that's when he started it. They went south before going over."

Anne gave her head a quick shake. "I still don't understand how this happened. I mean, for me to get this as

3

change in a Salt Lake gas station. It's a forty-one-year-old bill, for goodness sakes!" She read "Series 1935" on the front, in the lower-right corner, near the signature of Henry Morgantheau, Jr., Franklin Roosevelt's Secretary of the Treasury. "And it's got a 1944 date written on it. How is that possible we got it?" She spoke with a slow, deliberate rhythm, in awe of the moment.

"Someone must've had it and just recently spent it, maybe on accident. Maybe a kid got it out of his dad's drawer or something." Carl felt just as shocked as his wife, but he was not in the habit of revealing such feelings.

"I don't know. It doesn't make sense to me." She attempted to think through her frustration. "Oh, what do I know?" The self-deprecation for which she was known leaped to the fore. "This is too much for my brain."

Carl did not speak. He gripped the steering wheel a little tighter and sat more erect than normal.

The gray-haired wife intently gazed at her husband. She could see this was different from Carl's usual silence. She noted his narrowed eyes and clenched jaw. She felt the tension.

The Granada maintained a constant speed as it traveled into the desert, away from the city, on its way to California. While the car motored along, the driver's mind could not avoid the many thoughts which raced faster than the Ford. After a long five minutes, his mind reverted to 1937.

Chapter Two

The two sandy-haired boys wrestled in the dirt, yelling at each other as they tussled.

"It hit it! It hit it! I saw it!"

"Did not!"

"Did too!"

"I saw it bounce off the top of your marble!"

"No, you did not!"

"Yes, I did! I saw it!"

"All right, all right!" the younger boy shouted. "I'll just give it to you. Mother will kill us if we rip our clothes." The fight ended.

"Okay." Fifteen-year-old Eugene Morris Peterson released his grip on his brother, rose to his feet, and extended a hand. "It's been a long time since we wrestled."

"It's been a long time since you cheated," thirteen-year-old Conrad Gilmore Peterson sniped as his brother lifted him upward. "Bud, you get to help Mother with laundry."

"Why me?" The youngster known as "Bud" looked incredulous. With two Eugenes in the tiny town of Puposky, Minnesota, the nickname came quickly in grammar school once he got tired of being called by his middle name.

"You cheated. Besides, I will *never* do laundry ever in my life. Ever," Conrad chirped.

"You've helped Mother before."

"Yeah, but I don't like laundry. I'd rather help with the dishes."

Bud's attention turned to a man walking toward them from the south.

5

"Laundry is for girls," Conrad continued, unaware of Bud's focus.

"It's Carl!" Bud shouted.

"Well, I'll be. It is Carl!" Conrad yelled as glee flooded the air.

The boys ran from where they played in front of Our Redeemer's Lutheran Church and toward their approaching brother. "Carl!" they yelled as they ran, enthusiasm on full display.

A wry smile crossed the eldest brother's face. Before he could be hit with the full force of the rushing boys, he thrust out a hand.

Bud and Conrad came to abrupt stops. The middle boy thrust out his hand and gave a hearty handshake. Conrad followed suit, understanding they were to shake hands like men, not—in Carl's view—hug like children.

"How long are you back?" Bud asked, excitement unconcealed.

"Oh, for a good while, I s'pose."

"Don't you have a car yet?" Conrad wanted to know.

"Not at the moment. I had one, but I had to sell it."

"You walked from Duluth?"

"No, no," Carl protested. "I hitched a ride to Bemidji. Then I walked."

"That's fifteen miles!" Conrad gasped. Puposky, north of Bemidji by just under fifteen miles as the crow flies, received its name from the first three syllables of a Chippewa phrase meaning "the end of the shaking lands," a reference to the soft soil which often sank when walked upon.

6

Carl stopped for a few brief seconds to stare at the church he helped build. "Oh, I've walked farther than that, Connie." Carl smiled as the three brothers headed home. "How's Mother?"

"She's swell," Conrad cooed.

"I don't mean 'do you like your mother?' I mean, how is her health, goof. How's she doing for dough?"

"Things are pretty skinny," Bud said with a touch of sadness. "And she's had it tough, 'specially with her feet and leg."

Carl sucked in a deep breath and sighed. "Well, I can help with the dough a little."

•   •   •

Hulda Peterson stood up in her garden when she heard voices. She took one last glance at her blueberries, which were coming along nicely, then squinted to see who approached her and her beloved garden.

"Carl." Her voice carried the flat statement along the slight summer breeze.

"Mother!" Carl gushed as he reached her. His tight squeeze caused her to let out a short laugh.

"You're as tall as a Norway pine. I think you grew a little while you were gone."

"Maybe so. I just thought my britches shrunk," Carl chuckled. Just shy of his twenty-second birthday, he had reached the six-foot mark and was not going to grow further; it would be decades before he would lose his slender figure. He was in

7

excellent condition; working outdoors suited his physique—other than his fair Norwegian skin.

"I think the taller and older you get, the more you look like your father." The comment was as close to ebullience as she would get. Life had taught her to keep her emotions steady, even with her five children.

"Where's Elsie?" Carl asked as he looked over the property. The land on which they lived jutted out into what the locals called "the point"—its boundary formed by Puposky Lake. He watched as his young brothers rushed to the water pump to stroke refreshing, cool water onto their heads.

"She's visiting Thelma and Ray." Hulda volunteered little, as though words were like possessions had been her entire life: scarce. Her taciturn nature had rubbed off on Carl and Conrad.

"Everyone well?"

"Everyone's well."

Carl knew he would have to resort to prying information out of Bud and Conrad.

Hulda studied her eldest son. Her rounded nose held her tired blue eyes in place. Her perfectly-shaped lips were not in the habit of curling upward. She was tough, but not lacking compassion; strong, but not lacking kindness. If the situation called for a smile, she would comply; but, the forty-three-year-old had experienced enough hard times and tragedy to make happiness a distant, almost foreign destination. Her economic situation pressed down on her with unrelenting force and gave her a fatigued countenance.

When her husband, William, died eight years earlier, carrying on for the sake of her children was never a question.

Giving up did not enter her mind; so, she plodded forward, raising proper young men and women, with the faith, morals, and principles on which she was raised.

Not long after William passed, Boys Town had contacted her, intimating just enough to frighten Hulda into believing they wanted to take her two young boys. She would not cower; she would not let any of her children go, under any circumstances, no matter how hard she had to work.

Self-sacrifice is what her generation of women did. It was engrained in their psyches: the family comes first. So beholden was she to what loved ones wanted, she still wore a hair net—because William liked it. No matter that he was buried a mile or so away. William liked it, so she wore her hair as he wished.

The wind flowed over her thick brown hair with a gentle touch. She watched for just a moment as Carl strode toward his brothers, then without a word she returned to weeding and watering her blueberry plants and checked them to ensure the leaves maintained a healthy green hue. Like the gardener, the Northern Highbush were hardy; blueberries able to withstand almost anything.

•   •   •

Hulda and her three young men sat together for a meager dinner of chicken and carrots; but, it was not meager to them. Chicken was the norm; the creatures were not raised to be pets at Mother's house. Vegetables were home-grown to save money—they possessed more chickens and vegetables than dollars. The effects of the Depression were less painful living on a farm.

"I hope you didn't cook chicken on the account of me, Mother," Carl said with a bashful tone. "You could've saved your chickens for another time."

"Nonsense. My son has come home," she stated with a firm riposte. "Besides, we have more."

Carl nodded as he put another piece of the cooked bird in his mouth. He dared not tell her that he had long ago tired of chicken; but, this was a difficult time for everyone, and he knew better than to express anything to his mother which could be interpreted as ungrateful. "Be glad you don't live in the big city," she would say on occasion. Carl took the message to heart and understood having chicken for dinner could be considered "rich" by others, who lacked their own ability to provide at least some of their own food.

"Tell us about boxing in Chicago, Carl!" Bud gushed.

"Yeah! I want to hear those stories again," Conrad added.

Before Carl could swallow his bite of carrots, Hulda ended the conversation. "We will have no talk of fighting at the dinner table, young men."

"But why'd you quit?" Bud wanted to know.

"Even though I've got good hands, I want to keep my head," Carl grinned as he explained the realities of life as a boxer.

"Then tell us about what you've been doing in the CC camps," Conrad happily changed the subject as ordered. "What was it like building that great big Paul Bunyan and Babe the Ox?" To Conrad, the stories were all fascinating, and all similar:

10

they were about life outside of little Puposky, with its population of 288 at the last census. Besides the city of Bemidji, which was home to nearly 9,000 people, Conrad only knew rural northern Minnesota.

Carl paused before answering, thinking of the right words. Economy of words was a family affair. "I was part of a team. A bunch of men were involved." He watched young Conrad's reaction. "It was work, like any other job, 'cept the result was bigger."

Unsatisfied, Conrad probed again. "You had to have done something interesting, didn't you?"

"Sure I did," Carl replied. "I helped map the border with Wisconsin. I made friends with a bear."

"A real bear?"

"A real bear. Black bear. When we were out in the woods every day, this big sow kept wandering into our camp. Scared most of the men." He glanced at his brothers before continuing. "I was afraid somebody was gonna shoot her, but fortunately nobody had a gun. So that sow wandered my way when I talked to her, and I petted her. You shoulda seen the look on the boys' faces."

"You're pullin' my leg!" Conrad laughed.

"Of course he is!" Bud scolded.

"No, I'm not. It really happened."

The boys studied his face, waiting for a smile to crack or a laugh to betray the truth, but none was forthcoming.

"For real?" Bud broke the brief silence.

"For real."

"Some people just have a gift, Eugene." Hulda called Bud by his birth name. "Carl's always had a way with animals."

11

"Wild animals, snarling dogs…" Carl added as his voice trailed off.

"Wow!" Bud's energy did not subside while Conrad stared with amazement.

"The men in the camp were shocked. After that," he continued. "She came around a couple more times, and each time I scratched her on whichever shoulder she turned my way. Then she'd wander off."

The boys stared in wonderment; chewing stopped.

"Finally, we had work elsewhere, and I didn't see that sow anymore."

Bud looked at Conrad as he posited his interpretation of their brother. "You know how Mother just knows when people are coming over, even though she shouldn't know it? It's the same with Carl and animals, only different."

Carl smiled. "Yeah. Just like that." He took another bite of chicken.

Hulda, amused by the boys' reactions, cracked a small smile.

•　　　•　　　•

Carl stared at a framed photograph of his father, which had maintained a home on the table nearest the main room's window for the better part of nine years. Hulda, holding the infant Thelma, stood on a porch in the background of the photo. Taken in 1914, a year before Carl was born, William was at the forefront, surrounded by extended family. Carl thought he remembered being told his Uncle Gil stood next to his father—his arm partially visible—but he could not be certain. Cancer consumed Gilbert Peterson in 1922, and Carl's memories of the man were only disjointed stories and incidents, woven together like a tattered blanket.

William's mild resemblance to Abraham Lincoln was amplified in the photograph as he raised his chin and stood erect for the camera, projecting prominence. With a similar build and facial structure as Lincoln, his suit added to his stately appearance. His deep-set eyes stared outward, beyond the camera, as though looking into the future with a fierce intensity and courageous anticipation. His gaunt face gave him the look of a man etched from stone. His long neck held a white tie and shirt, and his broad shoulders hinted of physical strength. His mental strength was never questioned.

The dark jacket, with only one button fastened, and hands held behind his back portrayed the look of a relaxed man, yet his forlorn expression belied the casual dress. His light-brown hair swept backward and upward, while his thin build gave him a taller appearance.

He had worked hard all his life, and was a strong, stern man set on raising a good family when cancer got the best of the forty-six-year-old. As one of Carl's uncles put it, "Nineteen-Twenty-Nine wasn't a good year for nobody."

In the same photo, Hulda, holding her first child, possessed a bright young face with eyes which leaped toward the camera, as though the battle to hide her past as a playful prankster played out in plain sight. Despite her bizarre ability to foresee certain events, the destiny of her husband remained unknown to her at the moment of the photograph in 1914. While she seemed to be on the verge of a smile, none was forthcoming. Her fat-cheeked daughter was oblivious to the camera and the commotion which always preceded use of the fascinating, yet still uncommon, invention.

Carl could not ignore that his mother's face in the photo exuded a happiness and vivaciousness which he could no longer see in her. The thick brown hair grew a little thicker then, and her fiery eyes had flashed brighter, despite the photo's low quality.

Hulda Josephine Peterson was now the anchor of her burgeoning family, the backbone which allowed the family to move forward. That 1914 photo captured not only her steely fortitude, but a kind heart. Most did not know she was destined to marry William and raise her brood in a way different than most people—at least in the United States—experienced. Right after her birth, her parents promised her to William by way of William's parents. That she would marry William—her elder by eleven years—was never in question. It was predetermined, out of her control.

When her husband died, she vowed not to remarry, remembering her own stepfather, an abusive traveling salesman. She did not want to take the chance her children would experience the same fate as she and her siblings had. She had the opportunity to re-marry. For a time, she maintained a platonic relationship with a man to whom she gave shelter in an out-building on the farm. He had shown an interest in her before she married William, and now he held the same interest.

Hulda's mother had left her husband for a salesman, and that act of infidelity stuck in Hulda's mind, never to be forgotten. The resulting abuse was never forgotten, either. She feared even the possibility of subjecting her children to such cruelty.

Carl continued to stare at the photo of his parents, his sister Thelma, and two of his cousins, until his mother entered the room.

"How long are you staying?" Hulda inquired. They both knew the reason for her question.

"Oh! That reminds me." He reached into his wallet and pulled out three twenty-dollar-bills. "This is for you. I did some handyman work on the side."

Hulda's eyes moistened. She was in the habit of turning down charity, but she raised her son to understand his duties to family. Carl was fourteen when his father died; she had an extra void to fill for five children, so it became his duty to be the male role model for his brothers—when he was around. When that "other man" started coming around the next year, fifteen-year-old Carl left, first heading to his uncle Adolph's house, then later finding work wherever he could, be it in boxing rings in Chicago or forests in Wisconsin.

"I'm gonna stay for a while. I'm gonna marry Anne." His firm statement convinced Hulda that his wish would be fulfilled. "I'm sure I can't live with Uncle Hap again," he added, referring to Hulda's brother, Adolph Gustafson. Nicknamed "Happy," the choice not only fit the man, but given the current state of geopolitics, "Adolph" undoubtedly was not the best Christian name at the moment.

"Okay. Are you going to be able to afford yourself and a wife?"

"I'll manage."

Hulda knew better than to be sad a portion of his income would now go elsewhere. She, too, would "manage," just as she had for so long on a $20-a-month pension, plus odd jobs and Civilian Conservation Corps payments.

"I'm about to lose this place," she said, a quiet falling over her.

Carl came alive with anger, frustration, and a sense something had to be done this instant. Before he could speak, though, his mother gave great effort to calm him.

"Carl. Nothing can be done. I've sold so many of our possessions just trying to make ends meet, but it hasn't stopped the bleeding."

"But how can you lose the place?" Carl demanded. "You *own* this place!"

"You already know the answer to that," she scolded. "Taxes. Because I haven't been able to pay the taxes, we're gonna lose it. The bank and the government can figure it out between them." She was not made aware for years that she lost the farm because of only $40.22 in unpaid taxes.

Anger gave way to emotional exhaustion. Carl had supplied his mother with as much money as possible. When he kept for himself what little he earned, he felt guilty. Working in the Civilian Conservation Corps camps made it easier not to spend; the government gave the young man five dollars a month and sent the remaining twenty-five home, to Hulda.

All to no avail.

"When?"

"Any day I'll get a notice about it."

"Where are you going?"

"I've made arrangements for me and the boys to live in the old train depot," she said, referring to the shuttered Puposky train station, which would become the family's home for a while.

Carl shook his head.

"As soon as we can, we're gonna rent a house in Bemidji. I'll have room for a garden, so that will save us money."

"Okay."

"Carl," Hulda tried to soften her steady tone. "It'll be best if you find somewhere to stay while you're here."

Carl nodded, his head hanging slightly. "I understand."

Hulda turned and left the room—left Carl to his thoughts and emotions, the latter of which remained hidden away, somewhere deep inside him. Carl turned to the photo again, of a father who was alive and a mother who was young. Times were tough then, too. It just felt worse now—maybe because people labeled it a "depression." Maybe because he was experiencing it himself rather than hearing about it. Either way, Life was cutting a hole into the Peterson clan, and Carl resented it.

Chapter Three

Nineteen-thirty-eight was a difficult year in the United States. The entire world suffered through the Depression to varying degrees, but that did not make the average person—the "forgotten man," as he came to be called—feel any better.

The U.S. economy experienced a dreaded "double-dip" in 1938, which saw the employment rate reverse its positive trend. The New Deal was already in full swing and made little impact. The upside of make-work projects was employment, food on the table, and renewed dignity. The downside was government jobs stimulate the economy to a lesser degree than private sector jobs. Taxpayer money spent to create government jobs limited the multiplier factor of money which flowed into the federal treasury; economic recovery takes far too long when tax money leads the way.

By 1938, the U.S. economy proved unable to recover the way countries such as France, Australia, and Germany had rebounded. Australia's unemployment had a higher peak (29%) compared to the U.S. (24.9%), but six years after the 1932 peak, Australian unemployment was at 8.7%; France, 8%; Germany, 2.1%. The U.S. stood at 19.8%.

Tariffs remained high, leading to the extension of the retaliation of the early 1930s by our trading partners. Higher tariffs on foreign products and outright embargoes of American products put a knife through the hearts of U.S. farmers, who were then paid by the federal government to *not* grow their crops.

In the meantime, Americans were forced to ration food and other needed items. Instead of freeing the economy, the

Roosevelt administration kept it bound up with injurious rules and regulations, unable to move or grow. By the president's own admission, he did not know what to do.

Despite the best efforts of F. D. Roosevelt's so-called "Brain Trust"—the alleged best and brightest the government could summon—the failure of the New Deal hit the country like an economic kick to the gut. In 1937, the stock market lost a third of its value. In 1938, unemployment jumped from 13.2% the prior year. Gross Domestic Product shrunk. Industrial output dropped. Deflation, once thought to be defeated, once again bared its economically potent teeth. Those who suffered had to endure more. Those who were in the middle of recovering returned to scarcity once again.

By May of 1939, unemployment again hit the 20% mark.

Employment from make-work projects was good for families in the short term, but the bad times were extended by the incessant experimentation by the Brain Trust. Historically, steep economic downturns—called "panics"—were short-lived, but government's best intentions found ways to make this depression last longer in the name of "helping."

For Hulda Peterson, economic catastrophe was inevitable. The year 1929 saw not only the famed Stock Market crash, but William's death. Now, nine years later, she could escape neither the economic collapse nor the personal loss. Money was difficult to come by and her property on "the point" was gone. Unpaid taxes, which she could not afford, uprooted her and her brood. The picturesque setting and 160 acres were never owned by the family again.

She took odd jobs, cleaning or caring for others, to offset the financial deficits; she still had children to raise and mouths to feed. In 1938, her youngest child, Conrad, had reached his fourteenth birthday and Bud and Conrad edged ever closer to the day when they could sustain themselves.

Hulda knew more challenges were coming. She could sense it.

•   •   •

The light leaking from the barn interrupted the blackness of night. A closer investigation revealed music, laughing, and frivolities. The wooden barn, on its way to dilapidation, lay void of farming equipment, which had been moved outside to accommodate the party. Soon it would be time for harvest and many of the attendees would find work.

Extra bales of hay, meant to be used as feed for farm animals, now served as a small stage for the frolicking musicians. A lanky man tapped his foot and moved to the rapid squeals from his fiddle. A young guitar player wore overalls but no shirt. The red-faced trumpeter rocked his shoulders back and forth. The zither player strummed an instrument brought by his parents from the Norwegian motherland. The accordion player lost focus numerous times as he chatted with friends and watched a particular young lady dance.

The cool August evening failed to protect against sweat as the partiers danced to the music of an eclectic selection of songs, from Louie Armstrong's *When the Saints Go Marching In* to the Will Glahe hit *Beer Barrel Polka*.

Polka tunes and Norwegian favorites were mixed in with tunes from Minnesota favorites "Slim Jim and the Vagabond Kid" and "Skarning and His Norwegian Hillbillies" — songs

known to the locals courtesy of a Minneapolis radio station, which relayed content to the northern stations.

The ensemble had not previously played together, and at times the amateur musicians drifted off-key or simply did not know how to play what bandmates were churning out. They rotated resting with the revelers, who welcomed the occasional ballad to bring relief to their feet.

While a few of the men and women were over thirty, most were in their twenties. In this area, crowds considered to be large by those who lived in "the cities" would never materialize. That over thirty people younger than thirty years of age congregated meant friends from Bemidji peppered the crowd.

Beer and whiskey flowed and the music and dancing continued, but behind the barn a lone figure with a tin can of Hamm's beer leaned up against the building, out of sight, taking in the waxing Gibbous moon. Five days prior the man celebrated his twenty-third birthday; tonight, he drank through his thoughts.

Carl stared at the darkened farmland and the distant water of Turtle Lake. The calm water lay too far away to be observed in detail by moonlight, but his mind was elsewhere when he opened his final beer—number six for the evening. As he placed the can opener back into his front pocket, he returned to deep thought.

"Carl!" The angry voice cut through the night. He neither needed to look nor ponder the source of the voice.

"Carl Peterson!" Anne paused before hitting him with her strongest line. "What do you think you're doing?! I've been looking all over for you!" The darkness hid her fierce countenance. A clip bound her curly brown hair together, allowing it to only reach past her shoulders. Her soft, high cheeks, usually stuck in a smile, pushed back tighter against her face as she snarled her words.

His mind worked but his mouth struggled. "I wash jus' lookin' at the moon," he slurred.

"Oh, goodness gracious! You're loaded!" She paused before inquiring, "Hooch?!"

"Hamm's. Hell, I've had more than these." Carl smiled but she did not.

Anne's veins flowed with Norwegian, Swedish, and Danish blood, but now the Danish took over—at a boil. He was surprised he could not see her blue eyes, which he knew were on fire.

She yelled at him for a full minute as he stared outward. Every time she asked whether he was listening or thumped him on the shoulder — harder each time — he nodded or said, "Yes."

After she slammed a piece of scrap metal into the barn siding — Carl never saw her pick it up — he turned to her. "You know what? You have the ability to sober me up." He grinned, then continued slurring, although improvement became more noticeable by the sentence. "How do you do that?"

"Oh!" Anne shouted. She picked up the same piece of metal, which lay a few steps away, raised it, and lunged toward him. "I have half a mind to split you in two!"

Carl leaped backward. Miraculously, he kept his feet. "Well, I'll be damned if it ain't workin'! I'm soberin' up."

One last shout of "Oh!" and the young woman spun on her heels and disappeared into the darkness.

"Well, nuts," Carl mused aloud as she left his sight. "Now wouldn't be the best time to ask her to marry me."

•   •   •

"What are you gonna do now, Bud?"

"Get another job, I s'pose."

Bud, who was months away from turning eighteen, and Conrad, who had recently turned sixteen, strolled through the small park which featured statues of Paul Bunyan and Babe the Blue Ox, which their brother had helped build. Both young men were considered handsome according to the local young women. Conrad's soft features — which were soon to harden through age and experiences — and Bud's determined, masculine face made the young men hits with the ladies.

The young men walked along Lake Bemidji's shore, less than half a mile from their new home.

"I keep watching you bounce around with your jobs and I'm trying to figure you out." Conrad was not being helpful and knew it, but he did wish to understand Bud's plan.

"It's not easy," was all Bud could manage; his blues eyes had lost their glow.

"You quit school a year ago and you've only had odd jobs."

"A diploma wasn't gonna help feed the family." Bud shook his head in disappointment. The job market in 1940 gave no favors to Americans, young or old.

"I guess life has to go on, Connie." Bud suffered a momentary bout of sadness as the present situation raced through his brain. True to form, within seconds he mentally bounded back, energetic. "Look at Carl. He's got a wife and a baby on the way." His spirits lifted as he spoke. "Pretty soon you're gonna have a nephew or another niece. You can't be crying in front of a baby. You have to live your life."

"Mother says war is coming."

"Mother knows lots of stuff, but you can't worry about it. If she's right," Bud continued. "Then we'll deal with it when it comes."

Conrad saw things differently. "What do you mean, 'IF' Mother is right. You know she's right. She's always right about what she says."

"Yeah, just make sure you understand her words," Bud tried to explain. "A whole lot of people believe war's coming. If she said something like that, she means 'war's coming to the family.'"

"That'd be a rough job," Conrad responded, referring to the military.

"I'm gonna work and live and not let everyone else's worrying worry me." Bud scratched his head through his "curly top" haircut — a popular cut for young men who could pull it off — curls climbing over three inches above his scalp to form what looked like a pie made of hair.

"Mother says you may be working in one of the Dakotas."

"The Dakotas! Now why would I go there when there's work to be had here?" Bud's aggravation from the mention of traveling for work reflected his irritation with the conversation. His bright blue eyes flashed determination. "You just gotta find it. Work ain't easy to find these days."

The two young men continued their stroll, but they turned toward the town when they reached Bemidji State Teachers College. Across Bemidji Avenue and toward their new neighborhood, past house after house they headed for home. Because of their youth, they easily adapted to having neighbors — they even liked that whatever they needed was close — but they missed the open country and the easy access to the several lakes so close to their former home in Puposky.

Bemidji was a small but growing city; its nearly 10,000 inhabitants were just as hardy as the people Bud and Conrad had known all their lives. Much larger than Puposky Lake, Lake Bemidji was perhaps six times the size of the former. Lake Bemidji, with a road which ran along the lake's western edge, saw a considerable amount of human traffic compared to Puposky Lake, where "traffic" was just as likely to be wildlife.

The biggest difference, however, was the boys had felt as though Puposky Lake was their lake, with their property pushed to the edge of the water. In Bemidji, they could not simply run out the back door and launch a small boat for the latest fishing expedition.

Bemidji was a big city, as far as Bud and Conrad knew. They had heard stories about Chicago from Carl, and they read newspapers, which gave them a peek into New York City and other such faraway lands, but having close neighbors was big city enough for the country boys.

●　　　●　　　●

She was a wanderer. She could not stay in one place — just as liable to show up here as there. Difficult to find; on the

25

move; uncomfortable with rest. She was like a small boat without an anchor which lacked the ability to tie off at a slip — unable to dock, adrift. Maybe she was uncomfortable in her own skin — she certainly had reason to feel that way. Maybe she had silent, invisible ghosts chasing her, which also seemed plausible. Any explanation sounded reasonable when trying to sum up Johanna Lampe — the woman the family knew as "Grandma Thompson."

Johanna had married Charles August (Carl) Gustafson and bore seven children. When Hulda, the fifth child, reached age eleven, Johanna dumped Carl for Oscar Thompson, a traveling salesman. At the time, Johanna was working as a window-front model for various stores; live models would display the latest clothing or jewelry fads.

The affair, marriage, resulting child, and treatment by Oscar impacted young Hulda. Rather than following her mother's path of unfaithfulness or bringing another man around her children, Hulda-the-widow chose to remain alone when suitors called. She did not want her children treated the way she and her siblings had suffered at the hands of their stepfather.

Grandma Thompson and Hulda experienced struggles in their relationship far into adulthood. Conrad's advice to ignore the woman's words and actions did not prove to be an option at which Hulda excelled. The woman was Hulda's mother, so the daughter attempted to get along and thus treat the mother with cordial respect. But, stubbornness was a family trait; at times, cordiality was lost in the ensuing battle.

Hulda's father died four years after the divorce, and the salesman/stepfather died in 1932. Hulda named her eldest son, Carl August Peterson, after her late father.

The aging Johanna remained active and strong. Her big-boned frame gave the appearance of a woman who could carry a sack of feed on her back if needed. Her thinning gray hair did not reach her nape. Her weathered face seemed to be held in place by her narrow eyeglasses.

No one knew how Grandma Thompson spent her time; she just appeared. On one occasion, she walked across frozen Lake Puposky and showed up unannounced at the Peterson farm.

"Where is Grandma Thompson these days?" seemed to be a family theme. Curiosity of her whereabouts infected everyone who knew her. She would tell where she had been, but details of her adventures remained vague. People who wished to write her would ask Hulda about Grandma Thompson's location, but the daughter could not account for the mother.

One day she would return to Beltrami County to die, but until that day came, the question would get asked over and over: "Where is Grandma Thompson?"

•   •   •

Carl was sick of being sick. While not literally true, by his calculations he had gotten sick every winter the last decade. He was a man of the north — a descendant of the Norse — but he did not feel like it each winter when the cold north winds blew in the flu or pneumonia. In this instance, the latter ailment devoured him like a polar bear eating a seal, but his difficulty breathing could not eclipse his disgust at getting sick every Minnesota winter.

Spring was coming. The houseflies which had made their way into the small cabin proved the northern climate was changing and about to leave Old Man Winter behind.

Carl married in May of 1939 and wanted a place for his bride; living with Mother was not an option. Living with Hap, which he had done fewer than ten years prior, was unthinkable given Hap now had eight children. His need led to the only reasonable conclusion: he built a one-room cabin for him and his bride. The 300-square-feet cabin sufficed for the newlyweds. A "bedroom" in one corner, a "kitchen" in another, the newlywed cabin made Anne happy. They were married, they lived alone, and they had what they wanted from life. They both knew people who had far less.

Carl could have rented a house in Bemidji, but work was not a year-round undertaking unless he could find a job which continued through the snow and extreme cold. He needed a cabin which he could build with his own hands, owe no one, and live out the winter. If he could find work nearby, all the better. Once he found and purchased the land he needed, the rest was simple for the lumberjack. The cabin was completed in time for the Puposky cold season.

Carl possessed skills; this small cabin, with a fireplace to keep them warm, proved the point.

Now, in late winter/early spring of 1940, Carl focused on his one problem: he was bored. He was bored and sick. An unseasonably warm day had prompted the houseflies to hatch, and they buzzed around him as he lay flat on his back with pneumonia until his boredom evolved into annoyance.

Across the room from the bed, closer to the currently dormant fireplace, Anne worked on a bedspread she was crocheting. Alone with herself, she snapped out of her deep thoughts when she heard the .22 bolt-action rifle chamber a round. She froze. Crocheting could wait. She eyed Carl just for a moment when a blast filled the room.

"Got ya, ya little bastard." Carl's angry words flowed through a soft, smooth tone.

Anne watched in silence.

Another fly, startled by the cacophony created by the Springfield Model 1922 rifle, landed on the gabled ceiling. The exposed logs had perfectly absorbed the .22 caliber bullet, leaving only small splinters as a sign of the shot. Carl paused to ensure the housefly would not move at an inopportune moment.

Anne kept her tongue as Carl took aim. The next small explosion created the same result:

"Got ya, ya little bastard."

The silence lasted a long five seconds before Anne could no longer control herself and she erupted into an over-sized laugh. "That's the funniest thing I've ever seen you do!" she roared.

Carl looked at her with a frown. "I'm sick of those damned things!" He watched her bellow with laughter until he could not resist. He followed her into a laughing binge, which led to a horrible, dry coughing binge.

"That's the funniest thing I've ever seen you do!" Anne boomed as she repeated herself.

Carl fought off additional laughter, wanting to avoid the painful coughs. Before he could speak, he spotted another fly as it landed on the ceiling. He chambered another round and fired. A third fly disappeared. The explosion of gunfire caused Anne to laugh even harder.

                                •   •   •

Spring and Carl's pneumonia had passed as Conrad
enjoyed the warm air while on Hulda's front porch. Newspaper
in hand, Conrad sat in an old, metal chair, next to his mother, his
blue eyes buried in a ten-day-old story about the war which had,
in recent months, boiled over into a major conflagration. His
copy of the *Minneapolis Daily Star* had passed through several
hands before reaching the Peterson household. The sixteen-year-
old fed his hunger for information with a story of what would
become known as the "Battle of Britain." Luftwaffe bombs
rained down on Londoners while the island nation fought for its
life.

France had fallen and the British fought to stave off
surrender at best, annihilation at worst. The German war
machine had proven to be an unstoppable force.

The lazy summer afternoon had given way to a cool,
crisp Minnesota fall night. Conrad dropped his newspaper and
ventured to one end of the front porch, deep breaths filling his
lungs. The young man, not yet to his destined height of six-feet,
had not reached 140 pounds, and boyish looks complimented his
boyish charm. A quick wit provided a powerful bite to his
observations of life.

His thick hair had darkened by degree since childhood,
but was still light enough to appear blond in certain light. His
big smile did not flash often — not because of unhappiness;
rather, because his unconcerned attitude about everything in life
kept his pulse at an even rate. Conrad was a happy person, but
he did not feel the need to tell anyone.

Satisfied with the increased blood circulation and brief respite for his eyes, he opened the front door to enter the house. From her porch chair, his mother snapped her head in his direction as he passed through the doorway

"Did you hear that?"

Conrad made an immediate about-face and returned to the porch. He stood silent, but failed to understand for what he should be listening. "No. What?"

"The train whistle." Hulda stood, surveyed her surroundings as if in thought, and then announced. "Mother is on that train. I need to put on a pot of coffee."

With furrowed brow, Conrad re-entered the house, now aware of the train's call. Before he could let the door close behind him, Hulda grabbed it so she could follow her son.

Conrad knew the answer to his question, yet he wanted certainty. "Did Grandma say she was coming?"

"No," came the answer as Hulda mixed a raw egg with the coffee grounds, which took a bite out of the bitterness and made the concoction more palatable.

"Do you know where she's been? We haven't seen her in a while."

"No. Haven't heard from her in months."

"Ah." Conrad nodded his head, as though he understood. He looked around the room for a moment before making his decision. "I guess I'd better finish the newspaper in case Grandma wants to see it." His comment was more mutter than statement.

Thirty minutes later, when the inevitable knock on the door came, Conrad said nothing but shook his head. Seventy-one-year-old Johanna Thompson stood on the porch, waiting for

Hulda to open the door. Conrad did not bother to ponder his own mother's bizarre behavior — there was not a need to do so because there was not a rational answer which would explain it to the youngster.

As Hulda hurried to the door she asked, "Connie, you want some coffee?"

"No thanks," came the reply. Conrad stood to greet his grandmother as Hulda opened the door. He let out a low addition to the rejection of coffee. "I need something stronger than that."

Chapter Four

Most Americans possessed at least a passing knowledge of the atrocities which had taken place and were still occurring in the Orient. Japan was on the move. The inexorable militaristic tide of Japanese power swept through eastern Asia. Life held no importance — one's own life belonged to the emperor; the lives of others were treated like mere agitation — a gnat flitting around a person's nose and eyes — and could be dispensed with at will.

In the late 1800s, Japan had decided to become a modern nation, so the Japanese worked with astounding zeal and, over a ten-year period, became a modern nation. In the early 1900s, the government decided the samurai spirit needed to make a return to society, so it returned. More natural resources were needed in the mechanized world, so the government went about acquiring the resources required for the 20th century. The Japanese people believed they could accomplish anything they wanted.

The Japanese government did not find the need to purchase everything. The actions of the United States and European nations taught them, in the extended age of colonialism, strength was the ultimate virtue. Their turbulent 1920s taught Japanese officials only the tough survive.

When the turbulence subsided — the number of assassinations lessened and the young emperor matured as a man and leader — the military clamped down on dissenters. They still existed, but the military's authority could not be stopped — and it was a good idea not to question such authority.

Emperor Hirohito left the day-to-day workings of government to the politicians, but he wisely — in the context of the ever-evolving Japanese political landscape — maintained direct control over the military. The Imperial Japanese Army and Imperial Japanese Navy battled each other in a stereotypical inter-service rivalry, but Army and Navy alike served — worshipped — their emperor.

Japan ravaged China in a style reminiscent of the Ancients. Like the Roman fury at Carthage or the Vikings unleashed on a countryside occupied by frightened English peasants, Japan plundered, raped, and murdered. In the Chinese capital of Nanking, Japanese soldiers made a game of murder. Death by bullet, sword, drowning; decapitation, thrown off bridges, dismemberment, or left to die a slow, agonizing demise: the "rape of Nanking" was both literal and figurative, so thorough were the three months of destruction of human lives and possessions and buildings. Experiments were conducted — on individuals and the masses.

Cruelty was best served slowly.

The subjugation and destruction of China continued into the 1940s, but by late 1941, the Japanese government decided they were not going to control China as they wished, and military forces were needed to expand the empire throughout the Pacific — and to fight the Western powers, if necessary. They had killed many Chinese — upwards of 250,000 people in Nanking alone — and had conquered key areas of China, but they did not fully control the populous nation.

At some point, films of atrocities made their way to the Western world; on celluloid, for all to see. Young Japanese Army recruits were taught how to properly use their bayonets by stabbing bound, living Chinese prisoners. The rest of the world did not know how widespread this particular training method was, but the evidence ruled out the possibility of Allied propaganda.

Japan needed sugar, so they took Formosa. Their ten-year excursion in Manchuria brought much needed iron while China fulfilled their need for coal and timber. Along with Manchuria, control of Korea gave them a buffer — a feeling of security — against the hated communists of Russia.

As 1941 progressed, so did the military plans. Hirohito portrayed himself as a lover of peace, but he supported war with the United States.

Japan was a growing colonial power. Their leaders respected the British, French, and Americans in this context; however, they truly admired Germany. They valued the military discipline and power of Kaiser Wilhelm II's military earlier in the century and Nazi Germany's tactics, military strength, and action on behalf of racial superiority beliefs. Long before war with the West, Japan had developed their own secret police which rivaled the Gestapo in brutalities committed: the *Kempeitai*, or "Law Soldier Regiment."

Even the Dutch held a Pacific colony. Japan fervently wanted to be one of the colonial powers; but, the Western powers did not want Japan to attain such status. They both did not trust and metaphorically looked down on the Japanese.

After almost a year into the Tripartite Pact with Germany and Italy, Japan was ready for an expanded war, and Emperor Hirohito maintained firm control of the military.

The Japanese government hated Americans, both racially and politically, and Americans undoubtedly lacked fondness for the Japanese. Japan had a host of reasons to dislike the U.S., including immigration laws which they interpreted as anti-Japanese, repeated objections to their military and human rights actions around southeastern Asia, a ban on shipment of scrap iron to the island archipelago, and in mid-1941, an oil embargo and freezing of Japanese assets. When other Western nations, including Britain, followed suit, war became inevitable.

With a monstrous rate of growth reminiscent of creatures in science fiction movies of the time, Japan grew until it could kill indiscriminately, take what it wanted, and leave behind, in each country, a puppet government which would serve Tokyo's needs.

The West tried to stop Japan as it grew more dangerous, but the more pressure put on them, the more the Japanese resented the West and wanted more — and later *needed* more — respect, resources, and buffer zones against enemies.

The United States government believed it had to stop the growth of this Asian monster, and the Roosevelt administration did everything short of war. Historians would critique every move by the administration, but no one knew the Japanese could reach as far east as they did. American officials assumed Guam or other similar islands would face the Rising Sun's wrath.

Secretary of State Cordell Hall would receive a great amount of criticism for seemingly leaving the Japanese with no other choice but war; but, what is overlooked in this context is Franklin D. Roosevelt's vicious hatred of the Japanese. His quotes and writings left no doubt he believed, as many Anglos did, the Japanese people were an inferior people. Hull, too, may have been lulled into doubting Japanese fighting abilities, which many of his day did.

Japan either had to stop growing, stop killing, and stop conquering, or they had to fight the Allies. With an emperor's acceptance of war, a prime minister who was also an army general, and a plan designed by an officer — Isoroku Yamamoto — who had been educated in the United States, the government could claim they were pushed into war, but they actually wanted domination; the Pacific Ocean out to Hawaii would be theirs. *They* were equipped to lead the Far Eastern world and points east.

Or they would die trying.

To many Japanese people, fighting was the only answer — and most soldiers were willing to fight to the death. Surrender was neither part of the military's psyche nor in the militarized public's jargon.

With both sides viewing the other as an inferior people, and with diametrical political and social beliefs destined to clash, only one question remained: "When will war break out?"

Indeed, war was inevitable.

As the push for domination of the Pacific increased, and American insistence, among other demands, that the Imperial Japanese Army leave Manchuria, the calendar turned to December Seventh.

•   •   •

Over four dozen young men and boys stood in line, all with similar attire: white t-shirts, boxer shorts, and socks — mostly black or brown.

"Knutson!" A slender corporal with a regulation haircut barked.

"Yes, sir!" A young man — a boy, really — leaped out of the line.

"Knutson! You're fifteen-years-old. Get out of here!" The corporal may as well have been a full-bird colonel to young Knutson.

"But, sir. Please. Sir. I just — "

"Don't sir me, Knutson. You are a civilian and you will remain a civilian for at least two more years. Now get!" The fire in his eyes left the boy with no options.

As the fifteen-year-old fled to fetch his clothes and exit the building with wounded pride, a twenty-six-year-old sat quietly as he dressed, deep in thought and unsure of his future. He had a wife and a baby daughter, but providing for them caused a struggle with not only the family budget, but his heart. He internalized everything; he did not express emotions with ease, except for anger, and perhaps frustration. Happiness, sadness, fear — his emotions were not for the consumption of others.

Carl wanted to serve his country. He wanted to accomplish something. More than that, he wanted his family to be comfortable — "rich" never entered his mind. Life in the military would mean Anne and Carla would receive a monthly stipend. He was not intending to look the Grim Reaper in the eye, but if he were killed in action, Anne would receive a $10,000 payout.

All his problems came back to one subject: money. The WPA jobs were helpful — they paid a decent salary — but he lacked confidence the jobs, or even the program, would still be available next week or month.

He had no fears of being fired. Years earlier, when he laid railroad track, he watched as a co-worker made a mistake, was fired on the spot, and the next person in the nearby line stepped forward to transition from unemployment to earning a paycheck. Carl had survived those times. He maintained a self-confidence in his own abilities; he possessed skills and talents. Nevertheless, the matter of income nagged at him, stalking him like a timber wolf following a lone child strolling through the countryside.

Carl marched out of the recruiting office and took note of three boys about to step inside from the sidewalk. Bemidji residents and numerous country dwellers were in the process of answering Uncle Sam's call, but Carl could not. All because of two lousy knees, injured over the years.

Yes, he wanted to fight Hitler's forces. Yes, he wanted to stop Imperial Japan and pay them back for Pearl Harbor. But he also wanted some consistency, some stability, to take hold of his life.

And he needed a better income to provide for his family.

•   •   •

"Mother, you look glum."

"There's nothing wrong with me."

"Mother, I can tell when something's bothering you," Thelma responded. The slender young woman wore a hairnet similar to her mother's and her face reflected much of the same wear and exhaustion which she saw in her mother.

"My health is a lot better than yours," Hulda replied, with the knowledge the subject of "health" had not been raised. "I'm not raising children. I have wonderful grandkids. I'm not glum."

Hulda's eldest child stood and strode away from the kitchen table. Now a mother herself, she turned and looked her mother over, skepticism flowing from her eyes. With two daughters of her own, she had learned the art of detecting deception.

"You're not happy and I can tell." Thelma looked down at her seated mother. "What's got you worried?"

Hulda waited a long five seconds before answering. With her decision in place — she would open up — she looked at her twenty-eight-year-old offspring as the latter moved to return to her seat at the kitchen table. "It's the war." Hulda responded in perfect English, with no linguistic indication remaining of the little girl who was removed from school until she could learn the language of America. Knowledge solely of the Norwegian language did not suffice in the early 20th century, even in an area filled with Norwegians.

The younger woman fought back the urge to respond. She knew her mother would use interruptions to change the subject. A facial expression of both care and impatience controlled her face.

"Thank the Lord Carl couldn't get into the Army," she began. "Those bad knees were good for something." Again a beat. "He's married with a daughter — awful lot of girls in this family." She paused again to move her thoughts forward. "What's a man doing volunteering when he has a wife and daughter?" Another pause and her mind returned to trepidation. "Connie wants in the Army because jobs are scarce and you know Bud's going in. He's working on that now."

Sadness sullied Thelma's countenance. "They'll both get in."

"I'm hoping Bud's bum knee will keep him out." She looked around Thelma Beckstrand's kitchen. The old house could use a lot of work in most rooms. Cupboard doors, the ones which were intact, failed to close smoothly and the wood flooring could benefit from sanding and refinishing.

"And Connie."

"Yeah. Connie, he'll get in. He's healthy. Lazy as all get-out, but he'll grow out of that real soon."

Thelma laughed. "He's not lazy. He's working hard, doing farm work, right now."

"Oh, I know," Hulda chuckled. "He's a hard-working boy — when he wants to be. But if he don't want, try getting that bean pole off the couch."

Knowing Hulda did not criticize or complain about other people, it never occurred to Thelma that Hulda could be serious about Conrad; she was not. Hulda did have her moments of frustration with her children, but Conrad was growing up in front of her eyes.

"He's out of high school now, so he can't be a slacker."

"He's a good kid," Hulda smiled.

"What's Carl doing in the WPA?"

"I haven't heard. Unlike his brothers, he doesn't write much and I haven't seen Anne lately."

Carl's time in the employ of the Work Projects Administration remained a mystery at the moment, but the lack of good, private-sector jobs held no mystery.

"Where's Bud right now?"

"He's at a camp near Cass Lake," Hulda answered, referring to a Civilian Conservation Corps installation. "He said he'll be going to either Montana or North Dakota pretty soon. I told him it'll be North Dakota, but he wasn't very happy to hear that."

41

Thelma resisted the urge to ask her mother how she knew where he would wind up next.

"My family is scattering out," she muttered as she stared over Thelma's shoulder, off into space.

As if reading Hulda's mind, Thelma volunteered, "The economy is getting better. There are more jobs now."

"That's because there are fewer men to do those jobs," the elder woman lamented. "As more men go overseas, we may not have anyone to fill jobs. Then what are they going to do?"

"I keep hearing the war's gonna be short," Thelma said with as much comfort as could be mustered for such a subject. "I'm sure Connie will go in after he graduates, but maybe by the time they get him trained there won't be a war."

Hulda frowned.

"You never know," Thelma protested.

"I know Bud and Conrad will end up going off to war — it's inevitable."

"Maybe the war will end soon."

"I doubt it."

"Are you scared?"

"Concerned, not scared." Hulda let loose with the passion of a traveling tent preacher. "I've had a squaw chase me with a knife. I've had a bear follow me through the forest at night. I've had bears poke their noses in our cabin at night when I was a little girl, when we didn't have windows — just blankets covering the openings." Hulda's piercing gaze exuded resolve, not anger. "I'm not scared. I'm mad I can't control what's going to happen to my family. Concerned about what might happen to at least two of my boys."

A silence hovered over the mother and daughter, and both decided to let such silence carry away their thoughts.

•   •   •

Minot, North Dakota, did not hold any records for remoteness, but to Bud, it should have. When a Civilian Conservation Corps friend decided a weekend with friends in Williston was in order, Bud jumped at the offer to take the 125-mile trip. A day of digging potatoes at his camp was enough to make anyone want to flee.

After showers back at the barracks and with weekend passes in hand, the two young men hit the road, heading west on U.S. Highway 2, in time to arrive in the small town of 5,800 during the Friday night revelries of its young citizens. The town was much smaller than Minot's population of 17,000, but it was far from the hot July potato field. Bud and his new-found friend Stanley, in their borrowed 1938 Ford Coupe, pulled into the parking lot of the Williston, North Dakota, skating rink.

The sleek, rounded black car, with its fat white walls and unusual headlights — not quite round but not quite tear-drop — growled like a leopard ready to attack as it slid to a stop only a few feet from a small group of young people.

"Stanley!" a young lady called out, impressed by the car and happy to see him.

"Look who just blew in," one of the boys called out.

"Hiya, kids!" Stanley climbed out of the two-door as he greeted the group.

"How's the hard work? They turning you into a he-man?"

43

The group of seven was now nine, with four girls and five boys.

"Nah, I can't kick," Stanley answered Kendal, who was about to start a job with the railroad. "They're paying me, so everything's swell."

"Look at that. Stanley's rich. Look at that car!" Harold Hilb, who was usually called by his surname, laughed with a loud snort.

Seventeen-year-old Stanley laughed and shook his head. "No, that's not mine. I borrowed that from a friend. The CC's is pinching my jeans."

The group laughed again, but Chrissy's attention was focused elsewhere. The brunette eyed Bud as she questioned Stanley. "Aren't you gonna introduce us to your friend?"

Bud had only wandered as far as the front bumper.

"Oh. Sorry." Stanley looked at Bud, then gestured toward the group to carry his friend's attention from right to left. "This is June, Eddie, Sandy, Harold, Hazel, and Kendal." He paused as a wry grin enveloped him.

Chrissy glared at Stanley as she fought a smile from overtaking her. With an exaggerated display of disdain, the darkness hid her pretty blue Nordic eyes and the twinkle which floated Bud's way.

Stanley laughed a loud, hearty laugh. "And this fiery dame is Chrissy Anderson."

Bud's step toward her provided concealment for his moderate shyness around women. "Hello," he said with a gentle tone and smile.

Chrissy froze for a moment before blurting, "I envy the girl who gets you some day!"

44

The group laughed, except Bud and Chrissy. Embarrassment painted her cheeks red before she could finish her exclamation. She physically recoiled in horror at her boldness, taking a step away from her new acquaintance. Bud's smile eased her tension as he closed the added distance.

"I'm Bud Peterson, but you can call me Pete."

A side conversation broke out about the group's evening objectives, the amusing exhibition by Chrissy forgotten.

"We're here, let's go roller skating," Hazel posited.

"I was thinking we could head to The Orpheum," Hilb added.

"Or Zig Zags," June suggested.

"We just went there last weekend," Sandy argued with a mild tone.

"Same with the picture show," Kendal responded, referring to The Orpheum.

"Wait. I've got it." June's face lit up. "Ice cream."

Several responded with favorable exclamations. Ice cream it was, but neither Bud nor Chrissy noticed. There was enough light in the parking lot to allow him to look into her eyes. "You're a funny mix of bold and shy."

She dropped her head to hide the red glow trapped in her cheeks.

"It looks like we're going somewhere," June hollered at Chrissy, her best friend.

"Do you want to ride with us?" Stanley asked Bud.

"Chrissy and I are walking," Bud informed him, his eyes never leaving his new interest, a teasing smile pursuing her as he spoke. "I want to hear all about Chrissy."

The word spread they were walking, and soon the nine young people hiked through the parking lots of nearby establishments before crossing the somewhat busy street — somewhat busy for a town of such a small size.

"This is a nice town," Bud volunteered as they walked, his shyness evident.

"What? Williston? Well, aren't you a funny cuss!"

"Me? It's a nice big town that —"

"Big? Are you nuts?"

Bud chuckled. "I'm from a town of a couple hundred people. I — "

"Are you handing me a line? A couple hundred people?! How can you stand it? There's not enough to do here as it is."

He dropped his head in mock despair, though his blue eyes flirted with her the entire time. Before he could respond, her bubbly energy let loose again.

"I'm gonna call you 'Curly Top.' That's better than 'Bud' or 'Pete' or — what's your real name?"

"Eugene."

"Or 'Eugene.' I like 'Curly Top' for you."

A nervous laugh punched the warm night air as he searched for words.

"You don't like it?"

"It's fine," he laughed. "It's fine. Call me whatever you want. I'm fine with Curly Top."

Chrissy leaned her head into his shoulder as they walked, then pulled it away and looked up at him, smitten. "Oh, Pete. You're a swell catch. I'm not gonna lose you or have to throw you back, am I?"

The couple laughed as they lagged behind the group. The journey to the ice cream shop ended too soon for both of them.

Chapter Five

Hulda found work with an old friend outside of Minneapolis, acting as nanny to two little blonde girls, and received enough compensation to keep her there for many months. She took opportunities to return home as often as possible, mostly to check in on Conrad.

She stayed a few days with Thelma during this particular trip up north. Daughter Elsie and her husband, Jake Buzick, visited, with their daughters, four-year-old Joanne and one-year-old Judy, in tow. Conrad joined the rest of the family, which only lacked the presence of Bud and Carl and his family.

Conrad sat alone and watched. The girls played together — four-year-old Valrae and three-year-old Beverly — both Thelma's children — joined Elsie's daughter Joanne in a game of hide-and-seek, which took them outside, then back inside to hide. In the kitchen, Hulda sat at a table and listened to Ray — her son-in-law Ray Beckstrand — berate the owners of big businesses as Jake attempted to counter every verbal thrust his brother-in-law could make.

To calm Ray, and to establish a positive mood for the get-together, Thelma changed the subject. "Has anyone heard from Bud lately?"

"I got a letter from him the other day," Elsie volunteered.

"Still in North Dakota?"

"Yeah, but now he's thinking about joining the Navy. I guess he has some friend who tried talking him out of the Army," she continued. "He says it's pretty skinny going, with most of his paychecks sent home. He's got a girl in Williston now, and — "

48

"He's got a girl? That's great!" Excitement, and surprise, overcame Ray.

"Bud's a handsome young man," Thelma replied.

"Yeah, but he's so shy," Jake jumped in, knowing the subject as well as the others.

"Well, not shy. Reserved," Elsie corrected.

"Well, okay. Same thing, but okay," Jake laughed.

"It's that one," Hulda pointed in the general direction of her youngest son, Conrad, though she could not see him. "I'm concerned about. He's downright scared of girls."

"Why?" Thelma asked.

"I don't know. He's so danged shy it wrenches at your gut sometimes," Hulda added.

"Bud's not near as bad." Elsie wanted the subject to stay on Bud rather than politics. "He'll talk to girls."

"Bud hasn't dated much because he's always chasing jobs," Hulda explained. "Bud and Carl are a lot alike — they just don't talk much. But Connie..." Her voice trailed off.

Ray could not contain himself any longer; his wide grin had held back his words until now. "If those boys get in uniforms, they'll be fighting the girls off them. You know how women are."

"We do love a man in uniform," Elsie laughed.

"We have to get Connie married within the next few years." Thelma's evil grin caused laughter to erupt. "Get him married and have ten kids. That would open up his personality."

Hulda laughed as she countered her daughter. "No, it would do just the opposite. He'd go into a room somewhere and hide until everyone went to bed or the house quieted down."

49

"Then we'll find him a quiet girl." With a playful twinkle in her eye Thelma added, "Now who can we set him up with?"

"Harriet," Elsie piped in.

"Jo," Thelma added to the short list.

Hulda, recognizing the silliness of the conversation, shook her head and closed her eyes.

"Oh! What about — " Elsie stopped.

Conrad entered the kitchen without a sound. Thelma and Jake, with their backs to him, were startled when he spoke. His quiet voice and laconic delivery required the listener to catch every syllable.

"You people are nuts." With that, Conrad turned and marched back to his encampment on the couch, straight-faced the entire time. He resumed his quiet reflections and observations as Joanne ran by, desperation pervading the young girl's face as she fled her cousin.

Throughout the morning, the girls' energy burned off, the cooking became more frantic, the men migrated to the living room with Conrad, and only light banter preceded dinner. Every ten minutes, Conrad piped up with the question which concerned him more than any other: "How long until dinner, sis?" Every ten minutes the same answer was returned from Thelma: "Only a little while longer."

•   •   •

At long last — at least to Conrad — the family sat at a table, gathered for their midday dinner, ready to feast. A small, round table had been carried to the edge of the kitchen — it would not have fit in the kitchen itself due to the lack of space

— for the girls to sit, except Judy, who was stationed on her mother's lap.

Nobody moved until Thelma and Elsie put the last of the food onto the table. Then, as a pot of potatoes came to a rest, Ray instantly reached out, only to have his hand gently slapped by his wife. Ray returned a glare to Thelma's playful smile.

"We have to say grace," Hulda announced. "And since I wasn't allowed to cook today — "

"Except the apple pie," Thelma reminded everyone.

"I will do it," Hulda continued.

The rest of the family followed the matriarch's lead and bowed their heads.

"Dear Lord, we thank you for this wonderful food. Help us to remember times like this instead of times when we're hungry. Thank you for our country." She almost stopped, but then plowed forward. "And please keep our boys around the world safe. If I could be so selfish, I know I'll have boys overseas pretty soon, so please keep them safe." Hulda paused. Her voice had cracked at "I'll have boys overseas," but a resurgence of strength flowed through her. "And God, please keep everyone in this room safe from evil. Amen."

No one spoke. All eyes fixed on Hulda. The frequency of her premonitions — her bizarre gift or ability or whatever it was — baffled even her family. Was she having such a moment now? Or was she simply being a mother — a mother fearful of the future; fearful of what she was learning from the newspapers; fearful of how long they would be able to engage in these occasional large meals with plenty of food to go around?

51

After a long, quiet five seconds, Ray broke the silence. "Carl would hate this. Chicken. He told me he's sick of chicken."

Conrad only had one thought to add to the moment. "He's nuts, too."

• • •

One thing Carl knew with certainty: he had married a tough woman. Loving, sweet, and short-fused, Anne had a lot in common with her taciturn husband, minus the stubborn silence and the ever-present can of beer. She did not mind that Carl drank, just that he drank too much and too often. She was not wired to be as silent as her husband, either.

Besides toughness, one of the numerous qualities they shared was bluntness. Carl, ever to the point, began to lay out his case to his wife of three years. "Anne," he began, pausing only to be sure she was listening. "You know those letters I've exchanged with Uncle Hap?"

"Yeah. I've read them."

"Well, then you know they got jobs out there in California. I've told Hap I'm gonna join him in the shipyards."

"You mean move there?"

"Yeah, then send for you after I find a place."

"Carl!" She fell silent before she could protest more. Her heart wanted something her brain knew was not reasonable.

"Dammit, Anne. I don't want to go and leave you behind. But what am I supposed to do? Winter comes and you can't work around here unless you got the right job for winter work. Work's tough enough to come by as it is."

"Carla and I can go with you," Anne pleaded.

"And live how? In a crate behind a grocery market?"

Anne pressed her lips together, as though this would prevent her from speaking further.

"I'll get you out to California," he continued. "Just as soon as I can. It should work out after a couple of months."

"Are you gonna stay with Hap?"

"We haven't talked about it," Carl replied. "But I'm sure that's what we'll probably work out."

Tears welled up in the young woman's eyes. "If you do this, promise me you'll find a place quick."

"I will."

She grabbed both of his arms just above the elbows and applied pressure to communicate her sincerity. "Promise me!"

"I promise, Anne. What the hell you think I'd do? Sure, I'm gonna find something fast."

"What about Bud and Connie? Are they going?"

"No. Conrad's working on a farm and Bud's back in the CCs," Carl answered. "He went into the Navy and got out faster than you can say 'U-boat.'"

She squeezed him with her strong Danish arms, then stepped back so their faces could meet halfway as he bent down to reach his lips with hers. After a brief kiss, he pulled her back by the shoulders. "We'll figure this out, one way or another."

As Anne hurriedly left the kitchen and rushed past her two-year-old, little Carla did not understand the tears meant her daddy would be leaving when winter came.

•   •   •

Bud stared at the words, as though they were a bat which could flit away at any moment, into the darkened barracks, never to be seen again. "Love, Chrissy," awash in the incandescent light of the angle-head flashlight, stormed his memory to form a lasting, eternal impression. He turned off the borrowed flashlight — which was against the rules to use after the call of "lights out" — and rolled over in his bunk. He had read the letter three times in succession and could almost recite the six-page letter.

Bud recalled her descriptions, written on 9- x 5½-inch beige paper Chrissy undoubtedly "borrowed" from a sibling's school supplies, as he attempted to drift off to sleep. Stanley had been transferred to Baltimore, the Andersons were squabbling with a neighbor, and Chrissy had another of her recurring nightmares about Hitler bombing the Anderson house. To anyone else, the content of the letter was pedestrian, silly. To Bud, it was music — a symphony composed by Mozart for a full orchestra.

"Love, Chrissy."

They had previously expressed their love for each other, but each letter he read warmed his heart further, as though the inner groans of a budding love would burn his soul. He drifted toward sleep as he recalled prior letters — from the silly stories of home life with brothers and sisters to her embarrassment at her excited exclamation when they met in Williston.

The September 25, 1942, letter was her twelfth to him — yes, he was counting — and he had written only four fewer. He watched and read as she transformed, in a matter of months, from a sophomoric young girl into a more mature eighteen-year-old woman who was outgrowing her high school ways.

Bud's time on North Dakota farms meant back-breaking work, usually from sun-up until sundown. Free meals of bland food and free board of austere living quarters and thin, worthless mattresses seemed to be part of the job description. The pay was the same as when he first entered the Civilian Conservation Corps: twenty-five dollars a month for his mother and five for himself. It was work. It was respectable. It was exhausting with little hope cast on the future — especially with a war going on.

Freed from the Navy, which did not agree with him at all, after sixteen days and back to working like an ox, he did not know at this moment whether he would be happy. His relatively light troubles, physical soreness, and tired bones all felt a little easier to bear when he thought of Chrissy or received another letter. Sleep greeted the tired but smitten young man in only a matter of minutes, and he slipped from consciousness with the knowledge he would be seeing her in a matter of weeks; but, nothing could top "Love, Chrissy."

Chapter Six

The German war machine powered on — until the winter of 1942. As the temperature dropped in advance of winter, October brought the beginning of the "beginning of the end" for the Nazis' brand of terror.

Having nearly ended the war with the Battle of Britain, Adolf Hitler's hubris got the best of him. Everything of which he dreamed had been achieved: German unity; dominance in most of Europe; and god-like domestic powers which saw him praised and loved by most of the German citizenry, including fawning women who wrote loving letters of adulation.

Hitler possessed a fiery hatred for communism but, out of practicality, entered into the Molotov-Ribbentrop non-aggression pact with the Soviets. Then, with satisfaction flooding his iron heart and a callous, heinous desire to control those nipping at his heels, he ordered his generals to open a second front, in the east. Nineteen-Forty's plans became 1941's aggression in the form of Operation Barbarossa, which became 1942's quagmire in Russia.

The Wehrmacht was ready by July of 1942 — or so the Führer believed. His sights were set on the city which had its name changed to honor the current dictator of the Soviet Union.

By believing he knew more than his generals, Hitler ensured his own failure. The Battle of Stalingrad — urban warfare at its most brutal — was underway. The winter of 1942-43 proved unkind to Germans and Russians alike, but most Russians had access to food. The Germans were captured or killed by the tens of thousands.

The once-mighty Wehrmacht began its decline. The arrogance which propelled a tyrant into power served to destroy the same creature.

Had they defeated the British, German domination in Europe arguably would have gone unchallenged. The United States was not ready to send massive numbers of troops to Europe in 1941, but by late 1943, the American economy had ramped up to produce enough war materiel for sustained warfare on two fronts.

Germany, however, could not sustain a war on two fronts; thus, the incursion into Russia represented a calamitous mistake. When the Battle of Stalingrad finally ended in German defeat in February 1943, it was the marker for the beginning of the end of the Third Reich. The trouble was, no one knew that at the time, and the Germans, including its citizens, were far from willing to relent. The war continued.

Meanwhile, World War I flying ace and Hitler's head of the Luftwaffe, Hermann Göring, spent portions of the war advancing through Europe, in search of coveted, expensive artwork. Reichsführer Göring, number two in command of Nazi Germany and one of the top tormentors of Jews, in time lost his boss' ferocity to a lavish, luxurious lifestyle. Göring did not lose his wickedness, just the zeal to be wicked. Food, wine, and art came easily; planning battles and committing genocide took more effort than he was ready to expend. Thus, Hitler stood alone, in firm control of the military.

The Second Battle of El Alamein had begun in August of 1942. It was a fight to allow the Allies to maintain control of the Suez Canal, which facilitated man and machine to flow freely from the Mediterranean Sea to eastern Africa and the

Indian Ocean, and vice versa. In the months ahead, the much-lauded General Erwin Rommel would be defeated by British General Bernard Montgomery.

The Sudetenland, Poland, and even France were just memories, dangling like medals in the collective Nazi memory. Germany had conquered so much, yet the signs were visible for anyone able to read them. After a violent, genocidal rise throughout the 1930s, the 1940s Nazis were beginning to falter — and the first significant misstep was Stalingrad.

By October 1942, John Wayne's first war film, "The Flying Tigers" hit theaters, and American boys wanted to fly rather than fight on the ground. Five days later, the Germans tested their first V-2 rocket. The war was changing, and so was warfare itself.

•　　•　　•

Bud stepped off the train not knowing whether Chrissy and June would be waiting. When he spotted her running toward him, like a young girl lost in a large department store as she finds her mother, Bud knew what he had. From their recent letter exchanges to the memories played over and over in his mind — of every second he could remember when they were first together in Williston and her brief visit to Minot — and from the feeling he had in his chest and stomach, he knew that he and Chrissy were destined to be together. He could feel it.

"Oh, darling!" Her squeeze suffocated him for a brief moment, but he did not mind — it was a good kind of suffocation.

A wide, gentle smile was followed by a tender tone. "I've missed you, honey."

"Oh!" Tears welled up in her eyes. "I've missed you, too!" She squeezed him again, just to ensure she did not forget the feeling.

"Hi, June," Bud offered with a shy, almost embarrassed grin as Chrissy pulled away, swung herself around, and held Bud's left arm with a firm grasp.

"Pete, it's good to see you," the young woman laughed as she glanced at Chrissy. "You'll have to excuse Chrissy. I don't think she slept a wink last night knowing you were coming."

Chrissy stomped her foot. "Junie! I told you not to tell him that!"

June laughed as the threesome walked through a small crowd of people toward a car.

Bud eyed the car with a questioning look.

"My dad said I could borrow it to come pick you up." She put her hands out as though she wanted to sell it to him. "You'll be staying with Hilb, but I told him I wanted to pick you up."

"Okay."

"He's not as impressed about you borrowing your daddy's car, Chrissy," June said with a mocking tone.

"Oh, come now."

"I like it," Bud had to beg to stay out of trouble. "I do. It's just that, well. I came to see you, Chrissy. I don't care if you came on a horse."

The three laughed as they climbed into the red 1934 Packard. The vehicle looked like something used in Chicago to carry gangsters to hits, only this Packard showed not bullet holes, rather signs of harsh wear bordering on dilapidation.

Billed as "America's most distinctive car," this two-seater was indeed distinctive in little Williston, but the luster had been long-since scraped off by rough roads hiding craters-more-than-potholes and driving practices which brought to mind Barney Oldfield more than family usage. The three young people squeezed onto the bench seat and Chrissy led them on a precarious journey for such a short drive, nearly causing two accidents on the way.

"I may not make it into the Army," Bud quipped.

Chrissy looked at him as she made a turn onto a neighborhood street, her bizarre smile looked more like she was ready for a fight than a weekend with her boyfriend.

"Uh, Chrissy!" June struggled to slip the three syllables from her mouth.

Chrissy cast a long, loving look at her boyfriend.

"Maybe you should watch the road," Bud said, a calmness dominating his voice. He nodded as he spoke, as though he could reinforce his words with the movement.

Chrissy jerked the wheel to miss an oncoming 1940 Ford. The car's black paint highlighted the headlights and grill, while the almost-pointed end of the hood gave the appearance of a bulbous nose sitting between the eyes of the headlights, the grill a monster's mouth. As Chrissy turned the car hard right, the metallic face of the Ford grew larger still.

Bud observed Chrissy's demeanor: she looked calm and wanted to project confidence and control, but a quick upward exhalation that lifted the hair on her forehead belied her true feelings. "Are we there yet?" Bud laughed as he teased her.

Before she answered, she swung the car for another hard right, this time landing them on the Anderson driveway.

"Let's not jangle about this. We're here." Chrissy nodded her head to add emphasis.

"Oh boy," June shook her head as she opened the passenger door.

Bud smiled and gave his head a slow, almost taunting shake to and fro.

"We're here," Chrissy stated again, this time without the emotion, adrenaline having lost some of its power.

• • •

The tall, wild Dakota grass had given way to the Williston climate many weeks prior, laying down to allow visitors to tread on top of a flattened sea of hay. Clumps of tall Cottonwoods, along with clusters of American Elm, littered the landscape and provided a layer of privacy for anyone who walked along the river's shore. A secondary wall of privacy presented itself in the form of an embankment as the river had cut deep into the soil over time. A relative tameness hung over the muscular Missouri River, energized by the injection of the Yellowstone River only twenty miles to the west. Four miles to the west, the Little Muddy River, a winding, twisted mess of a river just upstream from the confluence, released its volume into the mighty Missouri east of town, which at this location was building up to attain its "mighty" title.

Widening out at a bend, the Missouri reached over a mile across, but the low water level exposed large sand bars. Its width would once again become immeasurable next Spring, when the snow melted and the area flooded.

A large, yellow blanket covered a small section of a narrow strip of sand that only four months prior had rested under more than ten feet of water. The river rushed by, but without the occasional flexing of its natural power. The last flooding did its usual damage, and the townspeople dwelling nearby dried out, continued farming and living, and went about their business until the next time the banks overflowed.

Young Chrissy occupied the middle of the blanket, eschewing physical in favor of emotional comfort by maintaining contact with her suitor. Gone were her feisty demeanor and saucy attitude. The eighteen-year-old was maturing at an impressive rate — Bud could see it in her letters, hear it in her voice, feel it in her touch.

The loveliness of the moment, of the solitude, rocked — almost shook — toward a precarious position of imbalance. It started with a simple sentence from Bud. "I'm going to join the Army."

She pulled back her head. Her light eyes narrowed with pain. Her body stiffened. She wanted to let loose the torrent of words which dominated her mind, but she held her emotions firmly, like a stagecoach rider attempting to control runaway horses.

"It's something I need to do."

"Okay." Her voice conveyed not only concern, but the need for more information. "I knew you would. Everyone else is either going into the Army or Navy — you're doing both."

Chrissy chuckled at her own words but Bud maintained his serious tone and countenance.

"Look, Chrissy. I don't want to be away from you. I really don't. But the fact is, I'm scraping by in the CCs, I have no area of expertise because I can't get a job. I'm only doing work that's back-breaking, not skilled work." He paused to control his own emotions. "Nobody will hire able-bodied men my age because they figure we'll get drafted. And this five dollars a month ain't gettin' it done." He added another thought. "I'm working out in the fields sixteen hours a day sometimes. I hope I never see wheat again. I can't be a farmhand my whole life."

Chrissy closed her eyes. When she opened them, she struck a positive chord. "I heard you mention the Army when I picked you up from the train station. I was just hoping you were kidding."

Bud understood the roles were reversed; he was being emotional while she remained strong.

"*You* can get a job easier than me. You're not going to be drafted," he added. His emphasis on the first word verbalized the frustrations faced by young men across the country.

Tears filled her blue eyes as the whites turned red. She wiped away a tear with a finger just as he leaned in to kiss her. Crying, and speaking, ceased.

• • •

"I'll wait for you. I mean it."

Tears welled up in Chrissy's eyes. "I'll wait for you. It's only you. I promise."

"I know." Bud paused as he watched a piece of driftwood float by. "No question about it."

63

The Sun lowered, almost to the horizon as the yellow ball turned to orange, its brightness dimming while the inhabitants of Williston prepared for nightfall. A light breeze picked up on occasion, lifting Chrissy's light-brown hair for a brief moment, then dropping it back into place.

"We can stay as long as you like."

"No. We should go. I'm hungry." Chrissy stared into his eyes. Her expression gave the impression she might melt at any moment, becoming a liquid, Nordic version of herself, unable to move without Bud's help.

He met the expression with a smile. They stared into each other's eyes, thinking, absorbing, feeling. They also had no doubt who would break the silence.

"I feel alive," she cooed, her voice as soft and sweet as he had ever heard it. "How do we keep moments like this from ending?"

"Keep it in your heart, locked away but close to your thoughts." He winked, then smiled. "It will always be there. We'll always remember our times together because they mean so much."

A deep breath lifted her shoulders and head. "When will I see you next?"

"I don't know. The Army says because of the CCs I have to wait to be drafted. I'm not putting up with that."

She laughed with a small quake of her chest and shoulders. "My Pete is gonna make the Army take him, huh?"

"Aw, I don't know." He shook his head.

"But why will the Army take you but the Navy spit you out?"

64

"I guess I needed my knee in the Navy," Bud said with a chuckle. "The recruiter I talked to said my knee's not too bad for them. Go figure."

"What happened to your knee?"

"When I was a kid, we had a dog that ran into me real hard. We were playing and the collision tore up my knee pretty good. It's never been the same and I have to be careful with it."

"Don't they do a lot of marching in the Army?"

"Jeepers, I couldn't believe the timing. It only flares up occasionally, and it just happened to be at the wrong time, in the Navy." He paused as his train of thought jumped the tracks. "It's just as well; the Navy wasn't my kind of place."

"I hope you don't have to do a lot of marching with a bum knee."

"I'm wanting to go into tanks. I read a magazine article about that General Patton character. He knows how to get things done."

Sadness enveloped Chrissy's countenance, her eyes lost their sparkle and her lips sagged at the corners. After a few seconds of dwelling on the negative, a new thought reflected in her eyes. "Come on, Pete." She jumped to her feet. "Let's go find a place to eat."

Bud understood the need for a mood change and grabbed the blanket as he stood.

"Tanks, huh?" They strolled across the flattened tall grass. "You gonna shoot Krauts or Japs?"

"I don't care. I just need a job that pays better and I learn some skills."

The mood reflected by their love was over — for now. The love birds understood what they had in one another. Now, patience was required — and inner strength.

Chapter Seven

Bud would have shaken his head in amazement had he worked alongside Conrad on the railroad. Not only was the skinny kid adding muscle to his slight frame, he was working hard. On his way to six-feet tall, the five-feet, eleven-inch youngest Peterson had never reached 140 pounds until now. Fifty cents an hour meant he earned in a day what Bud earned in a month, not counting the money which went to their mother.

Whereas, according to government regulations for Civilian Conservation Corps guidelines, Bud was only allowed $5 of his $30-a-month salary, Conrad's private sector earnings pocketed him over $100 a month — minus Uncle Sam's 19% cut — and he vowed to make the most of the brief time before he received his military status designation.

"Peterson! Over here!" The railroad foreman's voice cut like that of a drill sergeant. "I need someone who knows what he's doing! Over here!" Every word gushed of urgency, even when no importance existed. The barrel-chested, blonde-haired dragoon stood at only five-feet, six-inches tall, but his explosive energy — and temper — added another foot to his aura.

"Yes, sir. Coming." Conrad marched with haste, hand-sledge dangling from his left hand.

The foreman eyed Conrad and forced back a smile. The eighteen-year-old who was skinny as a rail was working on railroad tracks; a certain irony existed between Conrad's personification of the expression and his job. "Look at this, Peterson." The fierce man pointed toward a sixteen-year-old boy operating a crane attached atop a flatcar. "That boy," he swept his hand in a dramatic arc toward a nearby flatcar. "Can't load straight. Look at that! Look at that crooked pile!"

"That crooked pile" was a leaning stack of 60-feet-long track sections, complete with both rails and the ties linking the two. The crane operator, on a car on the secondary track, lifted the section being replaced from the rail bed and deposited it in a neat pile, on a flatcar, to be shipped away. The crane then pivoted to another car, lifted a new, replacement section, and placed it on the rail bed.

"Peterson!" the foreman barked. "You think you can do a better job than Amundsen?"

"Uh. Yes, sir. I can."

"Good! Do it!" The stout man turned to the young Amundsen. "It looks like you'll be down here, putting in the fish plates for the new sections!"

"Okay, sir. Be right there." The youngster climbed the short distance to the ground.

"Mister! Anymore screw-ups from you and you'll be in one of them handout lines!"

"Sorry." Conrad could not help himself. He felt the need to apologize to the skinny sixteen-year-old as the boy passed him and replied with a frown.

"Peterson, stack those right, then we'll be able to move on to the next section."

"Yes, sir."

Laying rails was not "make-work" on the part of the railroad company — they could not afford such a luxury. Replacement became necessary over time because of wear and tear, particularly on lines supporting passenger trains. Today's rough ride could be tomorrow's derailment, but with Conrad's paychecks rolling in, he would not mind if they replaced every inch of rail in Beltrami County.

Each evening, when he returned to Elsie's house, he tried not to count his earnings before receiving his paycheck; but, he knew, with a little wisdom, the money could add up handsomely. If only it would last.

•　　•　　•

Bud stepped down from the blue, 1937 Super Coach emblazoned with a white swath from front to back and a white image of a striding dog. "GREYHOUND LINES" identified the company for anyone who for some mysterious reason failed to recognize the logo.

While not one of the newer models — those were used on busier routes around the nation — the bus felt comfortable enough for Bud.

He had worked for several weeks in the fields after his visit with Chrissy when the Civilian Conservation Corps told him to go home. After visiting with his family in Bemidji, he decided to return to the one person who kept North Dakota on his mind.

"Hello, Pete." Ernestine's curly brown hair bounced as she stepped toward Bud and wrapped him in a quick, friendly squeeze. Four additional people exited the bus behind him, and within minutes the bus would pull away, bound for Billings, Montana.

"Hi ya, Ernie!" Bud smiled at the sight of Chrissy's older sister. The only luggage he carried was a small bag with his clothing inside.

"Chrissy couldn't make it, so we're going to drop in on her at Andy's," she explained, referring to the local bakery.

"Suits me fine."

"I'm afraid it may be a little noisy for you at our house," she chuckled. "D.K. and Cubby are little balls of energy," she said, referring to her two- and six-year-old boys. "Emily's quiet, but not her brothers."

"That's what boys do, I guess."

"Yes, and little Covertt certainly takes after his daddy."

"Don't you worry about noise," Bud reassured her. "I grew up with two sisters and two brothers."

"Oh, that's right. You grew up in a small family. That must've been nice."

Bud eyed her in an attempt to determine whether she was trying to be funny.

"If you're okay with noise," she continued. "You'll be okay in a house with two small boys."

Bud wanted to inquire about Chrissy but feared his questions would come across as seeming paranoid, so he fought off the urge. After a nine-hour bus ride, including a stop in Fargo, he could wait a few more minutes to learn how his girlfriend was handling the long-distance relationship.

The couple had shared their feelings for each other in writing and in person. Nevertheless, Bud understood the effects of time and distance. While he knew their separation caused them to predominately remember each other's good qualities over the bad, he also knew she could meet someone else, just as she had expressed the same fear about him.

Bud realized he could make the relationship work, just as she could; however, with the indefinite time element introduced by The War, his heart at times felt as though it were being eaten away from the inside when he could only look at her photograph or re-read her letters.

As the car traveled the streets of Williston and Ernie continued with her small talk, Bud continued to focus on what he needed to do in order to guarantee the success of their relationship. His heart rate increased, his stomach knotted, and his muscles tightened as tension overcame him until his chest hurt.

•　　•　　•

The piercing scream made Bud feel embarrassed but satisfied. Chrissy's high-pitched cry of excitement, followed by the shout of "Pete!" brought with it public attention, which he loathed. On the other hand, he felt good knowing the moment was an exhibition of her true feelings. Of course, there were only two patrons in Andy's Bakery at the moment, so he was not embarrassed beyond recovery.

"Oh, Pete!" She ran around the counter, leaving a customer in front of the register. "Pete!" she cried again. "I've got you now," she let out as she wrapped him in a strong bear-like hug.

After a long kiss, she bounced across the small store and back to her position behind the counter, where she had been ringing up Mrs. Nelson before her eruption.

"I'll be right with you, honey," Chrissy said with a giggle to her boyfriend. Her attention turned to her customer, who appeared to be approximately sixty years old. "I'm sorry, Mrs.

Nelson. I just get so darned excited when my Pete comes to town!"

The older woman smiled. "I was young once. I understand." She looked over at Bud before turning back to Chrissy. "And he's a cutie."

"I know. Ain't he swell?!" Another emotional eruption appeared to be mere moments away. "And he has a brother — in case you have a granddaughter!"

Mrs. Nelson laughed as she took her bag of blueberry muffins and strode away.

With a look of embarrassment, Bud nodded to the customer as she left the shop.

"You're off the cob," Bud teased.

"I'm only goofy for you!" she responded with renewed energy.

Bud shook his head and attempted to conceal his laugh.

"Two whole weeks! I've got you two whole weeks!"

"And I'm gonna kick up my feet and relax."

"Ha, ha, ha. Fat chance of that happening, wise guy!"

The mild case of trepidation which Bud felt on the ride over to Andy's Bakery was long-since forgotten. Her feelings for him had not subsided — nor had his own for her.

•   •   •

The outdoor rink became an instant success each winter, with the only annual question being on what date it would open. In late November of 1942, the rink had been an attraction for the locals for barely a week. With daily temperatures struggling to reach 25 degrees, northerners found sunny days and windless evenings ideal for outdoor activities.

Bud and Chrissy glided around the ice at a casual pace and released hands only when a group of four boys skated near them during a game of tag, or they caught up with a middle-aged couple who exhibited lesser skills than the other two dozen people on the ice.

The Sun floated in the southern sky despite the one o'clock hour, its rays striking northern North America at a steep angle. The still air allowed Chrissy to keep her gloves in her pocket. Despite the lack of clouds, the Sun was not the brightest object visible — that distinction belonged to the faces of the young couple as they circled the ice.

"I've been here two days and it feels like it's going fast."

"I was just thinking the same thing," Chrissy agreed, the pain evident in her voice.

They skated in silence as they retreated to their separate thoughts.

"This makes the Army look like it's for sure."

"What does?"

"I've gone to six different places while you were working, trying to find a job."

"Six? I knew four. Wow."

"Yep. Six. Five of them listened to me talk, then asked my designation."

"First thing?"

"Not even asking me about my skills. As soon as I said '1-A,' that was the end of every conversation." Bud paused to grimace. "Then they'd say 'Well, I'm sorry,' and that was that. Every time."

"How awful!" Chrissy could not hold back her emotions. "People are acting as if the unemployment rate was zero!"

"Well, I guess they don't want to take time to train someone, then they're gone six months later."

Chrissy fell silent as the pair completed another circuit of the ice. She pulled him toward the side, where she leaned against the half wall. The wood-framed, three-feet-tall wall had been painted white all the way around the 200-feet-long ice rink, with the 2x4s covered by wood planks to provide a solid barrier.

"Why'd you stop?" Bud asked as he brought himself to a stop next to her and leaned against the short wall.

"I'm just mad," she stated with an even tone. "What's wrong with these people? I want to give them a piece of my mind."

Bud placed his hand on Chrissy's shoulder, on top of her jacket. "They're doing what's right for them, I guess." By his tone, she knew he was attempting to comfort her, but it did not work.

"I knew of four places. Where else did you go?"

"I went to a repair shop on Main. I don't remember the name of it."

"That would be a great place for you."

"I know. I did a lot of fixing things on the farm."

"What was the other place?"

"Oh, I don't remember the name of it, either," Bud confessed. "It was a little business, just starting out, that builds homes. They're thinking after the war there will be a lot of houses to build, but not yet." He paused. His face telegraphed he was deep in thought, but in three seconds he snapped out of it. "They said they got enough people for now. They seemed interested in me, even after mentioning '1-A,' so they at least told me stuff about their company."

Chrissy grabbed Bud's hand and they returned to making circuits around the rink. The four boys had grown tired of chasing each other, and a quiet blanket seemed to nestle over the young lovers. With only a dozen people skating, the two felt a cozy warmth overtake them.

"If I could find a job here I'd stay." He looked into her eyes as he continued. "But with my '1-A' it's not going to happen."

She squeezed his hand. "Honey, don't feel pressured. We said we'd wait for the war to end if we had to."

"I know," Bud said, his dejection obvious. "I'm sure I'll like the Army better than the Navy — I don't see how Stanley likes it so much."

Chrissy laughed. "He's a different one."

"Yeah. Good guy. Just the Navy wasn't for me."

Chrissy narrowed her eyes; then, as she was prone to do, blurted out her feelings. "Pete, you're just too practical! If you weren't so darned practical, we could solve this." Tears welled up in her eyes; one made its way down her face as she listened to Bud's response.

"Sweetheart, we've talked about that. We can't — "

"I know!"

" — just go run off and get married, then I go in the Army."

"I know."

"I mean, what if I don't make it home? Then you're an eighteen-year-old widow." He paused, taking in the meaning of his own words. "And that's just not right."

Her thin upper lip curled upward as she fought off additional tears. She released her grip and wiped her eyes with both hands. When at least some of the moisture had been swept from her face, she skated into Bud's side and thrust an arm around his waist. "You're right." She believed her words with her brain, but not with her heart.

Bud nodded with a response she never saw as the couple skated in silent circles. Through hand squeezes, smiles, and sweet glances, they both knew what the other was thinking, for the thoughts were the same with both of them.

Chapter Eight

Southwest of Minneapolis seemed like an odd location for an English-style country estate. The magnificent two-story brick structure, designed by an Englishman, rose up like a beautiful yet monstrous oasis in the middle of farming country and innumerable lakes which dotted the region.

The oversized white-framed windows, nearly floor to ceiling on the first floor and five-feet-tall on the second, added a touch of uniformity while the off-white Greek columns in the center of the front elevation stood like an exaltation of the past. The red roof and four tall brick chimneys, spaced evenly to form a square, reached heavenward, giving an onlooker the feel one was witnessing a display of power.

Trees of all sorts — native and otherwise — peppered the landscape. In some places, clumps of trees gave a natural feel, while other areas sported symmetrical spacing of bushes and trees alike, reminding a visitor of legalistic order.

The vast, vibrant green lawn had browned as Old Man Winter approached, yet the sea of dead grass captured the majestic property's essence as it flowed to the lake shore 300 yards from the main house. Sadness enveloped the owners every year when the emerald faded, but Minnesota life would allow no other fate for the lawn.

Snow from the smaller storms which hit in late October and November had melted long ago; but, the dry break would end soon, with reports of winter weather approaching.

Two acres of land to the east was devoted to the rows of apple trees which produced another source of income. The charming orchard became a favorite for the local children to use as a playground for games of tag when the pickers were not present.

The lake itself formed the southern edge of the 400-acre estate. Beyond the cultured turf and multiple brick out-buildings, across the paved driveway and down a slight embankment, an immense, empty field recalled the hundreds of thousands of soybean plants which, along with other crops, had become a lucrative source of income for the former New York banker.

Henry Koch — pronounced 'cook,' the 'right way,' he would tell people who tried to pronounce his name phonetically — had a complicated family tree which had roots in Germany and Austria, with Sweden, Finland, and Ukraine mixed in. After a successful career in New York City, as the financial capital of the world shifted from London to the Big Apple during World War I, Koch retired at a relatively young age, not wanting to join colleagues in the local cemeteries as the result of a heart attack or sclerosis of the liver. After making his way back to his home state, he decided it was time to marry, start a family, and pursue his love of oil painting.

He was raised as a proud American and lacked pride in his German heritage. His well-educated Swedish mother bequeathed to him a love of high society, British architecture, and Renaissance art.

Others performed the laborious work — in the soybean fields, pampering his cars, and caring for his lawn — while he managed his estate and spent his free time painting works of art which would achieve neither acclaim nor value.

Through the friend of a friend, Koch made the acquaintance of a single mother desperate to provide for herself and her growing family of sons- and daughters-in-law and grandchildren. Hulda had but one child left who lived at home, but even that arrangement had changed, for Conrad lived with his sister Elsie for his final year at Bemidji High School and remained since graduation. Nevertheless, Hulda needed more money on which to survive and pounced on the opportunity to make "some good money," as she put it.

Caring for the Koch children and handling laundry and kitchen duties proved to be a bigger pleasure than anticipated. Her youngest was an eighteen-year-old church mouse, so quiet was he. The two Koch children, with their loud shrieks of joy and anger, energy unmatched by any humans Hulda had seen, and vulnerable tenderness laced with interminable mischief gave her a new sense of purpose and energy, and change from the stresses of post-1929 life.

In time, she would leave this temporary job and return to her family for more than the occasional weekend visit; but for now, the work she performed felt more like a vacation from the stresses of reality.

Hulda sat in a tea room with Mrs. Koch. The olive-skinned, elegant woman, with her dark hair and eyes and a nose which pointed upward with a slight bend at the tip, looked the part of New York City royalty visiting a British manor. Somehow, she indeed was a visitor once she stepped off the manor, even though she felt at home on the estate.

Emilia, always in a dress — a grey one to match this day's sky — turned heads wherever she went, be it the social circles in Minneapolis or dead-heading her roses below her bedroom window. Smart but delicate, she lacked the wisdom, resolve, and self-assuredness Hulda possessed, which caused the two to grow fascinated by one another; they were each other's opposites in many ways.

"Oh, they all turned out well." Hulda answered her host, then took a sip of coffee.

"You're sure proud of them," Emilia offered as she placed her cup of tea on the table next to her.

Hulda shifted in her chair, as if to show discomfort. The high back held an unusual allure to her, having never owned such a piece of furniture, as was the case with most of the furniture in the house. "Proud of them? Oh, for sure."

"Yet you never speak of them much, especially your frustrations."

"I don't believe in talking bad about people — especially my own family."

"Oh, I would never dream of asking you to speak ill of your family."

Hulda paused, as though pondering the lady's words, before responding. "I believe you, but if I talk about my son Eugene," she began as she referenced Bud. "And I tell you how he's doing, then I might just start talking about all the things that worry me. Same with all my kids."

"From what I have heard, it sounds as though you raised them well." Emilia grew curious about the worries of a mother of older children since she would be in that place years from now.

"Oh, they all turned out well." She paused as she thought through her sentences before giving them life. "It's the finances and the war that've got me worried."

"Is there anything Henry and I can do?" The noble lady of the house conveyed her concern.

"You already are doing something. You're giving me a job."

"But I mean, can we — "

"No." Hulda interrupted. She did not like where the conversation was headed. There would not be talk of handouts. "No, thank you. We are slowly getting better." She struggled to soften her tone as a display of atonement for the sudden burst of sobriety and insolence. "I'm sorry I interrupted you, but things are improving."

"How so?" Emilia's positive attitude remained.

"My oldest daughter is married with children. They're doing pretty well. Her husband has a job with the railroad and they grow some of their own food, so that helps." She paused as she again pondered her words before delivering them. "My oldest son is married with a daughter and one on the way, and he's leaving for California any day to get a job working with my brother."

"It's so tough on our young men these days, what with the war and businesses not hiring them because of their classification."

"Yes. Exactly." Hulda paused to allow a smoother segue. "My other daughter is married and has children, and her husband has a job and is fine. Then there's my two youngest — sons."

Emilia's dark eyes dropped a little as she waited for the bad news.

"Eugene is twenty and can't find anything other than odd jobs. He's '1-A' and tired of waiting, so he says he's enlisting. At least, that's what he was talking about in his last letter." Hulda's cheery countenance faded as she considered Bud's dilemma. "He'll be all right. I always tell him he's brighter than he gives himself credit for."

When silence invaded the room, the lady of the house appeared to detest its presence. She felt empathy for the nanny of her children and wanted to hear her story. "And the youngest?"

Hulda smiled. Her countenance brightened and her eyes sprang to life. "Conrad." She let out a chuckle. "Conrad is a darling of a young man. He is the kindest soul, but he's so shy it's comical." She let out a larger laugh.

Emilia shared the chortle.

"My sons are good men, but Conrad is just so funny. He's been working since he was in high school, and he hasn't gotten a classification yet, so he's making money and doesn't spend too much of it, so he's fine."

"Will he be 1-A?"

"Oh, yeah. He will."

Emilia's face fell again. "I'm sorry to hear that."

"If my oldest son had his way, he'd already be in the Army."

"So, you could wind up with three sons going to war," the younger woman deduced.

"Two. The oldest has real bad knees." Hulda paused. "I think it's more of 'will' instead of 'could.'" Hulda's flat statement betrayed her lack of enthusiasm about the subject.

"Maybe they won't have combat roles," Emilia said with hope.

"All I can do is hope and pray. It's in God's hands."

Emilia nodded, unsure of how to react to the worried mother's predicament. Hulda raised her boys to be men, but the downside of what men must do weighed on her heart.

Hulda found an opportunity to return to her duties after the conversation devolved into small talk. She left the tea room grateful for Mrs. Koch's gentle and compassionate manner, but returned to work happy to no longer talk about what troubled her.

•   •   •

The school gymnasium proved the perfect location for the class teacher, even though she did not maintain a connection with the school. Countless large windows covered the 1920s-era brick building. The wood floor reached from end to end. Multiple banners hanging from the high ceilings decorated the small gym. The two basketball backboards hung so close to the wall an out-of-bounds area barely existed on either end. A red banner on the wall contained the lyrics to the school's fight song, along with a cartoonish drawing of a coyote, the school's mascot, with its tongue hanging out.

Tchaikovsky's "Waltz of the Flowers" filled every square inch of the gymnasium with a volume low enough so the high-pitched, Austrian accent could be heard by everyone. "Mrs. J," as they called Mrs. Jakobiec — no one could pronounce her name — overcame her high-pitched voice through snappy, terse directions. She marched around the basketball court as she counted.

"And one, two, three. And one, two, three. Young man, you are to lead the lady," she interrupted herself. "She is a lady.

You are the gentleman. Lead! And one, two, three. And one, two, three."

She eyed all eight couples in one visual sweep. "Beautiful! Beautiful, everyone! And one, two, three."

Bud looked into Chrissy's eyes the entire time. The blue-eyed couple seemed to float across the hardwood as they stayed in time with the others, yet they were in their own sweet world. With his right hand in the middle of her back and left hand holding her right hand, Bud's movements became increasingly effortless as the classical piece progressed.

"Very good!" Chrissy whispered.

A grin stretched across his face and announced his pride, but his words interrupted his concentration. "I haven't stumbled in — oops. Never mind."

Chrissy giggled.

"Come on, people. This requires you to focus," the accented lady bellowed as best she could with her screeching voice.

Bud sighed, shook his head like an irritated bull, then set his feet in motion in time with the music once again.

"And one, two, three. And one, two, three."

Chrissy fought off a laugh. For a brief moment, her left hand slid off his right shoulder and onto his triceps before she regained her composure and restored the proper position.

"It's been one hour, ladies and gentlemen," Mrs. Jakobiec announced. "You are doing quite well. You should be impressed with yourselves."

Bud flashed an expression of, "Look at us."

"You are not expert — that takes much work. But you are waltzing. Be happy you are waltzing after one hour."

As Chrissy stared into Bud's eyes, he blew her a playful kiss. Caught off guard, she laughed and stumbled for a brief second, but it was enough to throw off their timing.

"Aaa! That was your fault," she laughed, quiet enough to not be detected by their teacher.

Mrs. Jakobiec did not miss anything; she let out an immediate, stern count to drive home the point to Bud and Chrissy about focus. "And one, two, three! And one, two, three!" Her attention swung to another couple, which caused her to shout another shrill direction. "Gentlemen, do not forget this is a box step. Box step! You must make boxes! You can learn to slowly spin later. You are new. You are beginners!"

• • •

Twenty-year-old Bud and eighteen-year-old Chrissy bellowed with hearty laughs as they left the gymnasium. Small flakes fell onto their caps and coats as they agreed with each other about how much fun they had just experienced.

"And you thought your knee would hurt. You big baby!"

"Baby?! Who screamed when she almost fell to the floor?!"

"Listen to me, mister." She stopped walking and seized his arm, causing him to spin around to face her. She grabbed his coat with both hands and pulled. He dutifully complied and allowed his body to be thrust toward hers. He leaned down and touched his nose to hers.

"Mmm. This has been a fun day."

"A great day!" she agreed.

Bud moved his lips to hers. They stood, pressed together, in the middle of the parking lot — snow falling on and around them, a light wind pressing against Bud's back. Two different couples walking to their cars glanced at them, but Bud and Chrissy never knew of their brief audience. Mrs. Jakobiec had harangued Bud into focusing better; his focus now only lacked a count to three as time stood still.

•　　•　　•

"Why is there always a bus or train to take you away from me?"

Bud's only reply was a smile. His tall stack of curly hair tilted forward; his bright blue eyes shined brighter; his wide smile grew.

"What?" Chrissy giggled.

"I'm just watching your face, your eyes."

A blast of Arctic air kept the couple indoors. Chrissy's sister Ernestine ambled around upstairs, occasionally descended the stairs to add additional clothes to the stack about to be laundered, or discovered another item — such as the ash tray she carried on her last trip — broken by one of the children. Even though little D.K. was asleep in his crib, Cubby was at school, and her husband, Covertt Long, Sr., was at work, Ernie stayed busy enough to barely notice the loving couple.

At Bud's insistence, the pair sat in the living room, on wooden dining-room chairs, and gazed out a window at the snow which had fallen hours before the temperature plunge.

Chrissy stared back at her boyfriend. The only sounds were from Ernie walking upstairs and an occasional loud exhale from one of the lovebirds. Neither noticed the discomfort of the dining chairs.

"You're beautiful." Bud broke the most recent silence.

Her eyes moistened. Her breath quickened. As she fought to regain her normal breathing pattern, her expression changed. Bud made it clear he could see her thoughts had changed.

"What is it?"

She dropped her head and leaned into his shoulder, hiding her face.

Bud reached around her back and squeezed her right shoulder toward him. "What?"

"I just hate you're going off to war."

"But we don't know that."

She pulled away to look into his eyes. "You don't really think you'll be a desk jockey, do you? A clerk who types papers and files documents in cabinets?"

"No."

"And you said if you get your way you'll get in tanks. I read the newspaper." Her tone changed to anxiety. "I know General Patton is in North Africa right now, fighting alongside the Brits. If you go into tanks, they'll send you to Africa to fight Rommel."

"Wow. You really do read the papers." Bud did not hide how impressed he felt by her knowledge. She knew more about current events overseas than he did.

"Yes, I do," the tart response sounded angrier than she intended.

"They have tanks in Europe, you know."

"Well I don't want you going to Europe, either!" Her loud response surprised even herself. "Sorry."

Bud smiled again. "It's okay. But how about if I promise I'll come back."

"Funny!" She pushed his shoulder with enough force to cause him to transfer his weight to his left leg for balance, despite being seated.

"Let's go sit on the couch where it's more comfortable," he suggested.

The two rose to their feet and Bud carried the chairs into the kitchen. Furniture deposited, he joined his girlfriend on the couch.

"Now, about tanks and dying and war," Bud's serious tone grabbed Chrissy's attention. "I leave tomorrow morning, so let's put that out of our minds. Let's enjoy the time we have together until we see each other again."

Her eyes now soft, Chrissy nodded. "It's warmer away from the window."

Bud's grin signaled his appreciation for her changing the subject. "Maybe someday we'll move someplace where it's warmer."

"I doubt that," she laughed. "With the size of my family, I'd be better off to stay put." Indeed, she would eventually have a total of thirteen siblings. Fourth-eldest, the number of brothers and sisters younger than her was adding up.

"I guess we're so used to the cold and snow it doesn't matter."

"This morning, when I walked the kids to school," Chrissy began, referring to her younger siblings. "It wasn't terribly cold." She shook her head in amazement. "The radio says it's 18-below right now. That Canadian air is awfully cold! They should keep it!"

"Glad I don't have an outside job right now," Bud said with a laugh.

As the conversation continued, Bud's thoughts returned to his comment about not having an outdoor job. The problem was the lack of a job — any job. He knew the decision to travel to Williston was not a wise one, but he also understood this was the last time he would see her before he joined the Army. Two weeks was a long time without working.

•   •   •

"Aw, Anne," Carl's stern tone relented when her eyes moistened.

"Just go, Carl. Do what you have to do," Anne sniffed.

"Anne, don't be like that."

"I'm sorry," she fought back the tears. "I just wish you'd waited until after Christmas."

"Hon, if I did that, you'd want me to wait until you had the baby." Carl motioned with his head as he glanced at his wife's torso, which was yet to show noticeable signs of the second child on the way.

Anne took a deep breath. "I know. And you can't take a chance of a big storm coming and snowing you in."

"That's right." He saw hope of her emotions receding.

"I know, Carl. I know." Her voice was laced with the soft tone which signaled her surrender. "I don't have to like it, but I know."

"Look, as soon as the weather clears — maybe March — you can take the train out."

"Okay."

"April at the latest."

"That makes sense."

"Better then, instead of after you have the baby."

Anne smiled through her tears as she pushed her body against her husband's.

"And if it's a boy, we'll name him 'Emil Gilbert' after my uncles."

Anne stepped back with force as she swatted him on the shoulder. "Over my dead body!"

Carl laughed. The woman he married was back to normal.

"Boy I oughta…" She laughed as her words trailed off and she stepped into him again, this time for a long embrace and kiss goodbye.

Three or four months wouldn't be so bad, she reasoned as they strode out the door and into the front yard, little Carla in tow.

His "goodbyes" verbalized, words were no longer needed for Carl. Anne, oblivious to a cold December wind, waved and called out "goodbye" multiple times. Carla waved with a comical, childish hand movement and mimicked her mother's repeated goodbyes.

With tears pouring from under her glasses, she watched her husband walk away until he was out of sight. The journey to California held more significance than she could ever imagine. Step One for the Peterson clan to branch out from the north country, out across the nation, was launched to wet eyes and bobbing hands; but, the impact on the future hung in the background, overshadowed by the meaning of the present. With her husband bound for California, the twenty-five-year-old, with a two-year-old daughter and a baby on the way, she would face her pregnancy and day-to-day life on her own. A strong woman, she held no doubt of her mettle. Nevertheless, the task posed a bigger challenge than she wished to encounter.

Carl disappeared from Anne's sight, and with only a little money in his pocket, he was destined to hop a train and ride to California alongside hobos.

•　　•　　•

Bud stared at his girlfriend with an expression which looked like anger, but Chrissy knew better. His intent gaze held a combination of determination and sincerity. He had every desire to marry her, but the circumstances prevented it. They both knew of the commonplace practice of creating "war brides," yet Bud felt a strong determination to avoid such a situation.

As Bud continued his stare, he wished — he ached — to change his mind; to marry her and bring her to Bemidji, to ensure they belonged to each other for the rest of their lives.

But he knew better.

"Here we are again. Another goodbye," Chrissy said with glassy eyes.

Bud only nodded.

Her unbuttoned beige wool coat covered her cold frame. Despite being inside the bus depot, the extreme cold made its way indoors in seemingly larger doses every time someone opened up the doors to enter or exit. "Come here," she whispered. She opened her coat wide, indicating to Bud that she did not want a hug over the thick coat.

Bud stepped into her and wrapped his arms around her, underneath her coat as she wished. He planted a gentle kiss on her lips before pulling his head back to speak. "In the Army, I'll go through times where I can't write as often. Don't get frustrated with me."

The first tear of the morning rolled down Chrissy's left cheek. She nodded with a brisk movement, avoiding the challenge of speaking.

"All we can do is pray everything works out." He stopped to look deeper into her eyes. "You know how much I love you; you can't doubt that."

A vigorous nod was her answer.

"When this war's over, there won't be any more military classifications. We can get on with our lives." Bud had more to say but his voice trailed off. He had so much more to say — his thoughts and dreams. He never even told Conrad his dreams, but with Chrissy, he did not wish to simply tell her, he wanted to *live* those dreams with her.

An announcement over the public address system told him the time to board for his trip to Bemidji, with a stop in Fargo, had arrived. All his words were trapped in his mind with no time to say any of them. No time, yet he had just spent two weeks with her.

The tears flowed down Chrissy's cheeks. Her difficulty seeing caused her to doubt what she presumed she saw: Bud's eyes were moist, as well. "Oh, Pete!" She squeezed him with an

92

almost ferocious grip. "Pete, come back to me. Please come back to me!"

The couple kissed, with no regard whether the people in the bus depot were watching or the entire town of Williston could see them. When they finally separated, they both said at the same time, "I love you."

Without another word, Bud turned and walked away, his small bag of clothes in hand.

He did not turn to look back at her until he took his first step onto the bus. Through the window, he could see Chrissy waving like an excited school girl. Bud smiled, then turned and disappeared into the Greyhound.

Inside the depot, Chrissy collapsed onto a chair and cried.

Chapter Nine

"Where've you been, little brother?"

"All over," came Conrad's laconic response.

Bud looked at him and laughed. "All over. What does that mean?"

Conrad shrugged. "I worked on a section gang from Blackduck to Funkley for a while, then they moved me to another gang working from Cass Lake to Bena."

"Wow! That's a long way. So, you were replacing rail?"

"Yeah, but we didn't make it all the way. Weather set in." Conrad frowned. "I still have a job, but they were having some problems getting material, so we're off until after Christmas."

"They really kept you on the jump," Bud sounded impressed at how hard his little brother must have worked.

"Every day." Conrad gained a sudden interest in his brother's life. "Where've you been?"

"I just spent two weeks with that dish, Chrissy, in Williston."

"'That dish?' That doesn't sound like how you'd describe your girlfriend."

"Well, she's a dish. I'm just saying it."

"You gonna marry her?"

"Probably will, probably will." Bud nodded as he spoke, but his voice trailed off as he considered his answer. He took a deep breath before continuing. "Connie, I'm definitely going to marry her. No question about it."

Conrad's eyes bulged. "Really!"

Bud felt a surge of pride in his chest and pushed it outward a bit. "Oh, yes. She is quite the dame, and we're head over heels in love."

"Maybe going in the Army isn't such a good idea then."

"Nah. It's fine," Bud said, absolute certainty in his voice. "I'll go in, do my duty, the Army will pay me, and I'll come back and get a good job finally."

Conrad smiled. "I can't believe it. But you didn't propose?"

"No. No." Bud shook his head. "We talked about it — more than once — but we know we can't afford it right now." Before he could continue, and get to the real reason of not wedding now, Bud took a sudden interest in his surroundings.

Thelma rested on her couch and listened to her brothers as they stood in the entrance to the kitchen. Bud never developed the habit of broadcasting his innermost thoughts and dreams, but this time he had let down his guard and hung his head in regret.

Thelma stared, heart racing, and waited for Bud to tell more.

"Forget it, Thelma!" Bud shot out. "You ain't hearing no more." He turned to his brother. "You, either."

"Hey! What did I do?" Conrad protested.

"You tricked me into talking to you."

Thelma could not bear the humor in silence and laughed with a derisive cackle designed to show Bud how ridiculous he sounded. "Conrad tricked someone into talking? That would be nothing short of a miracle!" She laughed more.

"Oh, ha ha, Thelma," Conrad said, sarcasm flowing.

"One of you has been here for two whole hours," Thelma laughed. "And the other has been here for only a couple weeks, but you both sound like you've reverted to bored children."

"Hey! What's that supposed to mean?" Conrad asked sounding every bit the eighteen-year-old.

"Yeah. I'm with him." Bud feigned an angry expression.

"The way you two communicate is too much," Thelma explained. "You sound like two high school girls deciding if you're gonna share your secrets with each other."

"Oh, ha ha," Conrad responded again, mockery returning.

Bud filled a moment of silence. "Has anyone seen Carl?"

"No, he left for California a few days ago," Thelma answered.

"He's going to live with Uncle Hap?"

"Yeah."

"When's Anne and Carla going?" Conrad inquired.

"Probably early March."

"That oughta give him enough time to get a job and start making some money," Conrad reasoned.

Thelma rose to her feet and made her way to the kitchen. "Gotta get dinner cooked before Ray gets home."

Thelma passed them and entered the kitchen. Bud snapped his fingers as an idea came to mind, "Thelma, we're going outside for a bit. We'll be back."

"Outside? It's freezing cold out there!"

"We won't be long."

Bud led his brother out the front door and into the cold; the thermometer read in the single digits. The winds had calmed, so neither man became overwhelmed by the frigid conditions.

96

"I'm fighting the Army right now. They say I have to wait to get drafted, that I can't volunteer."

They both walked down the three steps off the porch and onto the short sidewalk.

"Why?"

"Some cockeyed story about my commitment to the CCs. I'm not in the CCs anymore; I keep telling them!" Bud's voice shot up in anger.

"So, what are you going to do?"

"Mother said in one of her letters to be patient, but I need some dough," Bud said. "This is pinching my jeans and I'm fairly sore about it. I have to work."

An occasional, short-lived crisp breeze cut at their skin, but both young men were so used to it they failed to take notice. With temperatures above zero, both shrugged off the cold as they stood at the edge of the property, by the road. As long as the wind remained light, they would find no need for coats.

"What's to be sore about?" Conrad asked. "You either got money or you don't."

"That's easy for you to say. You've been making money."

"I'm going to give you ten dollars. That oughta help," Conrad announced.

"No. I don't need your charity. I need a job."

"I'm giving you ten dollars."

"I could use the loan." Bud's tone made it clear he had no choice but to relent.

Conrad paused to think. "Okay. A loan. Good enough. Did you not want Thelma to hear about your tough money picture?"

97

"No. If she finds out, then Elsie and Mother know. I don't want that."

Conrad nodded. "Okay. It's between us."

"Thank you."

With casual strides, the two climbed the steps onto Thelma's porch, then re-entered the house.

•   •   •

Conrad looked up at Bud, who sat across from him, as the younger brother prepared to take his first bite. The brothers felt uncomfortable while seated at the kitchen table, and the distress could be seen by all present, although the girls were too young to understand.

Ray sat at the head of the table, fuming. Thelma kept her head down, quiet.

"Next time, don't hurry dinner and it won't happen," Ray snapped, his Norse eyes flashed fire.

"I said I'm sorry, dear."

Ray let his fork drop onto the tablecloth with a sharp clatter.

Bud's jaws tightened. He had remained silent during every fight, but the worst always seemed to be at the dinner table, where Bud felt required to stay seated. He took a deep breath and spoke up for the first time. "The beans aren't all that crunchy, Ray. So, tell me, what's new on the railroad?"

The ineffectual segue caused Conrad to snicker, so he lowered his head and continued shoveling bites of chicken, potatoes, and green beans into his mouth.

Ray gave Bud a cold stare before relaxing. "Those Republicans are trying to stop Roosevelt from helping our economy, but my railroad is on Roosevelt's side. They're on top of things."

"How so?"

"They're paying good wages. They're not firing people for making mistakes."

"I thought the railroad executives were Republicans?"

"What? No. They're good men." Ray sounded appalled he could be working for people he deemed as opposed to the president. "What they need to do in Washington is come up with more jobs. Look at Carl." He pushed a small pile of green beans into his mouth with his fork, then continued speaking as he chewed. "Carl is a helluva carpenter now. Where'd he learn that?" He paused before answering his own question. "In the CCs."

"I thought he learned that from Uncle Hap?" Conrad chimed in.

Thelma's tension level remained high as she balanced a quiet anger with embarrassment.

"Nah, he didn't know how to do that stuff when he entered the CCs," Ray declared with confidence.

"He did," Bud said with a calm, plain demeanor. "When he moved out a while after Father died, he lived with Hap. Hap taught him a lot."

"I don't remember that," Ray snapped.

"You weren't around yet," Bud responded, again with a flat tone.

With a nervous motion, Thelma reached over and wiped little Valrae's mouth.

"Me too, momma," young Beverly wanted the same attention.

"I thought he learned it in the CCs," Ray said in a quiet voice.

"I'm sure he learned a lot of things there, but he's a good carpenter because of Hap." Bud gave no indication he was prepared to back down, despite his low-key attitude.

Ray crinkled his face, which seemed to prevent his vocal chords from functioning, and the family ate the rest of their meal in peace.

•   •   •

"Connie, I gotta get out of here," Bud announced as he stepped off the porch.

"What's the matter?"

"All that bickering."

"You mean that wasn't unusual?"

"No. Not at all." Bud stepped onto the edge of the road while his little brother walked next to him. The temperature was in the midst of a plunge to double-digits below zero, and the current temperature of -2 made the conversation a brief affair. "Ray snaps his cap about every day."

"That surprises me."

"I know," Bud answered the exclamation. "I was surprised, too."

The brothers continued their stroll, but in silence until, without warning, Bud spun on his heels and headed back toward Thelma and Ray's house.

"What are you gonna do?" Conrad asked, a hint of excitement in his voice.

"Warm up."

Chapter Ten

Christmas arrived, but without Hulda; she had to remain with the Koch family. It was just as well, she had figured, when a powerful snowstorm hit the Bemidji and Puposky area on Christmas Day. The minus-30-degree temperatures before and after the storm made travel all the more treacherous.

Being cooped up in a tension-filled house and watching his sister get humiliated for minor reasons drained Bud. He witnessed her battle against migraines and a descent which threatened to unravel her emotionally. The Peterson clan was a strong breed, but Thelma showed signs of wear.

Perhaps living with his sister's family is what raised his ire; or maybe it was his frustrations with the Army; or maybe it was the separation from Chrissy and his belief he might not see her again until he got out of the Army — if he could only get *into* the Army. Or perhaps it was all these factors which pushed him to take three walks in two days in the extreme cold.

The first walk was a frozen journey to the Army's recruiting office. The cold trek felt all the more unbearable once the wind picked up after sunrise. Now, the icy morning air felt downright nasty. Bud found windless cold to hold an invigorating presence, as though it were a thrilling energy, an infusion of life despite the air's bite. But with the current wind, Bud would soon be cursing under his visible wintry breath.

Bud entered the recruiting office wearing the heavy overcoat his brother-in-law Jake gave to him the prior winter, his neck wrapped in a silk scarf Conrad gave him for Christmas, and a wool cap which covered his head and ears. Bud was on a mission and in a snarling, yet hopeful, mood.

A man pushed his chair back and stood from behind his desk at the sight of the cold visitor. "Well, now. Young man, there's someone the Army wants right there!" His stentorian voice and forceful demeanor failed to make an impact on the twenty-year-old. Before Bud could respond, the robust — in physical appearance and personality — man of forty-four years limped from behind his desk. Bullets from a German machine gun in the Great War had missed his femoral artery by the narrowest of margins and maimed his leg at the Battle of St. Mihiel in the waning months of action. Had the war ended two months earlier, he would have gone home with his buddies instead of enduring a winter in a French hospital.

"You came to enlist in minus-24-degree weather? That says a lot about your fortitude, young man."

"Sergeant Lindgren, it's me. Eugene Peterson. Remember?" Bud knew the man could talk and wanted to limit the prattle.

"Oh, yes. Mr. Peterson, I do recall you," the sergeant's booming voice filled the small office. "You're back to hound me again, I see."

"Yes, sir. I am. I want to get into the Army as soon as possible." Bud's resolute manner posed no threat to the battle-hardened recruiter.

"I understand that, but some things in life are complicated, my boy." His ironic tone was obvious.

"Look." Bud marched up to Lindgren as he spoke, undeterred by the man's daunting build and face, which was highlighted by a thick mustache and reflected a challenging life. "Last spring, you blocked me from going to Alaska to work on

103

the road." He referred to the Alaska Highway, which had been completed a couple of months ago.

"It was an Army project," Lindgren deadpanned.

"You guys keep telling me I can't get into the Army because of my CC commitment." Bud's anger surged. "I ain't got no CC commitment because I ain't in the CCs anymore. Now take me, dammit!"

"Mr. Peterson, Mr. Peterson, let's be calm now."

"Oh to hell with calm. It hasn't gotten me anywhere yet!" Bud snapped.

Lindgren took a deep breath before retreating to his desk. As he poured his heavy, still-muscular frame into his chair he looked up at the would-be recruit.

"You've got a temper, young man. The Army won't like that." Despite his calm manner, the sergeant's voice still reflected a certain haughtiness which Bud disdained.

"I'm usually calm and reasonable, but this has gone on long enough." Bud found himself stirring in his emotional juices again. "I lost that chance to go to Alaska because of the Army's rules. I can't get a decent job because of the Army's classification. The Army owes me, mister, and sergeant or not, you need to make it happen!" The longer he spoke the more his voice increased in volume.

"All right, young man. Take it easy."

The coaxing led Bud to regather his wits.

"I can't take you now," Lindgren began. "But let me see if I can get you out with the next group." Bud started to interrupt, but the sergeant lifted his hand and held it out to the young man with a hard jerk, as if to say, "Silence!"

Bud obeyed the unspoken command.

"I will make a couple of phone calls, but I think I know how I can make this work."

For the first time since his angry entry, calmness dominated the recruiting office.

Lindgren continued. "That means I may — MAY!" he stressed. "I may be able to get you out in the January 20th group."

Bud should have been pleased, but he boiled inside as he hiked through the outdoor freezer that is northern Minnesota in January. Bureaucratic red tape had cost him jobs and delayed his inevitable entry into the military, keeping him in a constant struggle to make ends meet.

He knew the news appeared good, but he would not believe his good fortune — would not allow himself to feel satisfaction — until he was on a train bound for Basic Training. Bud reached his next destination with belligerence dominating his stride. He had a score to settle with the *Northland Times*, the area newspaper to which most of the locals subscribed.

"Can I help you, sir?" the young woman at the front desk inquired. Her blue and white dress was so thick it looked to be made from a burlap sack. Bud looked across the room at the desks — some empty and others staffed with male reporters, editors, and assistants. The air was filled with the dissonant symphony of typewriters clicking, bells ringing with a single "ding" from each machine as the typists reached their right-side margins, and muffled chatter among multiple clusters of tie-clad employees.

"Yeah, I want to talk to the main guy." Bud's stern tone could not be missed.

"We have a managing editor. Our publisher doesn't work here," the receptionist explained.

"I don't care about a title, just get me the main guy." What little patience he possessed dissipated.

"But sir, is this about what appeared in a news story? Or an ad? Or — "

"Listen, lady. You've been looking at me for twenty seconds and I'm no closer to seeing the main guy."

The young woman rose to her feet, the top of her head climbing to five-feet-two-inches off the ground, with heels. "Mister. I want to help you. What is the problem?"

"You stopped delivering my mother's paper."

"Oh. Okay. 'Circulation.' You need someone in circulation." Her voice sounded triumphant. This could only mean progress had signaled a forthcoming resolution.

"Yeah. Sure. Circulation."

"One moment, please." The young woman turned and walked past the desks of reporters and editors to an office door made of wood, with the top half consisting mostly of glass.

Bud could not read the stenciling on the door's window from his vantage point, but he did not feel the need to know anyone's job duties. He wanted action.

Within seconds, a large, overweight, bald man in his forties followed the receptionist to Bud. His solid black tie descended only halfway to his belt. Bud took note of the man's appearance as the newspaper man approached.

"Can I help you, son?"

"Yes. You guys stopped mailing my mother's newspaper to her. She's staying outside Gaylord right now," he said, referring to the small town southwest of Minneapolis.

106

"Come with me."

Bud obeyed the command and followed him to his office. Bud left the door open and stood in front of a desk while the elder man planted himself in his chair. Bud took note of the messy office, and noted the man's name: Matthew Wolff.

"Her name?"

"Hulda Peterson."

Wolff flipped through a thick book which appeared to be a financial journal.

"Let's see," Wolff muttered as he flipped through pages. "Peterson. Peterson." He looked up at Bud and chuckled. "We have no shortages of Petersons."

Bud responded with a frown. His lack of enthusiasm for small talk could not be missed.

"Ah. Yes. Hulda Peterson. Let's see." He scanned the information under her name. "Well, she sure gets around — well, I mean, moves around a lot." The newspaper man hid his embarrassment at the slip.

Bud's demeanor and mood did not improve.

"Yes, I see the problem. It seems your dear mother hasn't paid us since 1938."

Physical and verbal reactions burst forth together. "What?! You're nuts, mister!"

The sounds of typing faded from the newsroom as heads turned and necks craned to catch a glimpse of the sudden outburst.

Bud never noticed. "Listen to me, wise guy! I know she's paid. Hell, I've come down here myself before and paid it for her! Now fix your problem and send her newspapers! Got it?!" The final two words were less question than instruction.

"But Mr. Peterson, you have to — "

"Don't worry about what I have to do. You have to fix your mistake!" Bud signaled with his harsh tone he would not relent. His hands flailed with each word and he punctuated the end of each sentence with a stabbing motion with his forefinger, which pointed at the seated man. "Do it! If you can't, I'll come back down here, but I won't be as nice about it."

Bud stormed out of Wolff's office, but paused when he made eye contact with a reporter at his typewriter. "What are you looking at?!" The reporter snapped his head down to look at his typewriter keys, which caused Bud to resume his angry strides. He ignored the receptionist and marched into the cold, donning his scarf and cap with tugs of anger.

•   •   •

The radio personality announced a temperature of 20 degrees below zero in Bemidji — the air had warmed up by five degrees. It was January 4, 1943, and cold. The Minnesotans took the weather in stride; it would be just as cold again in forty-eight hours. Bud was bundled to the point of not allowing any skin, except around his eyes, to see the light of day. The mask which covered his face had but one opening, which allowed the wearer to cover his nose, or with a gentle tug, drop down to expose the nose and mouth.

Valrae wished him good luck just as a knock at the door interrupted her sentence. Bud, only steps away, ambled to the front door as the sound of cloth scraping against cloth followed him.

Conrad stood in the doorway, let out a low "harrumph," and entered the country house, which lay near Bemidji's edge.

"What's going on?" Bud broadcast his surprise at the early-morning presence of a young man who should be at his job.

"It's cold out," was Conrad's only response.

"You're funny," Valrae giggled.

"You can say that again," a sarcastic Bud quipped. He then looked at his brother and continued. "Shouldn't you be at work?"

"You're funny." Val giggled again. Her uncles looked at her and chuckled.

"Nope. Too cold, they said."

Bud stood by the door, buried in a clump of heavy outerwear. "Connie, what brought you here?" He struggled to remain patient with Conrad as he removed his cap and unzipped his coat.

"I walked."

Bud sighed with a loud exhalation.

"Oh." Conrad acted as though he just recognized his surroundings. He bent down and kissed little Val on top of the head. "I got my classification card in the mail. I came to tell you."

"1-A?"

"Yeah."

"Well," Bud began with a slow, thought-filled pause. "We expected this."

"Hey, where is everyone?" Conrad noted the tranquil house.

"Ray's gone to work and Thelma is taking care of the kids. I'm going to check up on Anne, see if she needs wood or anything else."

"I'd give you a ride if I had a car," Conrad smiled as he teased.

"Aren't you a clown."

Valrae giggled again, then ran out of the room to announce her uncle's presence.

"I have to leave, Connie. Sorry."

"It's okay."

"How's Elsie's pregnancy going?"

"Fine."

"She doing okay?"

"Yeah."

"Is Jake nervous?"

"No."

Bud smiled, happy he could get at least a smidgen of information out of his young brother.

"It's fifteen miles, and you don't want to walk back in the dark," Conrad said.

"I'm staying the night, probably at Emil's," Bud responded, referring to one of Hulda's brothers, whom the boys knew well. "He just don't know it yet."

"Tell Anne 'hello.' Give Carla a kiss for me."

Bud nodded as he began to repeat his earlier steps of adding to his body's protection against the cold. He grabbed a small bag of clothing and personal effects, bid adieu to his brother, opened the front door, and headed out into the frigid January morning.

・　　・　　・

The Sun peeked through and around low clouds and looked down on the solitary figure as he tramped across seven inches of snow and battled a mild breeze. The beautiful landscape caught Bud's eye on occasion, but the wind took away the pleasure. He did take the time to watch a golden eagle land in an enormous nest high up in a Norway pine. Eggs would inhabit that same nest before long, but for now the only goal for the bulky female raptor was survival.

Snow-covered roads provided little assistance to Bud, other than to help him tread a true course. Not a single car drove by as he navigated the wintry landscape — hitching a ride would have been nice. The clouds scattered to make way for brilliant rays as the low deck of clouds relented to the emerging indigo sky. The visual oppression of overcast faded into a bright landscape. Sound traveled farther and he began to notice more birds than twenty minutes prior.

A seven-month-old fawn, spots fading, followed its mother across the snow-powdered road two hundred yards ahead. An eagle — perhaps the same one he had watched land in its nest — soared overhead in search of its next meal.

The skinny Norway pines, reaching in unison toward the heavens as if in praise, shed chunks of snow which had clung to the west sides of their trunks; the breeze provided the needed force to release the snow's grasp on the bark. A small flock of geese flew on a southeasterly course, which caused Bud to smile and mumble, "You're a little late." The geese, locals which had lost their natural urge to engage in lengthy travels, searched for a source of water in the frozen terrain.

His strides consistent, his body protected, the young man took time to reflect on the many subjects which carried angst to his heart. His mother's financial struggles continued. A strong chance existed he would not see his darling Chrissy until after the war, whenever that might be. Now Conrad, with certainty, would be Army-bound, most likely. His elder brother lived half a continent away while his pregnant wife and daughter remained in Puposky. Elsie was in the midst of a rough pregnancy. Thelma suffered migraines and her emotional strength deteriorated at an alarming rate. And Chrissy again. Always Chrissy on his mind.

His anxieties, which he kept to himself, except for occasional discussions with Conrad, did not serve as the reason for his wintry walk, but they propelled him forward. A lot of concerns had to be hashed out, separated, and examined, like a jeweler examining a fresh discovery of gems. He used the walk to mentally prepare to embark on a journey far more daunting than an expedition of a few miles to the north.

His assumption remained, as it had since the first thought he entertained about joining the Army, that a job in a mechanics corps would provide excellent opportunity. He wanted to beat the Germans or the Japanese, but such thoughts were ancillary to his need for not just a job, but job skills which could sustain him for a lifetime. True, he knew how to use a variety of tools for carpentry, but none of the skills obtained in the Civilian Conservation Corps satiated his hunger to be an expert in a trade.

As a habit, he did not share his dreams and desires with others, but that likely would change after he married Chrissy — she was a girl like no other in his life. He lost track of time as he marveled about her sweetness, lively personality, and feisty spirit, though he suspected the journey took well over four hours through the terrain made challenging by the snow.

Chapter Eleven

The fallow land became a lucrative gold mine once Henry Kaiser and the U.S. government agreed on the location. Building cargo ships for the U.S. Maritime Commission served as Kaiser's entry point into an endeavor which led him to a bonanza. By 1943, residents of Richmond, California, struggled to recall the sight of open spaces present just three short years prior.

Richmond mushroomed into a city of over 100,000 souls, more than four times the pre-1940 population, thanks to Kaiser and other war materiel manufacturers. People came from all around the nation to find work at the four shipyards.

The first order of business had been the production of ships for the British war effort. The U.S. had been an important supplier of arms and other war materiel during the Great War, and now its official neutral status left wiggle room to stay out of the war while still being an influence, repeating its role of money lender and arms supplier.

Kaiser owned seven shipyards: four in Richmond, two in Portland, Oregon, and one in Vancouver, Washington. It was Richmond's which became the backbone for the Maritime Commission's efforts to provide ships, first for the British, then later its own country. The Richmond shipyards would go on to produce 747 sea vessels during the war — an unprecedented accomplishment. Kaiser's shipyards would account for over one quarter of all vessels manufactured for the American war effort.

Kaiser used assembly lines for construction — a method not previously attempted by shipbuilders. Separate sections of the ship were built in pieces — pre-fabricated — then craned into position to be welded or riveted together. This allowed workers to create the same piece of the ship over and over. Once the section or device was assembled, it would be moved to another portion of the shipyard for final assembly.

Kaiser foresaw the need for extra land for his welders and other assembly line workers. The four shipyards could not allow cramped working conditions, which would have slowed production.

The shipbuilder held another distinction: he provided access to a health-care plan for his employees. One message found on signs throughout the shipyards read, "Be a healthy shipbuilder," with a reminder that health care could be purchased for 50 cents a week.

A billboard on the grounds read, "Will you take the responsibility of bringing one new worker to the employment office?" Despite the great boom for the economy and families who needed income, the speed of the expansion overwhelmed local attempts to keep up with the housing needs of the employees and their families. Men and women resorted to sleeping outdoors and boats were advertised for purchase to serve as homes.

In Portland, they had "Rosie the Riveter;" in Richmond, it was "Wendy the Welder." The latter name failed to catch the fancy of the public, and the many working women received the unofficial title of the former. In Richmond, they welded the ships together, allowing for increased production rates.

Other companies built ships in other ports, but Richmond became the center of the new world for both the production of ships and the all-important scarce nugget: jobs. This was the new world in which Carl Peterson found himself when his uncle Hap helped him get a job at Richmond Shipyard No. 3.

•   •   •

"Don't you think it's time you bought yourself some clothes?" the man known as "Hap" asked. "You've been out here a couple of months."

"I got a couple of everything: pants, shirts, undergarments. Why do I want more?" Carl's question lacked humor.

The man larger than life to Carl laughed and Hap Gustafson slapped his nephew on the back as they walked toward the former's automobile. "Carl, you wore the same clothes to work yesterday."

"But I washed them last night," Carl protested.

"Maybe you wouldn't have to wash your clothes in the sink if you had more." Hap paused to consider his nephew's reasons for frugality. "I know how it is, Carl. We've all come from nothing and now we have a little money and don't know what to do." They dodged a 1939 Plymouth as they continued through the paved lot. "We send money home — hell, probably everyone here does — but we have to spend some of it on ourselves, for food and clothes."

The twenty-seven-year-old pondered the words of his elder before responding with a heartfelt question. "You think so?"

"Of course. You have to eat, sleep, and have a roof over your head and clothe yourself."

116

"No," Carl responded. "I mean, do you really think I need more clothes?"

Uncle Hap laughed again but responded with a simple, "Yes."

• • •

The apartment possessed a useless view of the alley behind the building, offered but one bedroom, which forced Carl to sleep on the couch, and was almost certainly a fire hazard with its one exit and hastily built wood framing. But it was perfect for Carl. This marked the second time he had lived with Hap — the first being when Carl was fifteen and angry at the world, living with Hap and his wife and children.

Those days with Hap held invaluable importance for Carl: his uncle taught him skills, particularly in carpentry, which carried him through a lifetime. Now, here in San Francisco, he lived with his favorite uncle again.

Seventeen years and one day separated Hap from his nephew in age. His birthdate was either fortuitous or unfortunate, depending on one's point of view, for he found himself on a ship to Europe before his twentieth birthday, a soldier ready for war. When he contracted an illness and landed in a French hospital rather than the front, he missed action and returned to the States with little to show for the trip, for better or worse, other than a Spitz dog. He named the mutt "Fleur," which hunted and killed woodchucks on his farm. Fleur had multiple litters and her offspring possessed the same lust for woodchuck flesh.

Hap was the sixth of seven children born to Charles and Johanna Gustafson, and the fifth of six to live into adulthood. He was born four years after his sister Hulda. The uncle, born in Buena Vista, Minnesota, and the nephew, born in Climax, Minnesota, shared the small apartment, but neither minded the arrangement. Both understood the other's predicament: Hap, with a wife, nine children, and another on the way on a farm near Bemidji, and Carl with a pregnant wife and a daughter, were in such desperate need of good-paying jobs they traveled nineteen-hundred miles from their families.

Adolph had earned the nickname of "Happy," and people called him "Hap." Happy chance it was a loudmouth fascist dictator who shared Hap's first name did not also share his nickname, thus the moniker not only suited, it benefited him.

Though indeed happy, Hap maintained a low-keyed, calm demeanor and lacked the effusive, loud personality some expected of a man nicknamed "Happy." He mostly kept his opinions to himself and preferred action over words — a life-long workaholic.

Standing over six-feet-tall, deep-set blue eyes and thinning gray-black hair gave the Great War Army sergeant the look of a professor or accountant, particularly when his pipe hung from his mouth. His hairline in rapid retreat, he lacked enough hair to cover the top of his head. Despite the look of scholar or businessman, he possessed a fifth-grade education. Despite the education, he possessed a keen mind, able to complete calculations in his head when working on jobs. He could draw plans for building something — furniture, a shed — pause, and mentally determine how many board-feet of lumber was needed. His accuracy was uncanny.

While sitting on a rickety wood-framed chair given to him by a co-worker, Hap lowered the letter in his hand to his knee.

"How's Aunt Violet handling things?" Carl asked.

"Oh, about as good as can be expected, I s'pose," Hap answered. "Lorraine will be three this summer, and Ma says the little tyke is getting around pretty good, running herself into trouble."

Carl laughed as he considered his little cousin.

"Vernon turned sixteen a couple months ago and he's already talking about quitting school," Hap added.

"Money's scarce," Carl responded with a wistful tone. "I know it's best he stays in, but you can't blame him for thinking about money." He paused before adding, "Everyone else okay?"

"Yeah." Hap smiled. "Gordy, Arnie, and Stanley are learning as they keep the farm going." He continued as he named his children in order of their birth. "Arlene, Bob, and Lorna are helping take care of Lyal and Lorraine."

Every member of the family had a middle name which began with the letter "V." Vernon was Charles Vernon, Bob was Robert Vance, and so on. His wife, Violet, was known by her middle name.

Carl nodded as he recalled his interactions with his cousins.

Hap paused before he slapped his knee and stood with a burst of energy. He dropped the letter onto his chair and announced, "Let's go get a beer!"

Carl stood as he chuckled, "I thought you'd never ask."

"I know a great little bar in San Pablo, and we can grab a sandwich while we're at it."

"Let's go," came Carl's boisterous reply as he headed out the door.

•　　•　　•

Tired, but energized for a relaxing beer together, Carl and Hap walked to the old Ford. Eating at home saved them money, but it was time to spend a little. Hap had decided he wanted Carl to drive, so he climbed into the passenger side of his car. Parked on the street, the Ford was crammed into a tight space.

As Carl closed the door and fired the engine, a burly man walked up to the driver's side window, shouting.

"What the hell does he want?" Carl asked with a sigh.

"I don't know."

Waving his arms and pointing behind him, toward another car, the thick-haired stout man continued to shout as Carl rolled down his window just enough to hear and be heard.

"What is wrong with you?! Can't you park a damned car right, buddy?! When I tried to move my car, you caused me to hit the car in front of me!" Every sentence screeched from his mouth like a stream of demons hurtling out.

"Listen, mister," Carl started to explain he was about to move the car.

"You listen to me, buster! Who do you think you are to block me in this way?!" He flapped his arms with effusive energy. "You're paying for the damage to that guy's car and mine, not me!" Only sturdy cars rolled off the Detroit assembly lines, so damage to a car's fender from a small bump from another car would certainly be inconsequential.

120

"Listen, mister," Carl tried again.

"No! You listen. I want you out of that car right now so you can see the damage you caused! Then, I want you — "

"Mister! Shut your mouth for a minute!" Carl snapped.

The burly man stopped speaking.

"I'm tired. I've had a long day. We just want to go get a beer, so let it go. You hit a car, you hit a car. Not my problem."

The burly man wagged a finger. "I told you, get out of this car so you can see what you caused me to do!"

Carl shook his head slowly, as if in resignation. "Don't make me get out of this car. I told you, I don't feel like dealing with you right now. If I get out, it won't go well for you. Now scram!"

The burly man exploded with anger, his words bellowing through the street and down the sidewalks for all to hear. When he saw Carl's door open and heard the engine stop, he let out a triumphant harrumph and walked the short distance to the sidewalk. When he turned around, Carl neared him, and the loud burly man announced, "If you don't take care of this, I'm going to kick — "

The sentence never found its conclusion. With one punch, Carl dropped the man, unconscious before he hit the sidewalk. Annoyance, rather than anger, dominated Carl's face as he looked at the man for half a second before returning to the car.

As Carl climbed in, Hap did not say a word.

Carl fired the engine and turned to his uncle. "Well, I tried to tell him."

The old Ford pulled into the street, on its way to deliver the two Minnesotans to the beers which awaited them, leaving the unconscious man behind.

•   •   •

Hulda took the envelope from Mrs. Koch's out-stretched hand with suppressed glee. The return address showed Elsie was the letter writer. Hulda strode into the plush dining area and stood next to an oak table which could seat a dozen. The chandelier caught Hulda's eye every time she passed it; its sparkling reflections of light casting a dazzling display to the beholder, even before the light was activated. The thick, plum-colored carpet and wainscoted walls, with oak baseboards and crown molding, added to the reason the house itself was the most lavish she had ever seen.

Hulda did not notice the chandelier this time. Instead, she paused with her back to the table as she opened the envelope. She froze and her heart felt as though it had stopped when she read the first line.

Dearest Mother,
It is hard for me to write this letter, but I just couldn't let somebody else do it.

Her eyes never scanned the top right of the page, which would have shown her the letter was written in Bemidji on January 28, 1943, according to Elsie's own hand. Instead, her eyes devoured the words on the page like a hungry wolf would devour an elk it had stalked and mauled.

You see, Mother, our boy was born yesterday morning,
but he only stayed with us for 10 ½ hours.

Hulda stumbled to a wooden chair, with its beautiful craftsmanship sitting in wait for the next person to rest on the exquisite furniture, and lowered her body as slowly as possible.

He weighed only 3 ½ lbs. Although he was supposed to
be a premature baby, he didn't act like one. According
to Dr. Whittemore there had been something wrong all
along. Well it's pretty hard to take, but we'll have to
believe it's all for the best. Doc said there was something
wrong with him inside. He passed away quietly in his
sleep and he bloated so terribly I never saw him alive,
but after he was wrapped they brought him to me. He
looked just like Bud.

Hulda set the papers aside and shook.

With elbows on the table in front of her, face in hands, numbness overcoming her, Hulda watched as large teardrops began to dot the table. Part of her emotions were blocked, yet part of her felt the onrushing ache of the soul. She normally would have been horrified to see the amount of moisture splashing on the table, but lacking such ability at the moment, she saw, but did not process, the presence of a tiny pond of tears.

Five minutes passed before she moved, although it felt far longer to her as she lost track of time. She used a handkerchief to wipe her eyes and blow her nose. She walked with a painful amble into the kitchen, then returned with a dry rag to clean up the table top. Within seconds, the evidence had disappeared, but Hulda's moist, red eyes and rosy cheeks broadcast her emotions and provided confirmation of long, silent weeping.

Still numb but mental capacity returning, Hulda started again on the letter, wiping her eyes on occasion.

Thelma took Jo Anne. She asks too many painful questions. Judy is such a comfort. She's so full of life and affection for 'Mummy.'

Hulda paused to smile at the mention of her granddaughters. Four-year-old Joanne lacked the ability to understand the events, while Judy, not yet two years old, was removed enough in emotional development that, for her, it was just another day. The innocence of children tugs at everyone's hearts, but now, with the loss of an innocent, it was only with great difficulty a painful smile managed to sneak past the new tears which streamed down Grandma Hulda's face as she pictured the young, sweet girls from her memory.

Well, Mother, Jake said he'd write later. He was pretty broken up over this. He had named the little fellow Dennis William, and he had made arrangements to put him in the hospital for a month. No expense would have been too great for him.

Hulda and Jake had their struggles at times — the former's forcefulness and candor would be difficult for any son-in-law — but she felt a glow of warmth knowing her daughter received the care of her husband.

Conrad was here through it all, and I know now that nobody will ever really know how he's going to take anything. I expected him to bolt and run at the first opportunity, but he stayed around, helping with anything he could, so quiet you didn't know he was in the house.

With the matriarch over 200 miles away, the family managed to function as designed. Everyone present came to the rescue with love and commitment and worked to make Elsie and Jake's loss a little more bearable. Thelma and Conrad, along with a family friend, Mrs. Gunderson, made contributions to ease the pain.

Hulda retreated to her bedroom so no one would see her next silent cry. The tears and redness could neither be hidden nor turned off. After grabbing a fresh handkerchief, she sat on the side of her bed and re-read the letter. Unaccustomed to outward displays of emotion and the desire to be pitied, she felt alone, almost confused. She needed comfort but would be left longing. Hulda remained painfully alone.

A list formed in her mind: she was not there for Elsie, she was not there to help, and she was not there to be a rock for the others. She was not there. When those thoughts penetrated her mind, she pushed them back, remembering the true pain belonged to the entire family. They had lost a loved one — loved even though most of the family never saw little Dennis.

The remainder of the pain was for her daughter and son-in-law, who lost a child. Such a loss was something Hulda had never experienced and desperately hoped not to, ever. She took comfort as she thought about Elsie's strength. The intelligent, witty, vivacious young Elsie had grown into a strong woman, and perhaps grew much more over the preceding few days.

Her mind could not help but return to the passing of her husband, a little more than thirteen years earlier — thirteen short years. Hulda had become a widow with five children less than ten days before the great Stock Market crash. Now, a similar pain, although not quite as intense or hopeless, had returned as she considered what her daughter was now feeling.

Everyone in the family helped to some degree except two: Carl, who by virtue of his location did not know of the sad tragedy yet; and Bud, who had left the area a week prior, bound for a new adventure.

Thinking of Bud's life trajectory sent a chill through the mother and kept her in despair. She did not know how, but she understood Bud's life had been altered forever, though she did not know if that alteration would be for good or ill.

She tried not to think about Bud and again thought about her first grandson, whom she would never see; yet, as she suppressed the tears and dried her eyes again, memories of Bud's departure a week prior forced their way into her soul, as well.

Chapter Twelve

At long last, from Bud's point of view, Uncle Sam *finally* came calling. With the worry about landing a job now a memory, he found other concerns: his physical condition; neatness; promptness; and overall discipline. All those worries had paled compared to his previous money woes. Now, he could relax — at least mentally.

On the south bank of the Mississippi, where the great river cut a southern path through Minneapolis, only to turn to the north and head into St. Paul, near the point where the Minnesota River found itself gobbled up by the mighty waterway, sat Fort Snelling, an almost-ancient installation. The fort had been established well before Bud's family arrived in America, so the description of 'ancient' applied as far as he was concerned.

Bud lacked the liberty of time, and did not feel the need to learn, about the fort, the area, or anything beyond recovering from each day's exercises, tests, chow, sleep, more exercises, and more tests. He did not take the time to cross the bridge linking his new home to St. Paul; his only concern lay with writing his mother, girlfriend, and any family member who wrote him first.

On a Saturday evening, before the call for "lights out," Private Eugene Peterson, with his new "high and tight" haircut, lay fully dressed in his bed, Army stationery and pencil in hand, working on a letter to his mother. Bud felt so enamored with having a title that he wrote in the top left corner, above the U.S. Army letterhead which featured the Great Seal of the United States, "Pvt. Eugene Peterson."

On this last Saturday of the month, Bud hid from the cold Minnesota night. He paused writing multiple times to collect his thoughts and relay them with as much flair as his tired body and mind would allow.

> *... got my uniform too. Yes, and we got 2 shots today one in each arm. Gosh! I can't   lift my right hand up to my shoulder even.*

> *He chewed on the end of the pencil for a moment before continuing, abruptly dropping it as he fought to overcome the devilishly persistent feeling of fatigue. Undeterred by his lack of consistent punctuation, he continued his struggle to find adequate words.*

> *I'm sure the Army will be O.K. I took out the full $10,000 in insurance and $18.75 in   bonds   a   month.   I'm sending you both policy duplicates. The bonds are made out so you   can cash in on when, if ever, you may get hard up for cash. Pretty good, eh?*

Bud stopped to consider his mother always felt "hard up" for money, and with good reason. If not, she would be living in Bemidji, or even Puposky, rather than a rural area only fifty miles from the Twin Cities, working to fill the needs of a wealthy family in exchange for that much-needed cash. Thoughts complete, he continued.

We had another interview today. Yesterday I took a radio aptitude test, a mental test and a mechanical aptitude test. Don't know how I made out tho'.

I am in good hopes of getting in some mechanics corps.

Bud decided not to complicate the letter with an explanation of what the fort accomplished besides training raw recruits. Of course, he never had time to visit the soldiers who were there to learn Japanese.

Please don't worry about me because it's better for you and easier for me if you don't. I'm in an organization now where worry isn't at all necessary. Uncle Sam's Army.

He scribbled one final paragraph for a sign-off, filling the back page of the stationery, then contemplated the dissipation of most of his worries. He still took time to remember Chrissy and the letter he had written only minutes prior, and worried about his mother's financial situation, but he knew his monetary contribution to her would be enough to fill one little piece of the puzzle. Soon, Conrad would contribute, as well, giving both brothers deep satisfaction. For now, he counted on the lack of worry in Uncle Sam's Army.

• • •

Now, five weeks into his military service, Bud found himself outside his northland stomping grounds, having left Ft.

129

Snelling for Miami Beach, Florida — but not in tanks, as he had hoped. Instead, he trained as part of the Army Air Corps.

"'A-ten-SHUN!'" Bud barked to his squad of twelve men. Each man looked the same, with a few variances of skin tone: Army boots which rose above the ankles; khaki socks covered by khaki pants; khaki t-shirts; dog tags draped around necks; inexperienced faces covered with occasional flashes of fear in their eyes; and, underneath the khaki garrison caps rested barely enough hair to avoid being labeled as "bald."

"Listen up, men!" Bud called out. "Put your hats in the barracks and immediately fall back in."

"Uh, Bud." One soldier attempted to explain Bud's error as they jogged the twenty yards to their barrack. "It's a 'garrison cap,' not a 'hat.' "

Bud looked at the young man, smiled with one side of his mouth, and shrugged. "I gotta remember that."

•   •   •

Despite several weeks in the Army, the men were about to learn Uncle Sam meant business. As gunfire roared, Bud shouted his orders to his squad. The blasts of semi-automatic rifle fire pounded together to form a wall of sound, heightened by the air being ripped by a fully-automatic rifle. Privates and corporals who had been around for twice as long as Bud's class fired across a pit 50-yards long and 70-yards wide. The three-feet-deep pit allowed plenty of space for a man to safely crawl underneath the lead flying overhead. The earsplitting rage served as a perfect attack on one's ears, just as the Army

130

intended — like a rider training his horse to accept the sound of his pistol, but seemingly multiplied by ten-thousand.

The overpowering shock of sound was so intimidating, most of the soldiers still would have crawled if the pit had been dug ten feet into the Earth.

Thirty yards away, as they stood in a perfect line, Bud stood to the side in order to see his squad. "Men! On the other side of that pit, and that gawd-awful sound, is an ammo depot. We're to capture the depot." Bud paused as a World War I-era M1918 Browning Automatic Rifle ripped the air. When it stopped after three seconds, he continued. "This is not a race! We go across as a team. When we climb out of the pit, we are to rush the ammo depot as one unit, no one ahead of the other." He raised his voice another ten decibels as he continued. "Do you understand?!"

"Yes, sir!" the twelve men shouted back.

"Good! Now, we're not going to march up. You can be at ease until it's our turn."

The guns fell silent as another squad stepped into place.

The line fell out and the men moved forward, closer to the pit. They watched as the squad in front of them, on-deck to face the pit, plugged their ears with their fingers when a sergeant gave the order to resume firing at what was left of the wood-and-paper targets across the pit. The squad leader darted through his group and slapped hands from ears.

"Oh yeah," Bud said, reminded by the sight. "Can't put your fingers in your ears."

Most groaned but complied with Bud's lackadaisical order.

"Hey, Peterson," a man six-inches taller and thirty-pounds heavier called out as he stepped close enough for Bud to hear. "How do you like being the squad leader?"

"Fine, until today," Bud said with a flat tone.

"This is what you wanted, isn't it?" Every word came out with as many decibels as possible.

"No. I mean, sure. It's fine," Bud yelled back. "I just took all those tests you did and this is where they put me."

A sergeant motioned for a cease-fire and the sound stopped, although not inside the heads of the men, where it rang with a high-pitched fervor. The group in front of Bud moved into position.

Bud looked at his teammate and gave one final explanation. "I needed a job." He turned and looked across the pit in front of them as the preceding group disappeared from view. "I guess I didn't think about all the noise."

The man took Bud's statement as a joke and laughed. Bud smiled and added, "I guess we'll be doing some laundry tonight. And it won't be just cleaning off the dirt."

The horrendous wall of sound resumed. Each man clung to his nine-pound M-1 rifle and gripped it as though he wished to strangle it — no fault of the gun.

•   •   •

Conrad sat motionless on a chair at Thelma's kitchen table. His eyes followed Valrae as she opened the ice box and took a quick drink of milk before replacing the bottle. With a furtive glance, the little girl closed the door and scooted away,

132

unaware that the quiet man sitting alone witnessed her misdemeanor.

The amusing distraction provided by Val and her small smile which followed gave Conrad cause to break from his thoughts and allow a slow smile of his own. Before he could return to his contemplation, Thelma entered the kitchen.

"Oh. There you are," she announced.

"Hi."

"What are you doing in here?"

"Just thinking."

"What are you thinking about?" She made her way to the table and took a seat in a wooden chair.

"Hey, how's your head?"

Thelma took a big breath and sighed before answering. "The migraine is mostly gone." The troubled tone became evident as her thoughts returned to the multiple days of grueling head pain.

"Good. Glad to hear it," Conrad smiled as he answered.

"Thanks for all the help you've been lately, especially watching the girls," Thelma said as Beverly ran into the room.

"I was just watching Val a minute ago." Conrad cracked a coy smile at his own little joke.

Conrad's statement derailed Thelma's train of thought as she gave him a quizzical look.

"Mommy, can we go play in the snow?" The little girl's blue eyes sparkled as she gushed with excitement about her idea.

"No, honey," Thelma answered. "The blizzard may be over, but there's too much snow out there right now to turn you and your sister loose without me."

Not yet four years old, the desperate child looked at her uncle then back to her mother. "Uncle Connie can take us out. He can watch us."

"No. We'll wait. Uncle Connie doesn't want to go out there, either."

"Aw, Mother!" Beverly moped as she left the kitchen.

Thelma laughed as she turned her attention back to her brother. "They can run you ragged if you let them."

"They're cute little girls." Conrad smiled again and then added, "I can't blame them for wanting to go out."

"Ray should be home after everything clears from this blizzard."

"It's fine. Don't worry," Conrad assured her. "As soon as this clears up, I've got to check up on Anne. Carl wrote Bud and told him to ask me to check up on her, make sure she's got enough wood and such."

"Why didn't he write you?"

"You know Carl. He probably figured he was already writing Bud, and that fills his quota of one letter a month."

Thelma laughed but was interrupted by an angry cry which pierced the tranquil afternoon from another room of the small house. Before she could react, there was another cry, but from a different voice. Thelma sighed. "I'd better see what those two are up to this time."

Before Conrad could protest and take action himself, Thelma bolted from her chair and out of the kitchen. He tuned out the tyke fight and returned to his thoughts. He stared straight ahead as his mind raced through his plans, which he had yet to announce to anyone.

With Carl in California and Bud in Florida, life had changed in a way he did not appreciate. He was used to Carl's absences, but not Bud's. He and Bud were close, and when Bud left for Civilian Conservation Corps work, they wrote each other often. Additionally, Bud usually was only a few miles away, in Cass Lake, or he came home semi-regularly when in North Dakota.

He glanced in the direction of the kitchen window. As soon as winter departed, he intended to follow in Bud's footsteps.

Chapter Thirteen

In August of 1942, Germany had committed itself to the Battle of Stalingrad. The move, insisted upon by Adolf Hitler, proved to be a singular catastrophe for the German war machine.

By November of 1942, the Russians succeeded in surrounding the city, thereby trapping 300,000 men of the German Wehrmacht and forcing upon the invaders the twin killers of starvation and exposure to the nasty Russian winter. Life in the obliterated city became scarce.

Hitler had declared his troops should fight to the death, while Stalin had threatened those who dared retreat with court martial and execution — and in Russia, like Germany, courts did not delay long.

When the German Army — frozen and starving — surrendered at Stalingrad in early February of 1943, a contemporary observer could not possess the knowledge a tectonic shift was underway.

Only 91,000 Germans surrendered; the other 209,000 had met their end in the frozen, foodless desolation. The Russian military later removed a quarter of a million corpses from the city.

Now, in March of 1943, the monster that was the Wehrmacht looked a little smaller and a little less ferocious. The German goal of destroying the manufacturing capabilities in the city named for the current Red leader — a goal they achieved — became a Pyrrhic victory in view of the massive German losses. From a strategic standpoint, Stalingrad was not any sort of victory for Germany, Pyrrhic or otherwise. It was a disaster.

What started as Operation Barbarossa fourteen months prior did not go as Hitler had planned, and by the time German forces in the city surrendered, against direct orders from the tyrant, the incredible suffering and loss of life had, by February of 1943, reached 800,000 Axis soldiers (German, Italian, Hungarian, and Romanian), 1.1 million Russian soldiers, and an estimated 40,000 Russian civilians.

The war on the Eastern front manifested itself as a frigid version of Hell.

In the Pacific Theater, all of 1942 and early 1943 had been a seesaw affair. Huge Japanese gains led to significant American advances. From the Coral Sea to Midway to Guadalcanal, the Americans made slow and inconsistent progress while enduring setbacks throughout the Pacific islands. With Pearl Harbor and the brutality of Bataan on the minds of American soldiers, and the honor of the Emperor weighing upon the other side, furious fighting continued.

From March 2 through 5, 1943, the Battle of the Bismarck Sea raged. The Japanese had attempted to transport 6,900 troops to New Guinea. Only 2,734 survived. Australian and American aircraft sunk eight supply and transport ships as well as four destroyers, but both sides were losing ships and men at alarming rates.

As that battle raged, Allied planners spent their time readying for a major June offensive, which would move Allied strongholds north and west.

In March of 1943, the fate of the war remained in doubt.

•   •   •

The mid-morning Sun reminded the Minnesotan he was in south Florida. The thick air pushed through Bud's fatigues and pressed against his body. Still in the process of acclimating to the moist air, his lungs heaved with laborious effort at each breath when engaged in strenuous activity.

Bud wiped at sweat on his forehead as he adjusted his olive drab helmet. The act was in vain, as the sweat reemerged the moment his hand slid across his head and replaced the droplets which fell from his hand to the ground.

"What do they use for air here? Pool water?" Bud grumbled before returning his focus to the exercise at hand. "Okay, boys. We can't go to the north. Their squad is expecting us to come up through there." He motioned at the map in his hands.

A dozen men, all dressed in the same manner as Bud — olive drab and camouflage from head to toe — either kneeled or stood behind their leader. Privates all, they knew success would look good in the eyes of their superiors.

"Now, the way I see it, Ferguson, you take five men to the south of that house over there." Bud pointed at a house two doors from where they stood as he talked to a tall, slender 180-pound recruit. The cut lawns and neat rows of hedges separating the houses gave the neighborhood the appearance of an ideal place to grow up. The upper-middle-class structures, with stucco exterior walls, tall front doors, and no shortage of windows, lined the street beyond the view of the soldiers. "Landela, you take the rest of the men and take a left on that street," Bud said to his best friend in the Army thus far, Sulo Landela. He motioned again, ordering the short, barrel-chested recruit. "Loop around, and you'll come around here." Bud pointed on his map.

"I'm gonna let them see me and when they come my way, I'll get out of there and Ferguson, you will meet them at an angle, like this." Bud drew with his finger on the map, showing the 90-degree-angled attack. "Landela, you guys will come at this from behind. When they see me, they'll be expecting I'm a scout or something. They won't be expecting a flank or rear assault."

The Army wanted the men to simulate guerrilla warfare, having the Battle of Stalingrad in mind, and had alerted the neighborhoods for days in advance. Despite being part of the Air Corps, the military brass wanted their soldiers prepared for anything in case a man found himself reassigned to infantry.

"Where are you going, Peterson?" A voice inquired.

Bud rotated his crouched body and pointed at the house only feet away. "I'm going right through there."

Several men laughed, but Bud meant his words. "Listen, I go through that house and you guys do what I said, we'll throw those boys off. They're not expecting us to loop around so far and they're sure as hell not expecting someone to waltz through that house."

Bud stood, so those kneeling followed his lead. "Everybody got your rifles?"

Low mutters of "Got it" and "Right here" followed as over half the group lifted up their "rifles" — wooden facsimiles of the M-1 rifle.

"Okay, then," Bud added. "Try not to destroy these people's flowers and bushes. I don't want Uncle Sam mad at me."

While Ferguson and Landela took five men each, Bud hustled across the lawn of the large house. His squad, for which he was responsible, disappeared. Within minutes, Ferguson's group would be climbing fences and hiding in bushes.

Bud reached the front door and paused. He looked at the doorbell, then took a quick glance at the word "Welcome" written on the door mat. An Army slogan well known to the men stated, "If you do your best when you are here the sooner we'll be in Adolf's beer." Bud took the slogan to heart.

He opened the door, entered, and walked through the spacious living room and into a dining room. As he stepped into the kitchen, Bud heard a gasp which turned into a shriek. The sound startled him, but not to the level of shock which overcame the lady of the house.

Eyes bulging, one hand over her mouth and another on her heart, a kitchen towel hanging from the lower hand, the brown-eyed, dark-haired woman struggled to maintain her composure.

Bud stopped to deliver an apology. "Sorry, ma'am. U.S. Army. I didn't mean to startle you. I wiped my feet."

The frightened housewife nodded with short, jerky movements.

Bud looked around the kitchen and frowned. "How do I get out of here?"

The lady pulled her hand away from her mouth and pointed. "Turn right."

He walked in the indicated direction, then disappeared from her view after a right turn, which led him to a large, open living area with access to the back yard. He paused before crossing the room and shouted, "Thank you, ma'am!" With that, Bud darted to a sliding glass door, opened it, and peeked out. He turned to take one last look and saw the woman now standing on the far side of the room, having followed him. He looked at the frightened woman and gave an embarrassed shrug.

The errant soldier left the woman's house and closed the sliding door behind him.

•   •   •

"That was fun!" Bud exclaimed as his group trooped down a suburban street, on their way to an Army transport truck. "We lost three of ya, but taking nine prisoners is dandy!"

"Dandy? I got killed!" Landela shot back.

Ferguson laughed. "But that ain't gonna get you out of the rest of Basic, so what good did it do you?" The others laughed and resumed swapping stories with their brothers-in-arms.

"Hey, Peterson." Hobbs, a short man with big ears, maneuvered toward his squad leader. "Did you finally hear from your girl?"

"Yeah, I was starting to wonder what happened, but get this: she's been in welding school in Bismarck, so she's been pretty busy."

"When this war's over, the women are gonna have all the jobs," Hobbs mused.

"Good luck taking a job away from Chrissy. She'll fight ya for it." Bud chuckled as his thoughts turned to the woman he loved.

•   •   •

With a little time on their hands, several of the men relaxed in their barracks, stretched out on their respective beds.

"When are you up for guard duty, Bud?" Ferguson asked.

"Ten 'til midnight."

"Lucky skunk. I got four 'til six," he said, referring to the middle-of-the-night shift.

"I've got KP tonight," Landela volunteered.

"How's Menahga?" Bud asked.

"Fine, as far as I can tell," Landela responded, referring to his home town, one hour directly south of Bemidji.

"Same with my family," Ferguson added.

"Are you from Chicago?"

"No, I'm from south of Springfield," Ferguson answered.

"Is it so dad-blamed hot in Illinois?"

"Not like this," Ferguson answered. "My clothes take three times as long to dry here, if they dry."

"I'll second that," Landela chimed in. "It's like stepping out of the shower and into a sauna."

Bud re-read a letter he received from Carl the prior day. He was receiving one letter a day, on average, and it helped keep the homesickness at bay.

"Hey, Peterson. Why were you limping on our way back from the urban warfare training?" Nothing got past Ferguson.

"When I was a kid, my dog smashed into my right knee and made a mess of it. The Army doc says I have some soft bone growing underneath the kneecap." Bud flexed his right leg and stared at his knee as he spoke. "I haven't missed drills or marches, so I'm okay."

"At least you've had it looked at," Ferguson answered as he looked at his own legs and flexed his knees.

"I'm not going into no hospital while I have all this military stuff to learn."

"You gonna be ready for the drill on the beach tomorrow?" Landela asked Bud.

"Of course. First, the parade for that general yesterday, now he wants to watch us drill. I ain't missing that."

'That general' was Major General Walter Reed Weaver, who had just returned from the front lines in Europe. At the Virginia Military Institute, his first captain was George Marshall. Weaver, a West Point graduate, had a wide-ranging military career, serving in various capacities from China to the Philippines to New York City. Stateside for the Great War, he was a leader in training men and an innovator rather than a field commander. At some point, he seemed to have held every conceivable training or operations top spot in the military, reaching brigadier general in 1940.

A hero in the southeast because of his leadership in relief work for the victims of the "Flood of 1929," he was a problem solver and a doer. He was now the commander of the Army Air Forces Technical Training Command. Nine months away from retiring, General Weaver made sure the Army Air Corps operated with efficiency.

"What was your rifle score, Fergy?" Bud asked.

"Eight bullseyes."

"I got eleven," Landela piped up.

"Eight out of fifteen ain't bad," Bud encouraged his friend.

143

"How did you do?" Landela addressed his question to Bud.

"Same. Eleven," Bud responded. "A hundred-and-fifty-yards is a lot of fun, but it's tough. Especially when it's not been your gun for the last bunch of years."

"You country boys sure can shoot," Ferguson lamented.

"It's because we do it a lot. Like anything else," Landela explained. "The more you do it, the better you get."

"Sub-machine guns in a couple of days, men." Bud's smile reflected his anticipation.

Ferguson fell deep into contemplation. His eyebrows arched downward and his squinted eyes conveyed either pain or thought, or both. He gazed across the room in silence.

"What is it, Ferguson?" Landela looked the man over.

"I was just wondering if I'd rather be in civilian life right now." He paused in further thought. "I kinda like the Army."

Bud did not feel the need to contemplate. "If they try and discharge me I'll stow away on some battleship." The two laughed, but undeterred, Bud continued. "I would. I couldn't get a job except the CCs, and that don't pay much."

"At some point, Peterson, we're going to be in the war," Ferguson said, reflecting his concern for his safety.

"Yeah, that may be," Bud countered. "Or, by the time we get over there, the war ends. We go home. The Army taught us some skills we can use the rest of our life."

"I'm happy I'm in the Army," Landela opined. "But I could do without all that shooting stuff. That's why I'm glad I'm gonna be in the air. They don't get shot as much as the guys on the ground do."

"I'm not worried about the war. It'll stop." Bud spoke with a firmness the other two could not understand. "And when I get home, I'm going to marry my girl and get a good job."

The other two shook their heads and all three slipped into thought.

"Interesting," Landela added, broadcasting his continued focus on the subject.

After another half a minute, the conversation died, so Bud decided to use his time to write a letter to his mother. He was behind with his entire family and friends, but writing to his mother was a good place to start — a fact which the drill sergeants drummed into the recruits on a daily basis.

Halfway into his letter, the silence met a sharp, deep cry. "A-ten-SHUN!"

The three men leaped to their feet and saluted as a drill sergeant stepped aside for the executive officer — the ranking soldier over the drill sergeants.

Furrowed brow, eyes darting daggers, body leaning forward serving to speed up his pace, the square-jawed soldier took every step as though charging into battle. "At ease, men," he bellowed, his voice so deep it startled most people. "Who is Peterson?"

A weak, almost squeaky response met the demanding question. "Here, sir."

"Peterson, scuttlebutt is you walked through a lady's house today. You then surprised your opposing squad and led them into a trap you set. Is that accurate, Private Peterson?"

"Uh, yes sir." Like most of his family, Bud never felt intimidated by anybody, but the Army was in the midst of

145

attempting to change that. "I did, sir. And it worked. I was gonna tell my drill sergeant but forgot."

The steel face cracked and broke into a smile on the verge of a gut-busting laugh. The executive officer caught himself and allowed only a small smile to cover the steel. "Good work, Private."

"Did the lady complain?"

"No, son. We didn't hear from her. The other squad was pissed, though. I told them, 'too bad.'"

Bud's face erupted into a large smile; his eyes glowed. "Thank you, sir."

The fearsome soldier turned to leave, drill sergeant in tow, but stopped at the door and addressed Bud one final time. "Next time, Private, don't forget to report it."

"Yes, sir!"

Chapter Fourteen

Thanks to the onset of war, and the need to provide war materiel for the U.S. war machine and the Allies, the poor and middle classes were recovering from the Depression. At least some were. Young men of fighting age who had yet to be drafted — those classified as "1-A" — struggled to find work and did not experience economic recovery.

With the unemployment rate under 5%, the logical result envisioned would be a roaring economy and enriched populace. Indeed, the economic activity ushered in by the war effort technically brought an end to the Great Depression. The problem was one of "Guns and Butter," as economists put it: if the economy is producing all "guns," then there is not enough "butter" to go around. People found it difficult to find non-war items; from automobiles to coffee, products were in short supply and, for everyday items such as sugar, in high demand.

By February of 1943, Americans were into their second year of shortages and rationing. Food, fuel, items made of certain products such as rubber, and clothing: all to some degree were in short supply. Uncle Sam feared the financially well-off would hoard items and make the lower classes suffer more.

The government's solution for the problem of scarcity was to create a system of rationing, complete with a bureaucratic agency to oversee it. The Office of Price Administration operated through over 8,000 local boards, which in turn distributed ration stamps and sniffed out non-compliant citizens.

The public became familiar with, and often perplexed by, "uniform coupon rationing," "point rationing," "differential coupon rationing," and "certificate rationing." Many families felt as though a doctorate degree was necessary to understand the byzantine system, but most people did not complain. They understood the benefit to their sons, fathers, and brothers who needed the food and tools of war. Reminders dotted public places. Besides the "Buy War Bonds" posters, some of the reminders employed guilt as a motivator. "Do with less so they'll have enough" and "Be patriotic, sign your country's pledge to save food."

"Victory gardens" sprang up to ease the burden on the food supply chain. Scrap metal drives helped keep the steel factories working. Rubber drives were held so the substance could be collected and then recycled. Rules were established about the number of tires a person could own — often five per car — and the amount of gasoline one could purchase. Allocation of tires and gasoline depended upon one's distance from home to work.

Most stamps in the War Rations Book authorized purchase within a specified time frame and limited the quantities which could be purchased, while other stamps lacked the time designation.

Each War Rations Book belonged to a specific individual, and the coupons could not be traded or borrowed. The threat of imprisonment or a $10,000 fine served as a deterrent to cheating.

Red stamps were used to purchase meat, butter, fat, and oils and included expiration dates.

Blue stamps covered various foods, including fruits and vegetables which were canned, bottled, or frozen, as well as soups, baby food, ketchup, and dry beans.

With items such as shoes and clothing rationed, caring for one's apparel grew in importance.

The labyrinth of rules and systems fed the rise of a black market. No matter the validity of the cause, some were going to make money and others would break the rules to avoid the shared sacrifice. Meat, sugar, and gasoline could be purchased illegally — for a hefty price.

By 1945, the government estimated 20 million Victory Gardens produced nearly 40% of America's vegetables. Classes taught women to plant, grow, and can their homegrown crops. Companies advertised their patriotism and Americans responded in kind. *Good Housekeeping* published a cookbook in 1943 for using rationed foods to keep the family well-nourished. Kraft Macaroni and Cheese sold 80 million boxes in 1943. What made it so popular? Two boxes could be purchased with one rationing coupon. Cottage cheese experienced increased popularity, with sales growing five-fold from 1930 to 1944. Oleo margarine replaced butter.

When Hulda came home to Bemidji in the late winter of 1943, she, like her fellow countrymen, faced the maze of stamps and regulations. People learned quickly, and Hulda was not an exception. She returned to gardening, monitored her stamps, and struggled to not overuse her food supply.

Hulda's prohibition against complaining served her well, for there was much to complain about if one chose to do so; however, with a son in the Army, she knew it was all for a good cause.

Unlike many people, Hulda maintained a healthy skepticism about the magnanimity of people. During World War I, she had knitted a sweater for her brother Hap and put money in the pocket, stitching it closed. As was common at the time, she then gave the sweater to the Red Cross for delivery to Hap's location in France. Not long later, as she walked down a local street, she encountered a man wearing the sweater, cash still in the closed pocket. She recovered the sweater and cash on the spot. That was her final interaction with the Red Cross; she never trusted them again.

Good causes and noble gestures came with occasional ignoble characters and actions, which bred skepticism and caution in some.

•　　•　　•

"Thank you," Conrad said as he stepped out of the 1938 Ford. The driver turned the automobile around and backtracked down Irvine Avenue, back to the main road to resume his journey to International Falls. Conrad was fortunate to have a car pass with a driver willing to pick him up. The government rationed gasoline to save the supply of rubber for the military effort — gasoline was not the concern.

From the eastern end of Durand Drive, the young man walked the final mile to his sister-in-law's cabin. The cold breeze nipped at his ears and nose and his eyes watered, but Conrad felt little annoyance from the 18-degree weather. The two inches of snow offered no resistance; most of it had been smashed by the few cars which had passed over the road since the small storm came through the area.

When in sight of the little house, Conrad watched as the door opened part way, then closed. As he neared the door, it opened two additional times and closed with the same haste.

Conrad understood what that meant, so he stopped and stared. No adult could out-wait him, let alone a child.

The door opened again, leaving Conrad with just enough time to stick out his tongue as it closed. An idea struck him and he ran to within ten feet of the door. When the door opened again, it shut at once with a loud slam.

The uncle stood ready to wait, but instead, the girl with light brown hair and an ornery smile welcomed him. "Hi, Uncle Connie." Carla Anne Peterson, not much past the age of two, stepped backward from the threshold as she opened the door wide and curtsied for the tall uncle, her light-blue dress draped past her knees.

Once inside, he bent down and gave his niece a hearty hug. "Where's your momma?" he asked.

"She's out in the commode." The little girl pointed behind her, referring to the outhouse. "She's chasing a fox away."

"Oh." Conrad now understood. "She's near the commode."

"Yeah."

Conrad turned to go check on her, but before he could step toward it, the door swung open.

The next sound Carla and Conrad heard began as a wordless reaction to the cold wind which morphed into a scream. The truncated scream melted into relief. "Oh! Conrad! You scared the dickens out of me!"

Anne, five months pregnant and the baby bulging seemingly more every day, stepped forward and wrapped her arms around her brother-in-law's neck. She stepped back from the quick hug.

"Thank you so much for coming, Conrad! It's so good to see you!"

Conrad smiled. "I'm here to check on your wood situation."

"Oh!" Anne's effusive speech habits did not veer into the dramatic, but she spoke with pleasurable intensity, often with exclamation points, and was the mirror image of the man standing before her. "Let me tell you something. You should've seen the red fox that keeps coming around here! I tell you, that little creature looks real crafty! You know what I mean? He's already made off with some of Knutson's chickens!"

"He won't hurt ya," Conrad said. "He's just looking for a meal." He turned to Carla and gave her an evil grin. "And they don't like the taste of children much."

"I hope not!" Carla shouted.

Anne thrust an arm around her daughter. "He won't bother you, honey."

"That's right. So, don't worry about him, Anne."

"Oh! I guess you're right." She nodded.

"What about your wood situation?"

"Emil helped me a while back, but he's not been doing too good lately."

"Mother has told me about it." Conrad found himself in a long conversation with someone he cared about — but it was still a long conversation.

"I could probably use some, although we probably only have another month of winter."

Conrad nodded. "I hope it doesn't extend into April." He looked around the kitchen.

"Here," Anne volunteered. "Before you cut any wood, let's get you something to eat."

• • •

"Thank you, Conrad, for cutting the wood."

An exhausted Conrad responded from his seat at the kitchen table. "You're welcome." Known for his constant thinking, he settled on a question which had to be asked now. "When are you going out to California?"

"That goofy husband of mine keeps telling me to come out now," Anne blurted, not hiding her emotions. "But he doesn't even have a place for us to live. I'm not living in a cramped apartment with a little one and soon another one — and with Carl and Uncle Hap, to boot." She almost came out of her chair with the last line.

"He'll find you a place."

"There's lots of people out there. There's not much in the way of housing."

"He'll find you a place," Conrad repeated, quieter this time.

"I want to get there as bad as he wants me out there." The pregnant woman stopped as she struggled with her emotions. "He's all fired up at me, but he's just gonna have to stay fired up!" She folded her arms and nodded with a slow, firm bob of the head. "With Mother as sick as she is and me going to visit her when I can, I can't leave Minnesota yet."

Conrad looked around the kitchen, then at the floor, nervousness flowing from every pore. "I've gotta get. I've gotta head to Emil's for the night."

"You sure?"

"Yes." Conrad rose to his feet and waited as Anne did the same. He gave her a quick hug, then walked to Carla, asleep in a chair nearby. He gave her a kiss on the forehead and, without hesitating, walked out the door.

Anne chuckled as she shut the door behind him. She was used to Conrad.

•   •   •

Carl and Hap marched through the large parking lot toward Shipyard No. 3. Carl held his left hand against his left cheek and growled as he spoke. "Damned thirty-one-dollar dentist bill and I still hurt like hell!"

"I told you, you should've drank some of my whiskey," Hap said with a rueful tone.

"Yeah, and I should've done it. Maybe I could've passed out and slept some." His face remained twisted in a snarl with the pain and lack of sleep. "I thought dentists are supposed to take away the pain?!"

"If it's not better in a couple of days, go back," Hap advised.

"Yeah, and knock him on his ass!"

Hap laughed, but he knew Carl meant it.

"And when the hell is Anne gonna get out here?!" His mood worsened. "I keep writing her, telling her to take the train, but she won't do it."

"Where are you going to live?"

"Hell, I don't know."

154

Hap laughed "Carl, you've had a bad week with your dental pain. You've gotta make sure you don't take this out on your crew or family."

"I'm supposed to do a shakedown on the Liberty we rolled out yesterday." Carl took a deep breath. "I'm not going to be a very good supervisor today."

Hap tried walking in silence to see whether that would help his nephew's mood. It worked for a minute, until Carl's thoughts burst into the air. "Where the hell is Anne?!"

Hap squeezed his eyelids closed in a long, forceful blink, then fought off a smile. He felt bad for Carl, but the two approached life from different perspectives.

The men walked in silence until they reached the entrance, bid each other farewell, and strode away in separate directions, to their own duties.

Chapter Fifteen

"Four dollars a month! I'll take it." The three men with deep southern accents held a lively discussion about the recent promotion they had received to Private First Class. From his bed, Bud tried to tune out the conversation as he worked on another letter — this one to his mother.

"Hey, Pete!" one of the southerners yelled, despite his proximity. The three men sat on two different beds, including one next to Bud. "Whatcha gonna do with your raise money?"

"I'm gonna send it to my mother." The man who, by his admission and that of others, could get along with anyone, did not feel social at the moment. His legs felt heavy and his neck ached at the strain of holding up his head. He only cared about wrapping up his brief missive to Hulda.

"I've got a question for you boys," Bud said, attention span shattered.

"What's that?" one of them asked.

"What the hell is 'terbaccy'?"

The three laughed as though they just heard the funniest joke ever.

"And what's a 'gran pappy'?" A coy smile broke out.

"Oh, Peterson!" the shortest of the three began. "We ain't got many Petersons where we live. You're a funny man, Pete."

"Are you saying you ain't never chewed terbaccy?!" The man with the deepest of the drawls asked, incredulous.

"No." Bud shook his head, then mustered his best drawl. "I'm saying I ain't never no-how heard the word 'terbaccy.'"

The three looked at each other in unison. "I do believe he's making fun of us, boys," the one with the deepest drawl opined.

"We don't make fun of the funny way he talks and says 'eh' and says his 'O's' funny," the short one added.

"And we ain't for damn sure lettin' some Yankee make fun of us," the third man said, though his playful tone did not match the threatening proclamation.

"That's the first time I've ever been called a Yankee," Bud laughed. "The Civil War's over. Goodnight, now." Bud put his head down and continued to write. As barracks leader, he felt the responsibility to not allow the jabbing and poking escalate into swinging and punching.

Bud would send the letter to Elsie's house, where Hulda had taken up residence, though likely on a temporary basis, knowing her. Elsie continued to struggle with the loss of her baby, so her mother's presence comforted her. Bud made only passing mention of his sister's emotions in order to avoid bringing up the sad situation.

After writing about the "rebels," as the others called the southerners, Bud continued:

Our officers believe in writing. Gee, I never have met such a swell gang of men as our officers are. They come right in the barracks and talk to us. In fact, I came in the barracks one day and two officers were sitting on my bed talking to the men.

Training held the most value at this point in the men's military lives. They continued with daily drills and exercises, but the emphasis now focused on the brain and learning skills the Air Corps required. They were not headed to North Africa or the South Pacific; they were in Texas to learn about airplane mechanics. Others in the camp were at different stages of their training, and many were in fact training for combat; but, Bud received from the military exactly what he had hoped for: practical skills for future employment.

> *When I start school I will go six weeks in the daytime then I'll go six weeks at night, and so on. I will be sent to a factory for six weeks when my course here is completed... I am getting along fine. I hope you are O.K...*

He finished the letter, ending it with "Loads of Love, your son, Bud," and left his bed to make his way to the mailbox. With a smile at the "rebels" as he passed them, he stopped at the mailbox and wrote "Free" in the upper-right corner of the envelope, where the stamp usually rests. Free postage further encouraged the men to write home.

Back to bed, this time to sleep, he settled in, tuning out a lively discussion. He decided not to wait for "lights out" and instead wished to get an early start on rest. The classroom would soon beckon. The specter of war settled far from the thoughts of PFC Peterson as he slipped into slumber.

•　　•　　•

Conrad spent his winter days helping his sisters and their children and by running errands. With his mother at Elsie's house, he spent more time with Thelma to assist her. However, at long last, from Conrad's perspective, the mundane was about to turn to challenges, tests of courage, and an active life. He joined the Army. He did so without the drama Bud endured. Conrad read the tea leaves, knew employment could not be attained with his "1-A" classification, and simply volunteered.

Conrad thought through every action and reaction, observed life around him before making decisions, and spent all his quiet time where he felt most comfortable: alone.

Besides his family, he knew he would miss the mental solitude the most. He said his goodbyes, watched his mother fight back tears as her youngest child left the nest, and at the appointed time journeyed to Ft. Snelling.

At his request, Conrad was not regaled with the fanfare of a party or a big family gathering to see him off. He wanted to leave the way he did everything else: with quiet conversations when he said his goodbyes, around as few people as possible at any given moment.

Unlike Bud, who wanted to go into the tank division but found himself in the Air Corps, Conrad wanted the Air Corps. He wanted to fly.

And now, his adventure could begin.

•　　•　　•

The Peterson family knew the Martins well, so news of "Sonny's" death shook them. Francis F. Martin lost his life in the North Africa campaign; but, the shock was not just a friend had been lost, it was the realization it could be their own family grieving. The Petersons cared about the Martins, mourned with them, and prayed for them; yet, in the back of every family member's mind was the thought that, some day, they could be grieving for Bud or Conrad. They would not allow that thought to come to the fore, but the prospect lingered, ready to strike — a coiled rattlesnake with the words "Killed in Action" as its venom.

Sonny was the first resident of Puposky to die in the war. He had lived there until the age of six when his family moved to Bemidji. In small towns and rural areas, not everyone knows everyone else, but everyone knows someone who knows any particular person. In the case of the Martins, their move to Bemidji only limited Bud and Conrad's friendship with Sonny; it did not end it.

In his first letter home after learning of Sonny's death, Bud expressed concern about Mrs. Martin, Sonny's mother, Cecilia. In fact, the family fell apart emotionally. The Martins had three children and now had lost their only son. Like their parents, the elder and younger sisters were devastated. The price of war remained high.

The Petersons felt fortunate Conrad was in Basic Training and Bud remained stateside — but that could change. It likely would.

In Bud's next letter home, in the context of Sonny's death, Bud wrote that he needed to "wake up." Uncle Sam's Army did not exist for the sole purpose of teaching men mechanics skills.

•   •   •

"Are you doing better, Carl?"

160

"No. Not really. You?"

Hap smiled. "It just seems like a long time because you want to speed up time but you can't."

From his seat at their table, Carl took another sip of his Lucky Lager and stared across the room, in the direction of the bartender. Bottles of whiskey — Scotch, Irish, Canadian, Bourbon, Tennessee, and Rye — covered the back wall. Anyone who entered the bar for the first time knew immediately this bar believed in variety. Japanese whiskey and German beers were absent, but no one complained.

"How was your shakedown today?"

"Oh, they all run together, it seems, the way we turn 'em out."

"Understandable." Hap looked at his nephew with concern. "Well, you don't want to talk about work and you can't talk about what's delaying Anne without blowing up, so what do you want to talk about?" The question sounded harsher than intended.

Carl's gaze turned to Happy as he snarled. "You tell me, Hap. I don't know that I want to talk about anything."

Before Hap could respond, Carl interjected. "I'm sorry, Hap. I'm just wound up tight, that's all."

"I know, I know."

"I just… I got a little girl who's not gonna know me soon and a kid on the way." Carl paused to maintain self-control. "I… I just want her out here, that's all."

"Wait 'til you get number ten on the way." Hap laughed, although he did not mean the implied knock against Carl's feelings. "I miss my wife and kids, but I just make the most of it. We work like crazy, anyway." He changed his tack. "Besides, pretty soon you'll be told you don't spend enough time at home, so enjoy things now. She'll be here before you know it and you'll be happy again."

"You're the happy one, not me."

"Yeah, but you just have to make the most of life. You love her, you want her here, and she'll be here." Hap realized they were discussing the very subject Carl should avoid. "It'll work out soon. Don't worry."

"The shakedown went perfect." Carl kept his eyes on Hap rather than any distractions in the bar.

"That's good. Good to hear." Hap struggled with the conversation, despite his deep understanding of the young man across the table.

Carl realized he had just snapped at the man who became a father figure after William passed away. He could never repay his uncle for how much he meant and did for him. He lived with Hap's family even after they added another child — their fourth, at the time. Carl had departed and found work as a lumberjack and later at a sawmill.

"Missy!" Carl raised his hand to gain the attention of a young waitress. The young woman made her way to the table. "Two more, please."

The young brunette took note of their beer brands, nodded and smiled, then hurried toward the bar until she found herself flagged down by another patron.

"This is on me, all evening." Carl frowned. "I shouldn't have snapped like that and I'm sorry."

Happy smiled. "You don't have to buy my beer."

"Maybe I don't, but I am."

One of the ways Happy earned his nickname included knowing when not to argue. Still eager to lift Carl's spirits, he changed the subject. "When this mess is over with and I get home, I'm gonna build Mother a little house on my farm."

"Grandma Thompson?" Carl asked, incredulous. "She'll stay there for two weeks then she'll fly again." Carl laughed, causing Hap to follow suit.

"I know." Hap shook his head. "But I'm gonna try. Every time I get a letter from Violet or Hulda, they mention they haven't heard from Mother lately."

"She's a free bird."

"Oh, yeah. Always has been."

The conversation shifted topics multiple times, but as they downed their beers, Hap succeeded in getting Carl's mind off his frustrations in getting Anne out to California.

Chapter Sixteen

The mother of three sons — each well over a thousand miles away; two daughters — both with their own challenges, physical and emotional; five granddaughters — cute little girls who warmed Hulda's heart every time she found herself in their presence; a widow — a little hole remained in her heart after the loss of William; Hulda pushed forward.

Good and bad, happy and sad thoughts crossed Hulda's mind as she enjoyed the cool breeze reaching Elsie's front porch. A sweater sufficed to keep out the dry air which nipped at her skin with its chilled touch.

The rest of the house lay still. It was a Sunday, and in hours, the house would be enveloped by the sounds of scurrying and chattering, eating and dressing, before Elsie's family and Hulda went off to church services.

Life in Bemidji did not present the same challenges as the Puposky farm. But a memory now, the farm had brought difficulties and satisfactions, pains and pleasures. She missed that life, yet could not imagine ever returning to it. Life had moved on.

Hulda's light-brown hair, ever in the hairnet, lifted and sank above her forehead as the gentle wind kissed her soft, Nordic face. She turned her head to watch as a blue jay squawked at a pine siskin for invading its space at an empty bird feeder near the end of the porch. Perched in an American elm in Elsie's yard, which reached over forty feet into the sky, a brilliant red northern cardinal sang out his "what-cheer, what-cheer" call. Other birds flitted about, in search of breakfast.

Despite her best efforts, her worries and concerns came out in each letter to her military sons. Carl could take care of himself, and his family, when Anne and Carla made the trip, but the odds were Bud and Conrad would, at some point, find themselves in the war. She lost sleep on a regular basis over the thought.

The three men were raised to be good, strong, and independent. Hulda possessed plenty of faith God would be with her children, but she knew bad things happened to good people. William served as a perfect example of that; the evil cancer which took him away from her cared not of her faith or strength. The killer came, took its victim, and seemingly moved on.

She feared war somehow claimed kinship with cancer. Good young men died in battles, by land, sea, and air, with no regard for family, feelings, or friendships.

She chuckled at the thought of her two sons in Texas. Their reports painted the distant state into a picture of a foreign land, and in many regards, Texas was just that. Suffocating humidity and tame winters, red dirt and clay with few trees and fewer lakes, Texas was indeed a foreign place to the young men from the North.

To those from rougher climes, California was just shy of the Land of Milk and Honey. Beaches, mountains, mild temperatures, year-round warmth — all within close proximity to any point in the state. Carl's description of factory workers sleeping outside in winter months seemed fantastical. The economy boomed in the land of plenty.

She forced a smile as she thought about spending a few days in California, once Anne arrived and settled in.

The worries of war did not force out all consideration of her standard of living. Once the Kochs returned from their extended vacation in Canada and a tour of several U.S. states, which replaced the usual trip to Paris, London, and other European cities, Hulda could return to work near the Twin Cities. Until then, she would seek out odd jobs helping families with children, handle laundry duties, or perform other similar tasks just as she had always done.

In the meantime, gardens kept the grocery bills down and the lack of mouths to feed eased her burden. Bud and Conrad sent part of their pay to her, an allotment which came as a tremendous boost to her finances.

She tried not to think about the insurance policies they had taken out on their lives — $10,000 each.

Complaints from Hulda only reached her lips in rare circumstances, but as she sat on the porch, watching the day brighten into a warm June canvas of blues and greens, and as small creatures raced about, she pondered how the allotments meant her sons were fighting not only for country, but their mother. She did not feel comfortable with their charity, but understood the necessity.

A nearby empty lot featured a quaking aspen, which danced in the morning breeze — a breeze which warmed by the minute. She watched as the boisterous blue jay, tired of chirping in front of Hulda, retreated to the aspen. The triumphant little siskin flew in the opposite direction to search for breakfast in the neighbor's yard.

Her mind returned to her sons in the military. Bud had gained weight after his admission into the Army, and his expressed satisfaction for his current situation made her view of his life more tenable. Bud's time in the Army was aimed at acquiring job skills; he made that point on multiple occasions. When a letter from Bud announced he had passed the physical to move from the regular Army into the Air Corps, she did not know whether to worry or feel satisfaction. Bud noted he was not destined to be a pilot but expressed happiness he would soon be flying.

Conrad, on the other hand, wanted to go into the Air Corps but was placed in the Medical Corps. If he did not beg, take tests, and remain persistent, his desire to fly would go unrealized.

The time had arrived to get ready for church. Hulda could hear activity in the house and knew it was a matter of moments before Judy or Joanne would rush out onto the porch, run to her chair, and throw loving arms around her neck.

Necessity of a sweater waned, and thoughts of removing it floated by as she thought of her family's various predicaments. The melancholy morning calmed Hulda and gave her time to think. All five sons and daughters had problems, but life behaved in no other way. The key was to meet the challenges.

The door opened and Joanne let out a gasp of "Gramma!" Hulda's deep thoughts and stone face melted into the loveable grandmother the girl knew. The sweet child did not have to worry about war and money and security. The tight squeeze of little arms around her neck helped hide a tear that escaped. It was time to forget troubles and focus on sugar and spice and everything nice.

•   •   •

"This will be the first and last time I come here by car."

"I can understand that," Carl agreed.

"And I've heard it used to be a lot worse than this, when they had more lanes of trolleys." Hap shook his head.

Carl glanced at the street signs, then down at the piece of paper in his hand. He repeated the cycle with every block conquered through the jumbled and tossed mess of San Francisco streets. He removed the Fedora from his head, perched there since their brief stop at a cafeteria for lunch. "I hope it's not always this bad," he said, impatient with their slow travel, as a man ran in front of a trolley.

"It's every day. You can count on that."

Carl recoiled. "I'm not going across that damned Bay Bridge twice a day, every day." His voice thickened at the thought. "I'm tired enough from work and school," he said, referring to the mandatory classes for learning on behalf of Kaiser's shipbuilding processes.

"Don't worry," Hap encouraged him. "The ferry terminal is just a few blocks away, south of Pier 1. It takes you to the Richmond Terminal, in Harbor Channel, right there east of our shipyard."

Carl lifted his eyebrows at the thought this apartment choice could work out. He fidgeted with a map before announcing, "Okay."

As he took in his surroundings, he saw a sign in front of a hotel which read "Rooms: 50-75 cents." A truck with the company name of "Simon Bros. Wreckers" on the door pulled to the curb to assist a motorist.

The slow drive, in which they avoided numerous trolleys and pedestrians, approached its end as Hap drove the old Ford south on Drumm Street, then turned right onto Sacramento Street.

"Here it is." A moment of relief and satisfaction overcame Carl as he found the building matching the address written on the piece of paper he held. On the corner of Drumm and Sacramento, an old store had been transformed into an apartment building, such was the demand for wartime housing.

"Look at that, Carl." Hap stepped out of the car and waited for his nephew to do the same. "Two blocks that way," he pointed north. "And one block the other way you're at Pier 1. If you choose this place, your kids will want to go down to see the ships every day."

Carl grinned. "Let's not get ahead of ourselves."

One block from busy California Street and two from the busier Market Street, Carl understood the location had its weaknesses, but noise was not one of them. Life in the Bay Area had diminished his opposition to city noise; the lack of silence had become a fact of life.

Once inside the one-bedroom apartment, a wave of relief flooded him. "Well, if she ever gets here, this will work."

"One bedroom, two adults, and two children? No problem," Hap laughed.

"Yeah, that's because you have nine kids."

"Tenth on the way." Hap grinned.

"Ten. Damn. Makes me want to curl up in a ball and cry." Carl smiled.

"Sometimes it does me, too." Happy laughed again, pleased to see Carl smiling more lately.

Carl's unhappiness at his wife's delay slipped into the background with her so close to delivery. He ceased his insistence she move out to California immediately and now waited with great impatience for the birth of his second child.

"If you don't move here," Hap began his question. "You'd move back to Puposky, wouldn't you?"

"Damn right I would. I told Bud that in a letter," Carl smiled. "And I think the word filtered to Anne. I was hot."

"You said it. You were hot under the collar."

Carl only shrugged.

A review of the layout with an eye toward the quality of construction preceded a discussion with the apartment manager about the date rent would be due. Carl signed a short document which served as the lease, then bid temporary farewell to the manager. At long last, Carl could stop worrying about Anne and when she would move to live with him and could focus on worrying about when his second child would be born.

•　　•　　•

The group of privates left the mess hall. Some were in search of rest in their barracks while others went off to perform their daily duties. In Conrad's case, he meandered to the supply room to report for duty. As men peeled away when they reached their destinations, others talked about the subject at hand: the food they had just consumed.

"What was that green garbage?" one soldier asked, amazement dominating his voice.

"Goop," another responded.

"It's why we call it 'wonder food,' boys," Conrad said.

"Yup," another private added. "We wonder what we just ate."

"And wonder what we could've had somewhere else," Conrad said with a wry tone. With that, he changed course and headed to the supply room.

• • •

"Why do you look so sleepy, private?" The brown-haired, brown-eyed sergeant eyed Conrad with suspicion.

"I ate a lot for lunch, sir."

"A lot? You griped about the food for five minutes when you got here! Why did you eat so much if it tasted so bad?"

"I was hungry, sir." No smile; no chuckle; pure Conrad.

"See that pile of bedsheets on the floor?" the sergeant asked as he pointed across the expansive room.

"Yes, sir."

"Right next to that pile are the shelves where we keep the typewriters and paper," the sergeant continued. "Get the typing supplies off the dock, bring them here, and rearrange the shelves so they're in good order." He issued the command to act with a flat but confident tone.

"Yes sir, sarge." Conrad responded as he ambled away.

• • •

The kid in the olive uniform, garrison cap resting on his head, looked comfortable in the pile of sheets. He opened his eyes to see his sergeant's back as the man put the finishing touches on organizing typing paper, typewriter ribbon, and a small section of new black typewriters on the shelves.

The sergeant turned and noticed Conrad looking at him. "Did you have a good nap, private?"

Like a newborn horse, Conrad came alive and struggled to his feet. "Yes, sir. Sorry, sir."

With enormous care and concern in his voice, the sergeant continued. "You slept for a half hour, son. I hope you're feeling better."

"A half hour? Sorry, sir!" Conrad apologized again.

"Have you been sleeping okay at night?"

"When I have time, sir."

"Well, young man," the sergeant smiled. "I completed your job for you."

"Thank you. Wow. Thank you!" Conrad paused, then asked in a tenuous voice, "Am I in trouble? Sir?"

The sergeant shook his head with large sweeps in an exaggerated denial, his face moving toward his left shoulder, then to the right, and then back again. "Oh, no. You're in no trouble, private. Not at all."

"Thank you! Thank you, sir!" Conrad perked up at the thought of how nice his sergeant could be.

"You're not in trouble, but after today you're not working in the supply room anymore." He paused for effect. "From now on, your new job is KP duty." The sergeant's tone changed in a flash. "Now go to the dock, get the shipment of paper that's come in, and stock the shelves where they belong!" His syrupy demeanor gave way to a bark and a growl. "On the double, private!"

Pale and alarmed, Conrad stiffened his skinny frame, saluted, then jogged away instead of sauntering at his usual slow, patient pace. He grumbled under his breath as he trotted away.

"They teach me how to stitch up shot-up soldiers but they want me to play in the kitchen!"

• • •

As much as he loved and appreciated his uncle, Carl found it comforting to have his own place. No longer did he feel his presence was an imposition. No longer did he feel cramped, even though limited living space was a normal existence to him. He continued to see his mentor and friend, Uncle Hap, as much as possible — that would not change.

His thoughts ended with an abrupt knock on his door. On a Friday evening, he did not expect anyone to drop by other than his uncle. He opened the door to see a young man of perhaps fifteen years extend his hand in presentation of an envelope.

"Telegram." The boy's words had scarcely escaped his mouth when Carl snatched the envelope from him. He reached into his pocket and pulled out a dime.

With a gruff, "Here," Carl handed the grateful boy the dime, failed to hear the youngster's utterance of gratitude, and shut the door. He ripped open the envelope to read the Western Union telegram, transcribed at 10:38 a.m. from "Benidji" Minnesota.

CARL A. PETERSON= 32 SACRAMENTO ST SFRAN:
    = DEAR DAD: ARRIVED SAFELY LUTHERAN
HOSPITAL EIGHT AM THIS MORNING I WEIGH
    NINE POUNDS BIG ARENT I MOTHER IS
FINE=
    JAMES WILLIAM

173

Neighbors could hear the ecstatic shout of the ordinarily taciturn, even-keeled man. The first boy of the family's next generation; Carl had a son, named for both of the baby's grandfathers: James William.

•   •   •

Celebrations reverberated through the Peterson and Gustafson families, as well as Anne's local relatives: the Christensen, Graham, and Strand families. They were happy anytime a child entered the family, but at long last, a boy had arrived for Hulda's clan. Elsie's young boy had died after ten hours, so although largely left unsaid, a sense of relief at little Jimmy's survival pervaded the family.

Carl could not get away from work, but in his new, enthusiastic mood, he sent his brothers a dollar each and told them to buy a fistful of cigars. Conrad used the dollar on a steak dinner instead and teasingly offered to catch a Texas rattlesnake and send Anne its rattler for the boy.

•   •   •

Bud and Conrad separately battled the Texas heat — the third-hottest summer in recorded history for the area — and Conrad even joked he missed the Minnesota mosquitoes.

In the news and in conversations throughout Texas, Bemidji, and Richmond, there was a war on. Nobody saw it but everyone felt it. However, the war presented itself as a distant thought to Bud and Conrad. Killing Germans and Japanese remained as remote as a blizzard at Sheppard Field or Camp Barkeley.

Everyone continued to feel pressures, particularly financial, yet the family saw progress. Bud's wish of using Uncle Sam to teach him skills manifested itself every day in his classes. Conrad's stinging yet humorous observations about his surroundings kept the family amused by way of letters. Hulda's inner fears never reached the surface, and the new grandson helped to forget her troubles.

Even Carl's consternation over his wife's delay in migrating to California abated somewhat. He wanted to see his wife, daughter, and newborn; but, while the consternation faded and frustrations remained, the promise of change comforted him. Having a second child was like putting salve on a wound.

As the calendar hurtled forward and Carl turned twenty-eight, he spent the first part of August with rising expectations of reuniting with his family.

Chapter Seventeen

The front of the postcard featured a glossy photograph of a complex of three-story brick buildings, with a smattering of trees on the grounds to give the small lawns, broken by sidewalks, a homey feel. Cars, mostly black, filled the street, parked at the curb. Across the bottom of the card were emblazoned the words "University of Minnesota Hospital, Minneapolis, Minn."

Hulda wrote her message to Conrad in pencil on the back, where it was overlaid by a Minneapolis postmark. She wrote her words at a 90-degree angle from the norm, forcing the reader to turn the card long-ways to read it.

Conrad, just a card today as I am too upset to write a letter. News is not good from here. No hope. Matter of time. Will write details later. Hope you get this.
Love from Mother.

The postcard, dated August 17, 1943, conveyed the heartbreaking news that Gertrude Graham, Anne's mother and Hulda's longtime friend, would not recover from her cancer. The recipient, Conrad, understood the meaning of the cryptic card without any extrapolating on the message of "no hope" or even referencing the name of the doomed patient.

Hulda and Anne each gave a pint of blood for the ailing Gertrude and her surgery, and over the weeks the dying woman received fifteen pints. The doctors tried their best, but as Hulda put it, there was no hope.

Anne felt emotionally crushed. She had a responsibility to care for her mother and a duty to reunite with her husband. The strong, normally upbeat Dane remained somber on the trip as she and Hulda traveled by train back to Bemidji. At long last, Anne understood the time had arrived to travel to California, and she outlined her plan to her mother-in-law.

Carl had written to Conrad that he was so upset by Anne remaining in Puposky he was considering quitting his lucrative Richmond job and moving back to Minnesota. The lull in his frustrations, which had abated when his son was born, ceased, and he returned to writing angry letters with outbursts of disgust. He had good reason, for he had not been made aware of Gertie's dire condition. Anne could never bring herself to write about her mother's failing health, and no one else informed Carl, on the assumption Anne had done so.

On the train ride back to Bemidji, Hulda volunteered to assist with Gertie. When Anne agreed, the die was cast; she was finally going to California.

• • •

The train had departed Bemidji station several hours prior. Most of the train consisted of various cargo cars, both box and flatbed, loaded with civilian and military equipment winding its way across the country, often to the coast, where it could be shipped overseas to the troops or to the vast military machine.

The lone engine spewed black clouds of thick smoke which trailed behind the forty-car-long assemblage. The first four cars transported people, many on their way to California to fulfill military orders.

The wood bench seats lined the passenger car, leaving room for an aisle in the middle. A series of large windows on each side presented the look of one large window. Anne, Carla, and Jim traveled in this holdover from the early 1930s. The next car afforded a more comfortable ride, with padded seats, more leg room, elegant amenities, but a bigger price tag.

"Where you going, ma'am?" an Army private seated next to her asked.

"San Francisco," Anne responded, excitement mixed with melancholy.

"That's a little baby to get him in that shoebox."

"When we get there, little Jimmy will see his daddy for the first time," Anne cooed.

"Terrific! I bet you're excited." The clean-shaven young man did not look old enough to shave, let alone go to war. His thin frame reminded her of her husband and brothers-in-law.

A private seated next to Carla piped up with a slight Irish accent. "You be sure to speak up if you need any help, madam."

"Thank you," Anne smiled as she noticed the young man's red hair — what little he had. "You have hair the same color as my brother Norman's."

"Thank you, madam. I hope he's staying out of this mess."

"Oh, no. He's in the Pacific, somewhere out there." She looked from side to side at the young men sandwiching her and the children. "Where are you boys from?"

"I'm from Brooklyn," the Irish soldier responded.

"And you?" she turned to the man to her left.

"I'm from Cranberry Township, Pennsylvania, ma'am." Knowing in all likelihood she had never heard of the town, he added, "It's near Pittsburgh."

"Oh. You boys are from a long ways away!"

"You must be excited to see your husband again," the Irish kid interjected.

"Oh. Yeah. I am." Anne's voice turned melancholy. "But I'm going to miss my family, and I know I'll never see my mother again."

The young soldiers looked at her with pity.

With a stoic attitude, Anne plowed forward. "She's bad off. Cancer." She forced a smile. "But it's okay. Soon she won't be suffering." She paused again before adding, "I went to see her in Minneapolis a couple of weeks ago and said my goodbyes."

In front of her, two soldiers turned around and joined in the conversation, which helped to pass time. When she needed to stand up, the Pennsylvania soldier took the shoebox full of baby and watched over the boy while the others entertained three-year-old Carla.

Despite uncomfortable seats, long distances between stops, and the late summer heat of early September, the trip proved painless. Carl would be reunited with his wife and daughter and meet his son, and Carla and Jim would grow up in California rather than in Minnesota with their extended families. Unfortunately, Anne's fear later proved accurate; she would never again see her mother.

Chapter Eighteen

Now in his fourth week at Camp Maxey, Conrad had long since tired of Texas. First, Camp Barkeley, outside Abilene; then, halfway between Paris and the Red River. The man who hated the heat ("sometimes it gets down to 85 degrees at night") had been stuck in the South for too long, as his northern Minnesota mind saw it.

While he found plenty about which to complain, he did love the Army food, despite his frequent jokes. In spite of rigorous exercise, the young man put on fifteen pounds in his first month, reaching 159 pounds. He no longer had to eat like a poor man.

Conrad opened a letter to his mother with his caustic humor on display:

Dear Mother,
Just a note to tell you the good news. It's so good I can't keep it. It rained today! No kidding, the ground is still wet.

Now, lying in his bunk with a cold, his condition causing him irritation of not just the body, he listened to President Roosevelt and penned a letter to Hulda. As FDR's radio speech — a fireside chat — played on a barracks radio, he kept his mother updated about life in the Army.

I'm not in a very good mood for writing tonight, but I'll see what I can do. For one thing, it doesn't look like I'll ever leave this place...

President Franklin Delano Roosevelt, unknowingly in the last twenty months of his life, used what became known as "Fireside Chat 26" for two different messages.

"Today, it is announced that an armistice with Italy has been concluded."

His familiar voice and accent and famous pacing provided comfort to many, irrespective of party affiliation.

"This was a great victory for the United Nations — but it was also a great victory for the Italian people. After years of war and suffering and degradation, the Italian people are at last coming to the day of liberation from their real enemies, the Nazis."

Mussolini's form of fascism needed no mention considering its recent death. In the context of Europe, only fighting the Nazis mattered now.

"But let us not delude ourselves that this armistice means the end of the war in the Mediterranean. We still must drive the Germans out of Italy as we have driven them out of Tunisia and Sicily; we must drive them on their own soil from all directions."

Men in the barracks grumbled or gushed and frowned or cheered with quiet, almost bashful reserve. Some believed war's end neared; others did not. Everyone wanted the war to end, but no soldier wanted to look weak. "Of course the president said the war is not over! What else could he say?" one soldier snapped. Nevertheless, the prevailing belief the war's end lay in sight carried the mood of many of the men.

"Our ultimate objectives in this war continue to be Berlin and Tokyo. I ask you to bear these objectives constantly in mind — and do not forget that we still have a long way to go before attaining them.

"The great news that you have heard today from General Eisenhower does not give you license to settle back in your rocking chairs and say, 'Well, that does it. We've got 'em on the run. Now we can start the celebration.'

"The time for celebration is not yet. And I have a suspicion that when this war does end, we shall not be in a very celebrating mood, a very celebrating frame of mind. I think that our main emotion will be one of grim determination that this shall not happen again."

With the chatter in the room, Conrad struggled, at times, to hear Roosevelt's smooth voice and musical delivery through the distant radio. The tall, lean soldier felt small and weak due to his cold, but felt comforted when he heard the Commander in Chief speak with certitude in his voice.

"Well, that's one step toward the end of this mess, anyway," Conrad wrote as he listened.

"We have seen the satisfactory fulfillment of plans that were made in Casablanca last January and here in Washington last May. And lately we have made new, extensive plans for the future. But throughout these conferences we have never lost sight of the fact that this war will become bigger and tougher, rather than easier, during the long months that are to come.

"This war does not and must not stop for one single instant. Our fighting men know that. Those of them who are moving forward through jungles against lurking Japs — those who are in landing at this moment, in barges moving through the dawn on the targets at roof-top level at this moment — every one of these men knows that this war is a full-time job and that it will continue to be that until total victory is won."

A man of few words, Conrad's brief letter closed with an insight into his youthful, amusing nature.

> *P.S. I am enclosing a picture I had taken in town the other day. The other part is half of one of my pals. I guess the booth was too small for both of us.*

With a brief comment about sending more photos, he ended his post-script, and thus the letter, with the words,

> *... if I ever get out of Texas.*

The nineteen-year-old had already said his piece about the possibility of "this mess" ending soon, then moved on. Redundancy and excessive analysis were not among his shortcomings.

The rest of the president's speech centered on the sacrifice made by American citizens and the need to bankroll the war machine. By that time, Conrad had finished his letter and moved back into the deep cave of his mind where he engaged in trenchant thought and examined the world around him. He had briefly left that world, listened to Roosevelt, wrote his mother, and retreated back to the place he found the most comfort.

Conrad had not heard from his brothers lately. For Carl, that meant limited time — particularly now, reunited with Anne; for Bud, that meant he had shipped out, and out of Texas. Conrad did not hide his jealousy, though it was more playful than serious.

Fortunately for the disgruntled visitor to Texas, days later the relative who invited him to the Lone Star state — Uncle Sam — would revoke the invitation and send the young soldier off to a new adventure in Utah, away from the arid climate he detested.

•   •   •

"Eye tests, aptitude tests, KP, guard duty," griped the young man who looked like he had been alive for thirteen years rather than nineteen. "Night vision class, they gave me the bends in that altitude stuff. I feel like I should get another stripe because the Army's taught me to waste time like a pro."

This set off a minor explosion of rants and complaints from the men crowded around the wooden table. Eight cut loose with the energy of a puppy let out of its cage for the first time in hours. The men, sporting the same haircuts, uniforms, and even shoes, were difficult to tell apart if seeing them for the first — or even second — time.

"Come on, Peterson," the soldier with the child-like face admonished. "Everybody's griping but you. Don't tell me you're fine with this?"

The men quieted down to listen to Bud, a man who spoke approximately half as much as the others. Some called him "Pete," others "Gene," and still others called him by whatever nicknames they had invented, including "Piccolo Pete," or the awkward "Bathroom Writer" for his penchant of writing letters in the latrine after "Lights Out." The eight waited and stared at the twenty-one-year-old man from the land of many lakes.

"I'm not digging up potatoes or harvesting wheat or clearing out brush or building buildings in the wilderness." Bud paused and looked around, amazed all eyes were on him. "And it doesn't look like I'll have to do KP for twenty hours straight like I did when I was in Miami Beach." Murmurs and grumblings flared up around him. "I'm not walking in 20-below weather and I'm out of Texas. Oh!" he added. "And my second trip to Florida beaches!"

Laughter erupted and a fellow twenty-one-year-old lifted his beer mug and shouted. "No more Texas!" Glasses clanked and the clamor of the drinking soldiers rose toward the high wooden ceiling of the bar. "Here's to Florida!"

They had just survived, and for northerners such as Bud "survived" seemed apt, what was the hottest summer Bud had ever experienced. They were ready for change.

"Here, here!" a soldier who answered to "Lefty" added.

"Wait a minute," a young man named Mickey Baskin called out. "You had to do twenty hours of KP duty?"

"In a row," Bud nodded. "And because of drills I was awake forty hours straight."

"Damn! That calls for another drink," Baskin shouted as he downed another beer.

A sailor at a nearby table flirted with the waitress — the waitress the Army men needed to bring them more beers.

"Hey, bathtub boy, leave her alone!" a loud Bostonian soldier at Bud's table called out. "We need her over here!"

The sailor stood and glared at the soldier, but slowly dropped into his chair as the petite red-headed waitress wagged her finger at him while maintaining a smile. After a few more words, she calmly strode to the table of Army drinkers.

"Listen boys," she lectured. "Don't you be starting no fights with anyone. You get kicked out of here and it gets reported to your CO. Remember that." Her sweet voice and tone belied the look in her eyes. The young men did not like the message, but they understood it.

"I ain't worried about my CO," Bud said, more tired than cocky. "Unless he ordered me to stand in line. Now that would be punishment!"

The men all laughed between swigs of beer while the waitress attempted to get responses regarding refills.

"I'd be lost if I got out of the Army," Bud continued with his line of thought. "Think about it, boys. We line up for chow. Line up for shows. Line up for pay. Line up for school."

The men roared with laughter.

"I've stood in a line so much," Bud continued. "When this war is over I'll have to bring you boys home so I can line you up four or five times a day." Bud paused to drink while the others laughed.

"I'm never standing in line again in my life," Lefty said and Baskin responded with a "here-here!"

"And it's everywhere, boys." Bud continued. "My brother tells me the same thing about his Army time, and he's not been in as long as we have."

A couple others shouted, "No lines!" and "To hell with lines!"

After taking another drink, Baskin, the man from Brooklyn, spoke up. "Look, boys. When we get done with all these tests, we'll be sergeants." He paused. "Well, the tests and gunnery school. Then sergeants."

Head nods led to laughter, which led the men to erupt in a cavalcade of noisy confusion.

"Besides, we get to shoot things and blow up stuff!" Baskin announced.

"I can go for that," Bud nodded before taking another drink. "I can use the extra pay that comes along with an extra stripe."

Because of the noise — laughter, in particular — Baskin took advantage of a seat which opened up next to Bud. Now next to each other, conversation became a little easier.

"Mickey Baskin, Brooklyn, New York." Baskin held out his hand.

Bud smiled. "Eugene Peterson, Bemidji, Minnesota."

"Bemidge — what? Where the hell is that?"

"Down the road from Puposky," Bud deadpanned.

Baskin stared at his compatriot for a moment before laughing. "That's a good one!" He spotted the waitress coming their way, a tray full of beers in hand. "Over here!" he shouted. "Me and…" he looked at Bud. "What should I call you? Gene? Eugene?"

"I don't care. Call me 'Pete.' Most everybody else does."

Baskin turned to the waitress, who continued to struggle with obtaining everyone's requests for refills or new drinks. He raised his hand to gain her attention. "Two here, Miss."

"I'm good," Bud protested. "I've had my fill."

Baskin glanced at Bud then back at the young lady. "Make it one." He gripped the handle of his mug and downed the last of its contents.

"What are we doing here, Bud?" Baskin asked in a loud voice.

187

"It's just another Panama City pub, I guess."

"No, no, no," Baskin laughed. "What are we doing here in This Man's Army, waiting to go off to kill Japs and Krauts?!"

"I couldn't find a job; that's why I'm here. They pay me and I get to help my country, too, is the way I figure it."

"Makes sense." Baskin paused before needling his friend again. "You know where New York is, right?" A friendly smile failed to dilute the sarcasm.

"You've got that newspaper everybody knows. *The New York Times.*" Bud eyed the younger man to gauge his reaction.

"Yeah. That's the one." Baskin nodded.

"Well, when we get back to base, I'll show you our 'Times.' It's the *Northland Times*. They don't report much crime, but they got snowmobiles for sale if you need one. Bet they don't got *that* in your paper." Bud grinned.

Baskin shook his head and laughed. "You're all right, Peterson." He looked away for a moment before attempting to make amends by extending the conversation.

"I'm still not sure about you," Bud said with a chuckle.

Baskin laughed as though he had just heard the funniest joke ever. "I'm not too sure about me, either." After reaching for a pretzel in a nearby dish, he added, "Okay. I'll play nice." He paused as he changed subjects. "What are you going to do when we get out of this mess? Go back to a job? Back to a girl?"

"If I would've had a job, I probably wouldn't be here until later this year or next year. I got a girl. She's in Williston, North Dakota."

"Willis — where the hell's that? People've heard of New York. Nobody's heard of Williston and Bemidj… whatever."

Bud noted the return of the northeastern attitude but ignored it.

"Actually, she's in Washington right now working as a welder." Bud eyed the shorter man. "You've heard of Washington, I presume."

"Yep. Both of them," Baskin laughed. "You gonna marry her when you get back?"

Bud nodded, then took a drink from what little was left in his mug. "Oh, yeah. I will."

"I don't got a girl." Baskin's tart humor faded. "But," he again came to life. "I'll have a swell job waiting for me."

"How old are you?" Bud's incredulity could not be missed.

"Nineteen."

"You look fifteen!" the twenty-one-year-old exclaimed, then picked up his empty mug and clinked it with Baskin's empty mug. "Maybe I will have another one."

•   •   •

The view from atop the Liberty Memorial gave Conrad a sense of freedom — freedom he did not possess, yet the feeling he had escaped the state he hated with a fervor. To the young man, Texas was everything Minnesota was not: hot, brown, humid, and a lousy place to be a fisherman. The slice of the state he encountered served up nothing but heat and humidity.

With Air Corps friends near him, he stared to the north at the Kansas City, Missouri, skyline. The ten-or-so tall buildings rested on the ground where Lewis and Clark had once stood, having climbed the hill to look out at the Mighty Mo —

the Missouri River. Over 130 years later, Conrad breathed in the cool September Midwestern breeze and watched as the clouds which had carried in a morning rain dissipated as they floated toward the northeast.

He and his friends had climbed the small hill from Union Station to see the World War I museum, although this was a time before the Great War had a number after its name. With only an hour free, they proceeded to the highest point they could: up the narrow staircase inside the obelisk and to the top, where he could see the horizon in every direction. Between his location and the river, he could see the back of a "Coca-Cola" sign on the top of a building. On the street below, cars rolled down a street named for General John J. Pershing.

After a few minutes of staring at the buildings, glimpses of the river, and the horizon which surrounded him, the time had arrived to return. Conrad descended back to Earth and made the short trip to re-board the troop train. Despite his intense shyness around young ladies, he did enjoy seeing the USO women at each stop. When the men had to stay in their train cars because of time limitations, the young gals handed out drinks to the soldiers as they reached out their windows.

Here, in Kansas City, the time for rest and relaxation had drawn to a close, so he opted for a drink of water before climbing aboard. He did not look the twenty-year-old blonde in the eyes when he took a cup, instead opting to view the concrete below his feet.

As the train ventured west, Conrad's thoughts of Salt Lake City were of the distance in miles and hours from Bemidji, but soon the chilled mountain air would change all that.

• • •

"Gentlemen!" the chief warrant officer thundered. "The purpose of this drill is to help you train your eye on targets while you bounce around in an airplane." As if on cue, the truck jerked with a heavy thud as it hit a sizeable pothole. The uncovered military truck left the four men in the flat bed exposed to the elements as they bounced along.

"You've all handled weapons, men, but please, handle your 12-gauge with care."

The convoy of five trucks, nose-to-tail but spread out by over 100 yards to the next vehicle, allowed the three privates-first-class to prepare to open fire. Strapped into chairs which were bolted to the truck's bed, the men understood they were one broken chair bolt or one stupid move from another man's shotgun away from disaster.

The first truck entered the firing range — at 50 miles per hour.

"Gentlemen, ready!" came the bark from the leather-skinned chief warrant officer.

Bud and two comrades glanced at the safeties of their weapons then settled the shotguns into firing position.

"A reminder, ladies!" the man in command ordered. "Do not fire because someone else fires! Only fire when the target is straight out from you. If you get your head blown off from the man next to you, we have to find a replacement. Don't make me have to do extra work!"

Bud stole a quick glance at the man. Nothing fazed Bud, but he had his doubts about some of the people he encountered.

"Fire when ready!"

The sounds of shotgun blasts 100 yards ahead of them, the wind blasting salty air in their faces, and the whine of the trucks' engines presented the men with a multitude of distractions, just as the Army wanted it. As quickly as he noted the absence of gunplay, the two men to his right fired with simultaneous blasts. Bud squeezed the trigger moments later.

Bud could not follow his shot at the targets fifty yards away, but given the timing of the truck's latest bounce, he only hoped he had not struck anything in the distance, far beyond the target. He glanced at the warrant officer as annoyance and embarrassment flooded his mind and cheeks. The cracks from his neighbors' guns caused him to yank his head back into position and attempt to get a bead on the next square, metal target.

After shooting four times — once each at four targets — the drill ended and the truck looped around to get back in line for another run at the target range. In the meantime, Bud reloaded his shotgun with the three-inch shells.

"How do I know whether I hit something?" Bud asked as the truck rolled to a halt, the long line stretching out for over two miles.

"The point isn't accuracy, private." The harsh tone was intentional. "When you do this from an airplane you'll be just as poor of a shot, but Uncle Sam will give you lots more bullets and a bigger gun so you can miss at 25,000 feet."

Unsatisfied with the response, Bud debated whether he should voice his counter argument, then thought better of it and waited for the next attempt.

•　　•　　•

"That was fun!" Bud exclaimed as he walked away from the truck.

"Fun?! My arm hurts like hell!" Baskin shot back as he moved his right shoulder up, down, and around in its socket.

"My arm hurts, too, and it's gonna be worse tomorrow. But, when was the last time you shot from the back of a moving truck?"

"Never!"

"I have, but only a couple of times."

"You have?" Baskin's disbelief amused Bud.

"Sure. Ain't you ever played around, shooting at a tree or a bottle by the side of the road or something?"

"No. We can't do that in Brooklyn!" Baskin's amazement had yet to subside.

"What kind of life do you live in Brooklyn?" Bud smirked. "What do you do for fun there?"

Baskin shook his head and did not answer. Men in groups of three strolled back to their barracks. Their superiors had made it clear that door-to-range transportation, and the other way around, was not a service one would find in the Army.

•   •   •

Two nights later, in a letter home, Bud made the announcement to his mother when he penned the news: a furlough had been granted and he would be bound for home in a matter of weeks.

Chapter Nineteen

Heinrich Himmler did not know what to do. The German Army was capturing Jews faster than they could handle, so he ordered the famed and feared *Schutzstaffel*, or "Protective Echelon," known as the "SS," to put together the *Einsatzgruppen*, or "Action Group," to follow the Wehrmacht and gather all the Jews they came across in newly conquered areas, strip them of their possessions, force them to dig trenches, and then shoot them.

The *Einsatzgruppen* units were effective killers, but they had multiple problems. First, the Army moved so fast that, in many instances, the SS teams could not keep up. Second, the cold-blooded killers were human, and over time their heinous actions emotionally affected many of them. Himmler, as head of the SS, visited an *Einsatzgruppen* in the field and witnessed the killings. He had to rush away, on the verge of vomiting.

Himmler could not do what he ordered others to do. He was a weak man with great power — a vicious yet cowardly creature who oversaw genocide. Despite his exposure to the evil he perpetrated through others, he remained steadfast in the propagation of such evil.

Their solution, alternatively "credited" to several different men, including Hermann Göring, led to the concentration camps. Instead of the messy approach in the fields of Europe, Himmler oversaw killing factories.

By the early 1940s, word spread about these extermination camps, as well as forced labor camps, but the stories sounded so fantastical many refused to believe them.

World leaders began to realize Jews were being killed, but the magnitude of the atrocities remained unfathomable.

Many observers of the time saw Hitler as someone who wanted to dominate much of Europe, and they saw him as a charismatic leader willing to risk his people for that dream. Most did not equate Hitler, Himmler, and their henchmen as genocidal sociopaths willing to sacrifice their country for an unachievable Aryan dream. That knowledge took time to discover, depending on the frequency of one's interactions with the Third Reich. Reports of killings did not equal mass murder to most people, who viewed life through their own lenses of decency and humanity.

Much of the world was at war against Germany, so even for those who received reports and understood the implications to various degrees, there were no options for further action — Germany already was being bombed and attacked.

Meanwhile, in places like Auschwitz, Treblinka, Sobibor, Chelmno, and Dachau, the murders continued with cold, inhuman efficiency which would one day astound the world. Horror had reached a new level: Holocaust.

•   •   •

The sounds of dance music enveloped the air throughout the gymnasium as young men and women danced the jitterbug to the song "Jukebox Saturday Night." The wall of sound hit Conrad when he opened the door, then it grabbed him, in the form of two lovely young ladies who each took an arm. He tried to resist but did not wish to be rude. Before he could protest — verbal protestation would have proved futile given the volume at which the band across the gym played — the pair of blondes escorted him toward the portion of the gym in use as a dance floor.

Walking in the darkened back of the gym gave the dance area a glowing aura, with the dancers lit up to match their boundless energy. Men in baggy pants and sports coats flailed in rhythm to the music as they spun spry, lithe young women in knee-length dresses that launched to their hips as they twirled.

Conrad slowed as he watched a man who looked to be his age dance in place, arms thrashing, legs moving, as though in a sprint. "My legs don't move that fast when I run," he said with amazement, although no one could hear him.

Before Conrad could react, the blondes — mission completed — deposited Conrad in front of a brunette. The brown-eyed beauty, in the light, yet partially backlit, smiled as she took in her first glimpse of the frightened Minnesotan.

"Hello, soldier. I'm Louise. Shall we dance?" She purred with caring eyes and a warm heart. She gently grabbed his hands as she walked a few steps backward in search of space to maneuver.

"I… I uh…" Conrad's voice trailed off as he briefly took in the frenzy of bodies around him. "I have to go."

He slipped his hands from hers and spun in one motion, launched himself toward the exit, and did not look back. In disobedience of a direct order from the commanding officer, he did not have fun, but instead chose to flee.

•   •   •

"The biggest bedroom in Utah," as the men had called their sleeping arrangements, was in darkness, with the exception of sundry lit flashlights scattered across the floor and the glow of hallway bulbs through the windows of the gymnasium doors. The large gym served as an all-purpose facility for the men's basketball team and winter school recreational activities for the University of Utah Utes. It was much larger than the gym that hosted the dance from which Conrad had just escaped.

The word among the soldiers was a thousand beds filled the expansive facility, although Conrad doubted the number; yet, while attempting to find one's own bed in the dark, the figure may well have been one million beds.

Using one of the many flashlights left in the hallway for returning soldiers, Conrad wound his way up and down rows of cots for five minutes before convincing himself that he had located the correct destination.

With echoes of "Jukebox Saturday Night" bouncing between his ears, the handsome, shy, comical nineteen-year-old focused his thoughts not on pretty young women; rather, on his struggle to attain good grades during the brief time he had spent at the university. Essentially a college student, he felt contentment with his surroundings: excellent food; a less militaristic routine; and the opportunity to better himself. He had his doubts about college and the courses he had to endure, but found a small amount of comfort in knowing that, based on the grades in his classes, every soldier struggled with grades and academic pursuits.

Physics and chemistry were the two subjects with which he struggled the most; when he headed off to the Army, he could not have guessed he would have bothersome dreams about mathematical equations and compounds. He faded off to sleep thinking about the classes he despised.

•   •   •

The .50 caliber machine gun pounded the air with bullets and the concussions from the miniature explosions could be heard for miles. Anyone around the gun who forgot his ear plugs only did so once. The unforgettable force as the rounds were fired sent shocks of air crashing into the operator's chest and into the bodies of anyone nearby. The round itself could create an unimaginable hole in a human body, and a well-placed round could cut a man in half.

Man's ability to kill had grown on a continuous upward curve since the beginning of the Great War almost thirty years prior, until that ability had become so dependent on technology wars could not be won without possessing millions of machines — from fighters and bombers to artillery and pistols.

This particular weapon, the M2 Browning, proved to be a prolific killer when in the right hands. The older brother of the 30.06 caliber M1919, the M2 fulfilled the Army's desire for bombers to have protection during aerial attacks. In this case, the 85-pound gun was mounted on a tripod in the middle of the plane on the starboard side, which allowed trainees to play the role of "waist gunner" in the exercise.

Wearing a thick pair of coveralls and a metal helmet, Bud obeyed the patience ordered by the instructor. At 6,000 feet, oxygen was not needed, so the trainer communicated without electronic aid. Instead, he yelled as loudly as he could.

"It's over 2,500 yards away, private. Wait 'til we get closer." The trainer paused before shouting. "And don't shoot down our plane!" He added for effect, "That pilot has a wife and kid."

Bud gulped before mumbling, "Yes sir." His voice failed to reach a volume which could be heard, but a nod signaled reception of the message.

"When I tell you it's 2,000 yards, you get that image locked in your mind," the instructor yelled. "You need to remember what 2,000 yards looks like."

Bud nodded again.

"You start shooting at a Zero or a Messerschmitt too early and you may be out of ammo a couple of passes later!"

Bud nodded as he kept his focus glued on the colorful 12-feet-by-60-feet target being dragged by a B-25 which flew parallel to their plane. The planes each banked with a slight roll to close more rapidly. He spread his feet to shoulder-width and bent his knees slightly, just as he had been trained in order to help lower his center of gravity and maintain better balance, thus improve his aim.

"That's 2,000 yards," the trainer yelled. "Fire when you're ready."

Bud noted the canvas drogue, connected by a cable, trailed the B-25 by over 1,000 yards. He felt confident that, if the pilot failed to make it home, it would not be on his account. He squeezed the trigger and held it tight. After ten seconds, Bud's plane banked to port, placing the target out of sight, and the trainer tapped him on the shoulder to signal the end of the exercise.

The trainer now only had to shout because of the airplane's noise. "You reacted well. You fired for over ten seconds, so about 80-to-90 rounds. I would recommend you let off the trigger when you get off the target."

Bud nodded.

"By letting off the trigger, you save ammo that has no chance of hitting the target. Re-find the target, begin shooting again."

Bud nodded, absorbing every word.

"It's not what most people will do in the heat of battle, son, but it's the smart way if you're in a sustained shootout." The trainer listened to his headset for a moment before giving Bud the news. "Peterson, congratulations. You hit the target. They'll confirm on the ground."

Bud nodded and allowed himself a small smile.

•   •   •

As Bud walked across the tarmac, away from a hangar, two men jogged to catch him.

"Hey, Pete," Baskin called out as he caught up.

"Peterson, how'd you do?" asked Lefty as he caught his breath.

"I passed." Bud's smile filled his face.

"Same here," Baskin volunteered.

"Me, too," Lefty added.

"So, do you think we'll all go to Utah?" Bud asked.

"Haven't heard," Baskin responded. "I just know I'm going home for a few days."

"Me, too," Lefty said.

All three men boarded the waiting bus. As they did so, a second lieutenant handed each an envelope and advised them to find seats. The men tore at their envelopes in curiosity. They settled into seats near each other and read the information from their superiors with quiet solemnity.

"Chicago!" Lefty called out. "I'm to report to Chicago in two weeks."

"Idaho!" Baskin said, then paused before adding, "Where the hell's that?"

"Ain't you ever heard of Idaho, kid?" Lefty laughed.

"Yeah. Its capital is Boise. I learned that in grade school. Now, where is it?"

Lefty laughed as Bud read his letter. "Idaho via Salt Lake City," Bud said in an even voice.

"You've got to be kidding me!" Lefty shouted, unhappy about the news.

"Hey, that's what mine said. Well, Peterson, it looks like we're off to Idaho after I get back from Brooklyn," Baskin said as he stared out the window and allowed his mind to drift to thoughts of home.

"I'll be close to my little brother," Bud said as he looked down at the floor. He smiled before repeating, "I'll be near my little brother."

"Well, goodbye to Tyndall," Baskin said. "Six weeks and we're gone."

"I actually liked this place, boys," Bud said, still beaming at the thought of getting transferred to a place close enough to see his brother. "Good food, swimming in the ocean every day. What lucky fellow from Minnesota gets to do that?"

"Me, too," Lefty replied. "I liked this place. I just hate we're getting split up."

"Well, it's not Brooklyn, but it'll do." Baskin laughed as he added, "I wonder if they have brisket or matzo balls in Idaho."

•   •   •

The uneventful troop train ride to St. Louis led to a transfer for Bud. Now on his own dime, he could not have gotten home if not for the money his mother and sisters sent to him. Embarrassment about the gifts faded the closer he got to the Bemidji station.

The nine-month absence saw the return of a different man. Although still in possession of his mildly introverted personality and laconic responses, he had changed in ways a mother would notice. He now spoke more than ever, albeit with his usual calm demeanor, and appeared to have shed his tendency to worry about the "little things," instead thinking in a more mature, organized manner. While his love for Chrissy had not dimmed — they continued to write letters to each other — he internalized those feelings in a more efficient way than just a year prior.

Sergeant Eugene Peterson had evolved into a man rather than the "young man" everyone remembered. The uniform did not cause the changes; it only highlighted what he had become.

•   •   •

"Mother, I really wish you'd move back to town. It's almost winter."

"Either way, I'll be fine."

Bud shook his head. Now out of his dress uniform and in civilian clothes, he helped his mother with her garden.

"Elsie wants me to move in with her family for the winter, and she wants me to get a house there," Hulda explained as she pulled carrots from the ground.

"What do you want to do?" Bud asked as he dug out a group of carrots.

"I'd prefer to live with Thelma. She needs me more." She paused as she struggled with a particular carrot. "Her darned Pernicious Anemia has been acting up and I'm afraid it's going to kill her someday."

Bud frowned as he worked.

"It causes her to be depressed, and a whole lot of other symptoms," Hulda added. "And it doesn't help she has those migraines so often."

"Then go live with Thelma," Bud insisted.

"Thelma and Elsie talked it out and they're both willing to take me, but they just care that I stay in Bemidji," she said as she held up a carrot for Bud to see, triumph written across her face. "That way, I can find work helping people with their kids or cleaning houses and doing laundry."

Bud rocked his head side-to-side as he considered both sides of the matter. "Okay. I see," was the full extent of his offered opinion on the subject.

"What do you think?"

"Mother, I think you should do whatever you want to do, but if the girls say you should live with Elsie, that's fine. If they say Thelma, that's fine, too." Bud continued his picking of carrots as he spoke. "All I care about is you not having to do everything for yourself and needing wood and things like that."

"Eugene," she began her sentence with her son's given name. She commonly used his birth name and chose to every time she was irritated with him. "I'm forty-nine, not seventy-nine. I can take care of the wood and keep up with the food supply and everything else that needs to be done."

Bud grinned at her determination before responding. "I think Bemidji is perfect for you. You should live with both of them."

Hulda fought off a smile. "You think I'm a geezer."

"No," Bud deadpanned. "I think you're a fuddy-duddy."

She threw a carrot at him, across the eight feet which separated them.

"Fat head."

Bud laughed. "That's two words you've used that the kids say. You're not the same mother I left for the Army."

Hulda shook her head as she laughed and resumed harvesting her carrots. "Next we're doing some more canning — fruit," she added.

"I could be on a fifteen-mile march right now," Bud said. "I'll take canning any day."

•   •   •

There was not much to move, especially when considering how much most women accumulate over forty-nine years. Furniture for a living room, three dressers, a dining set, and a bed comprised the bulk of the haul. Clothing, dishes,

204

flatware, cookware, and, oh yes, lots of canned food. Lots of canned food.

Hulda's move into the rental house at 701 Irvine Avenue came as a blessing. She could still be close enough to her daughters, but now had the ability to entertain family and friends. When her brother Emil came into town, or Violet and children, or countless other Petersons and Gustafsons in the area, she could be their host. The possibilities suited her giving personality.

The two-story house felt spacious, particularly when considering the years with five kids growing up in the house on the Point. A little more than five blocks west of Lake Bemidji and six blocks north of the railroad tracks — she enjoyed hearing the train whistles — the neighborhood remained quiet enough most of the time. She did not find herself yearning for the countryside in such a quiet neighborhood; the silence only interrupted by the occasional rumble of automobiles passing by.

The front door faced east, which was a nice feature in the winter. With only three windows facing west, she hoped the house would be easier to heat, provided it was properly insulated. The laundry room granted access to the outdoors by way of a door above three wooden steps. In the front yard, a small box elder tree grew far enough from the sidewalk to delay the inevitable deformation to the concrete its roots would undoubtedly cause. Another box elder thrived by the northern edge of her property, near the boundary with the 705 Irvine house. Only two other houses sat on her side of Irvine before 8th Street.

A concrete walkway led to the front door, which was located near the southeast corner of the house. An alley crossed

7th Street, which ran south of the property, and continued farther into town to the north before ending at 12th Street.

Hulda had heard, but did not recall, whether the house had been built in 1910 or 1912.

Indeed, the house was a blessing because she could afford the rent and, at least to her thinking, not be a burden to one of her daughters and family.

"Okay, that's the last of it," Bud announced as he carried a chair for the dining room table.

"When do you have to go back?" Elsie's husband, Jake, asked Bud.

"Tomorrow. I have to catch a train to St. Louis, then the Army will pay for my trip to Salt Lake. Then on to Idaho."

"Well, we're all glad you got to come home," Jake said before adding. "As soon as I can collect Elsie, I'm taking her home and we're all eating dinner at our house tonight."

"Hey," Bud said. "Thank you for the way you and Elsie chipped in to help pay for my trip from St. Louis. I will get you paid back."

"Forget about it, Bud. It was our pleasure," Jake averred. "You keep your money so you can go out and have a nice time occasionally."

"I'll pay you back — in time."

"Hey, you didn't see your girl, did you?"

"No. She's in Washington State, working as a welder," Bud answered. "Craziest thing, these dames doing jobs like that."

"I agree," Jake laughed. "They already boss their husbands around as it is, now they want to make the money."

Bud also laughed. "With Chrissy, she's a little firecracker, so it didn't surprise me none."

"Can you see Elsie or Thelma doing work like that?" Jake let out a hearty laugh.

"Actually, yes." Bud nodded, certain he could envision such an occupation for either. "I know Thelma gets sick a lot, but they're both strong as an ox. And they're tough."

"Well, that's true," Jake smiled as he spoke. "If Elsie's anything, she's tough."

As the conversation with his brother-in-law continued, the next day's departure loomed in the forefront of his mind.

• • •

"We've known each other pretty much our whole lives," Bud said with a laugh. "Hard to believe we're getting old."

"Speak for yourself, Peterson." With a grin, Clifford Pearson chastised his long-time friend. "When we're old and gray we can look back on these days, but right now, these are the years old men dream about."

Peterson and Pearson looked out at Lake Bemidji from a wooden park bench which apparently had not been designed for comfort. The chill in the November air found itself nullified by the Sun's warming rays. The lack of a breeze added to the comfortable afternoon. The inch of snow on the ground only played the role of afterthought.

Their laughter continued. "When did you get to be such a philosopher?" Bud asked.

"Oh, I was just listening to a couple of old men the other day," Cliff said. "Sitting around a table and talking about the 'good ol' days' or some nonsense like that."

"I don't think we've had any of those." Bud flashed a wry smile.

"It was kind of an interesting conversation," Cliff added. "They drifted into a whole lot of subjects." The big-eared blond, with beaming blue eyes and a look of innocence in his face, enjoyed every syllable of his conversation with Bud.

"I guess they knew my dad," Bud surmised.

"Your dad's name came up," Cliff answered. "My dad and his parents. Some relative of yours who was killed in a deer-hunting accident."

"My uncle, Charlie Peterson. It happened close enough to town that a bunch of people heard the gunshot."

"How old will we be before we start talking about the good old days?" Cliff asked. "We don't know anyone killed in a hunting accident."

The light-hearted banter continued for several minutes before the inevitable subject came up.

"Would you recommend the Army?" Cliff asked.

"Yeah. I like it. It's got its downsides, but overall, I can't kick on it." Bud paused to consider an additional response. "I was in the Navy for a short time before I got a medical excuse to get out of there. The Army Air Corps is good, though. I've learned airplane mechanics; they've taught me to use tools I'd never seen before." He gave the impression more would follow, but stopped, instead.

"I was actually considering the Navy," Cliff said.

"Hey, if you went into the Air Corps, that would be fitting," Bud added as the thought popped into his head. "You and I were part of the first group confirmed at the Lutheran Church when it was new. Your family and mine were charter members. We've done just about everything else the same."

"But I wasn't the church's first janitor," Cliff laughed.

Bud laughed and slapped his knee. "I think that job helped prepare me for the Army." After his laughter subsided he asked, "Wasn't your dad a deacon?"

"Yeah, him, one of the Strands — Gustav, I think — and a few other men." came the reply.

"And my Uncle Emil," Bud added. "Was one of the board of trustees, along with Bob Strand and some others."

A brief silence ruled the moment, until Cliff returned to thoughts of the military. "If we could know we'd end up together you could talk me out of the Navy." He shook his head. "But we both know it doesn't work that way."

Bud nodded with an expression of chagrin.

The old friends caught up on girlfriends, past jobs, and the status of various family members. For over half an hour, they did indeed reminisce like two old men. The twenty-one-year-olds — Cliff was three weeks older than Bud — had their whole lives ahead of them to create memories, but on one chilly afternoon, on a bench on the shore of Lake Bemidji, within sight of the Paul Bunyan and Babe the Blue Ox statues, the young men swapped stories and enjoyed their time together, forgetting much of the world was on fire with war.

Cliff joined the Navy three months later.

•　　•　　•

209

Hulda and Elsie watched in silence as Bud completed a quick inventory of his bag.

"Nope. Didn't forget anything," Bud announced in a triumphant voice. "The Army wouldn't let me run back home and grab something." He laughed in an attempt to ease the sadness the three felt. The thought remained unspoken, but all three knew this, or anytime they were together, could be the final time they would see each other. They understood the depth of the sands of Time shrank, shallower and shallower, as the weeks passed. When the hourglass emptied, Bud would find himself overseas. In the war. In harm's way. With either Germans or Japanese attempting to shoot him out of the sky. A soldier and airman, dropping Hell and having it returned by anti-aircraft shells or bullets from Zeros or Messerschmitts.

"Well," Bud began, his tone almost sheepish. "I left an out-of-work skinny mess and I returned as a waist gunner, ball-turret gunner, flight engineer, and sergeant. How about that?" His forced smile fooled neither mother nor sister.

Tears welled up in Elsie's eyes and she attempted to wipe them away with her fingers.

Hulda looked her son in the eyes as she spoke. "You left a boy and you returned a man."

Bud's eyes transformed from clear blue to glassy blurs. He lunged forward, grabbed his mother, and brought her to him so he could squeeze her tight.

"I'm proud of you, son," Hulda said, her voice cracking. "I love you."

He released his grip and looked at her, their faces eight inches apart, their eyes filled with tears. "I love you, too, Mother.

You held the family together all those years. I'll make it back in one piece; promise. Connie, too. Don't worry."

He could not look at her any longer. He stepped back, collected himself for all of two seconds, then moved to his sister and hugged her with a firm, loving grip. She kissed him on the cheek as they exchanged "I love yous," then he made her promise she would look after their mother.

A booming voice called out, "All aboard!" A brief blast of the train whistle seconded the appeal. Bud picked up his bag, looked first at his crying sister, then to his crying mother, smiled, and announced, "See ya in 1945."

He turned away. Strong strides carried him to the coach car. He looked back and gave a brief wave to the weeping women before climbing the two steps to enter the train, unsure of when he would be home next.

Chapter Twenty

The Salt Lake Tribune headline blared, "Russ Evacuate Zhitomir; Gain at Dnieper Bend." Several smaller headlines provided updates from other war hot spots, but the gruff old man appeared unimpressed. With a disgusted *harrumph*, a frail gentleman wearing a gray fedora folded the newspaper and held it in front of Conrad as he passed the younger man.

"Here ya go, soldier," the man said as he walked by. Before Conrad could thank him, three strides separated the man from the brothers. "Russ Evacuate" was enough for the unimpressed gentleman; the little-known locales of Zhitomir and Dnieper Bend held no importance to him.

Conrad read the headline to Bud before adding, "Guess he don't like the Russians."

Bud snatched the paper and leaned against a building, out of the way of the bustling crowd just blocks from the capitol. Next to him, plastered on the stone siding of the building, a poster with a tough-looking man glared at passersby. The short-haired man of about thirty years, his fist thrust forward, had an expression of controlled anger. In large, bright letters, underneath the cartoonish depiction of the man and his bulging forearm muscles, the words "AVENGE December 7" caught the eye. Below the "7," an artistic depiction of two ships, engulfed by an explosion, filled the bottom-right corner of the poster. Just shy of two years later, no one had forgotten; it was not possible in the current climate.

A Saturday afternoon in November, with a chill in the air, ordinarily would not be filled with so many people, but the soldiers who roamed the streets and shops, in search of postcards, eclectic memorabilia, and gifts for loved ones, and locals enjoying the crisp late-November day, gave the feel of the first warm spring weekend rather than late fall.

"The paper says it's gonna get near 50 today," Bud announced as he read from a brief article before turning his attention to the big stories.

"I'll take Utah warmth any day over Texas cold," Conrad deadpanned as he continued to look back at the strange, tall man who finally disappeared into the crowd.

"Look at this," Bud exclaimed, his voice reflected his rising energy as he spoke. "They say hundreds of Brit bombers whipped it on Berlin! How about that?!"

"Wow!" came the quiet response, which barely could be heard as a car honked at a jaywalker.

"They better leave some for me!"

"What makes you think you're going to Germany?" Conrad asked.

"Well, think about it." Bud stared at his brother for a few seconds, but Conrad's expression did not change. "I've qualified to be an engineer on a bomber. Unless we get a base within range of the Japs, I'm not going island-hopping."

"I guess," Conrad said, a sheepish look on his face.

"And right now, we ain't got no bases in range of ol' Hirohito."

"We don't? I don't pay attention. I'm too busy studying books to know anything about this war."

"Now, a medic, you could go anywhere. But a bomber?" Bud ignored the younger man's response as he let his question linger.

"Makes sense," Conrad responded.

Bud dropped the newspaper to his side. "You wanna see anything?" he asked, referring to the paper.

"Nah."

"Okay." Bud stepped toward a fellow sergeant who was in the process of passing by. "Here ya go, Sarge."

The Army sergeant, E-5, paused as he took the newspaper. "Thank you, Sergeant!"

The pair resumed their stroll, steps coming at a slow pace as they chatted.

"Did you ever think you'd go back to school?"

"Goodness gracious, no!" The look of horror on Conrad's face amused his brother.

"Well, don't feel bad about not getting into the Air Corps. Most people don't seem to get what they want in This Man's Army." The pair dodged a lady looking around as though lost. "I think I told you, I wanted to drive tanks," Bud continued. "Instead of on the ground, I'll be in the air."

"That's just wonderful. You didn't want the Air Corps but got in. I want in, but can't." Conrad's level of dejection bordered on disgust.

"How'd you wind up on course to become a medic?" Bud lacked empathy for Conrad's unhappiness.

"An officer pointed at me and said, 'You! You're a medic!'" Conrad displayed his passion as he jabbed at the air in front of him as he spoke.

Bud smiled. "You can't change it, Connie."

"I know, and that's what's got me so darned mad." Conrad sniped, though Bud was not his target.

"Well, if you want, when I get to Gowen, I'll talk to my new CO and find out if there's any advice he has or strings that can be pulled."

"That's fine," Conrad responded. "I appreciate it, but based on what I'm being told, as long as I'm here I don't qualify for consideration." He gave a half-hearted kick at the sidewalk as he spoke. "I guess they don't want to put all that money into me becoming a medic, then I go and change jobs."

"That's understandable."

"I know." Conrad's unhappiness hovered over him like a dark cloud as they strolled. "But I don't have to like it."

Bud tried to change the subject. "Hey, you said in your letter when I was home to save some of the girls for you." He chuckled as he continued. "Are you even talking to girls?"

"I can talk to girls," Conrad insisted.

"But I said 'are you' talking to girls."

"Yeah. Well..." Conrad let the thought hang in the air. They both knew what that meant.

"That's what I thought."

"I just get so darned uptight I don't want to be around them."

"I know," Bud responded with a trace of sympathy. "When you told me about running out on that dance I cringed. I know it's tough for you."

"I gotta quit doing that, don't I?"

"Yeah. You do." Bud laughed. "You really do. They won't bite, Connie." He paused before continuing. "Well, most of 'em won't."

215

"From what you described, Chrissy would rip a guy's head off." Conrad's delivery remained in harmony with his emotions: flat.

"Oh, she's a little spitfire," Bud smiled as he reminisced. "I don't want to make her mad. No, sir. But you know I'm just playing around when I say those things."

"So, you two are still a thing?"

Bud took a deep breath before answering as they stopped at a crosswalk for traffic to pass. "Had you asked me last month, I would've told you we were done. She wasn't returning my letters and I assumed the worst." They began to cross the busy street. "Then she started writing again. She said it was her schedule. She sounded as loving as ever."

"Well, I'm glad to hear it, but I have to say, I'm a little surprised."

"Why's that?"

"Just because of the distance. That's great you two love each other, but it's gotta be tough when you go so long without seeing each other."

"Oh. It is." Bud paused. "But it'll all be worth it when the war's over and I go to Williston to bring her back to Bemidji. We pledged we'd wait for each other, and I believe we will."

They strolled another block before either spoke. The break in the conversation felt natural to both of them; they did not feel pressure to speak for the sake of filling the air.

"You know I'm going home for Christmas, don't you?" His faster-than-normal speech signaled Conrad's excitement.

"Yeah, you mentioned that in a letter. I'm happy for you."

"Yeah, I'm happy for me, too," Conrad laughed as he patted his brother on the shoulder. "So, what do I do about Jo?"

"That's a good question," Bud said, referring to a family friend back home who had written periodically to both men. "She and Harriet both act like I'm serious with them. I probably spent too much time with Jo when I was home. I apologized to Mother about that."

"Too much time?"

"Yeah. I came home to see the family, not her." Bud paused to think about his next words before delivering them. "I mean, I like her, but I love Chrissy." His emphasis on "love" settled the argument before Conrad could take the conversation in that direction. "So, you know. I like Jo and Harriet, but they both have it in their minds, it appears, that I'm hot for them, but I'm not."

"Great." Conrad's sarcastic humor surfaced. "So, what am I supposed to do?"

"Play up Chrissy to them. Make them understand I got a girl."

"Didn't you do that?"

"Yeah." Bud hesitated. "Of course, but girls don't always believe men, and they can't take their eyes off men in uniform."

"What'd you do, wear your uniform every day?"

"Well, no," Bud responded in a defensive tone. "Just when everyone came over to Elsie's house for a dinner and snacks."

"Oh, good grief! No wonder they love you."

"Yeah, that's what Elsie said," Bud laughed. "She reminded me how women are about these things." He removed

217

his garrison cap, exposing his "high and tight" regulation haircut as he rubbed the top of his head.

"I got enough problems. I'm better off not to wear my uniform in public." Conrad's tone communicated the seriousness of his statement.

"Excuse me," a man of about forty interrupted. "Can I ask you boys a question?" His gray suit, matching fedora, and dark tie gave him a look similar to that of many other civilian men on this chilly day.

"Sure, bub. What can we do for ya?" Bud asked as he removed his hand from the top of his head.

"Are you boys Marines?"

Bud looked at the man and issued a flat question. "Is my hair that bad?" He again reached for the top of his head.

Conrad's laugh added to the man's embarrassment.

"No. No, that's not what I'm saying." Embarrassment turned to nervousness. "I was just gonna ask you a question about Marine life."

"Sorry, mister," Bud answered. "The only marine life I know about is when I swam in the Gulf of Mexico."

"Oh. Uh. Okay. Sorry." The man scurried away.

Conrad looked at his brother in bewilderment. "What was that all about?" he asked.

"Don't go changing the subject. Do you understand how cute girls think you are?"

"Really?" Conrad responded to Bud, but thoughts were still on the brief encounter.

Bud threw up his hands, causing a young lady striding past the two to stare for a moment. "Yes, Connie. Girls think you're cute. I hear it all the time when I'm home. Chrissy even told me that when the girls in North Dakota saw your picture. Some of her friends wanted to meet you."

Conrad sounded exasperated. "They do?! Why?!"

Bud shook his head. "Let's grab a bite. I'm hungry and you're hopeless."

As the brothers walked down the street, Conrad stared straight ahead, only glancing to either side on occasion. Bud looked around and enjoyed the sights. They were brothers. Bud did not reach five-nine, Conrad neared six-feet in height. Bud was mildly out-going, Conrad was not even close to "mildly." Bud displayed confidence in himself, Conrad exuded shyness. They both looked like their father yet had traits of their mother. They were so much alike, yet so different.

As they approached a small sidewalk café, Conrad asked his brother a question, his voice sounded pained. "Bud, how am I going to deal with Jo when I get home? She really likes me."

Bud responded with a laugh. To use words at this moment would have been a waste of breath.

Bud and Conrad exchanged glances: Bud smiled; Conrad frowned. The latter felt true concern about how he would act toward the women of Bemidji. The former found such a fact amusing.

•   •   •

Bud's temporary barracks lay two miles from the capitol and within sight of Conrad's "barracks," known by its common name of "The University of Utah." His brief time in Salt Lake City had been spent at the pistol range, enduring another physical, a shot for something — for what he did not know —

219

and other minor tune-ups to prepare a soldier in the Army Air Corps for war. "They must be bound and bent to find something the matter with me," he wrote his mother. With crowded conditions and undesirable meals, Bud's enthusiasm for being near Conrad's latest military post waned. The time they spent together on that Saturday afternoon meant a lot to both of them. They had strolled around town for much of the day, found time for a movie, and dined in two cafés. The reunion which did not materialize in Texas did in Utah, and both men wrote glowing reports of their day together to their mother.

The next day, Bud began the next journey of his military career by riding a troop train to Gowen Field in Boise, Idaho.

• • •

Being alone brought happiness as well as sadness to Hulda. She loved her granddaughters, but the silence she experienced as she looked out the front window allowed her to relax. At times, life proceeded at too hectic a pace to allow for thoughts. Watching snow fall brought a feeling of reflection to the soul, and Hulda did just that.

When she moved into town, Hulda did not expect to be alone on a holiday as would happen in Puposky. Instead of a mile to the next house, she found herself surrounded by homes.

But then a snowstorm hit her brother's house. Emil, and his wife Louise, were supposed to visit and share a Thanksgiving meal with her, but with certain roads impassable or simply dangerous, her elder brother had to miss Hulda's great cooking.

The storm only brought an inch of snow to Bemidji, but Hulda positioned herself at the window, content to look out. The thirty-two-degree weather did not feel cold to her, but enveloped by the warmth of her home, even with cold drafts in certain areas, she saw no need to venture out.

She took time to give thanks to God as she took stock of the good in her life, starting with her granddaughters and now one grandson. Her children and how their lives were progressing came to mind, and relief flooded her heart when considering Anne had finally made it to California.

She also prayed for what lay ahead. The only barrier to Bud and Conrad going to war was Time itself. Thelma's health continued to concern her, but Elsie had rebounded well from the death of her infant son, and Carl sounded happier in his letters.

Nevertheless, no matter how often she tried to push it out of her mind, no matter how many times Bud and Conrad told her not to worry, she worried daily.

She could have injected herself into Elsie's Thanksgiving Day plans with her family or have done the same with Thelma; they would not have hesitated to include her. Instead, she chose to stare out the window, watch the light snow fall, and pray and think and think and pray.

Hulda could not get comfortable in her own skin. A murky, vague worry stalked her and she did not know why. She had endured this feeling before: when, as a child, a bear followed her home from school, getting closer and closer as she neared her parents' cabin. She did not see the bear until she arrived home but felt its presence along the way.

That same feeling — of being stalked, pursued — nagged her again. She feared, this time, when she looked back it would be too late.

· · ·

"What?!" Conrad could not contain his disbelief.

"I'm sorry, son." The doctor's somber tone conveyed the seriousness of the news through his surgeon's mask.

The masked doctor's pronouncement stung the young soldier — not out of fear of the illness; rather, out of frustration for how far behind he could fall in his development as a medic.

"But I don't even know what scarlet fever is. I mean, I've heard of it…" His words trailed off.

"We don't know you have it, private." The balding doctor with a spreading waistline summed up the situation. "But you were exposed. That's all that matters. So, into quarantine you go."

"Does it kill you?"

"No," the doctor answered. "You get a fever, neck glands swell up, and you get a rash all over your body."

"I don't have any of that," Conrad announced, his confidence rising.

The doctor left the room without responding, but the door remained open, so Conrad could see him as he stopped just beyond the doorway, in the hospital's hallway. He gave directions, which Conrad could not hear, to a nurse.

Conrad looked around the room, discontent growing inside him. "This is nuts!" he snapped, as though someone could hear him. "Nuts, I tell you!"

The doctor poked his masked face into the room. "Son, it'll only be for a week or two. You need three consecutive negative test results and you'll be released."

Before Conrad could respond, the doctor spun and strode a few steps away to confer with the same nurse and to write on documents held by a clipboard.

Conrad stared and shook his head.

Chapter Twenty-One

"How do you just sneak off and skip a parade for a general?" the man asked.

"It's easy. I didn't wanna march, so I didn't." Bud's flat response made the explanation all the more difficult for a disciplined Army man to accept.

"You're a bit of a wild one, huh?" Fellow sergeant Lige McIntosh's question bordered on statement.

"It was chilly out," Bud reasoned with unconvincing logic. "I was in Texas too long. I'm tired of cold." Bud lay stretched out on his bed, fully dressed sans boots.

"You're a sergeant now, Peterson. You can't be doing that stuff."

"Sergeants don't march. That's for privates."

"You're hopeless," McIntosh, the top-gunner who split time with Bud as the crew's engineer, said as he shook his head and walked to his bunk.

"I'm also warm, and I'm not tired." Bud laughed, but his friend did not agree with the humor. Bud shook his head, then resumed reading a letter from Conrad and frowned. His brother's words made him sound two steps from the insane asylum — quarantine did not suit him.

The five-feet, nine-inch McIntosh, who hailed from Buffalo, New York, returned to Bud's bunk. "Look, I wasn't trying to kick on ya, but you're gonna mess around and lose some stripes if you're not careful."

His sober yet conciliatory words sunk into Bud's brain, causing the latter to reconsider. "Yeah. I s'pose you're right." His slow delivery revealed his thoughts, which grew deeper and more regimented. "The last thing I want to do is get myself in trouble."

"Or put your squadron in a bind."

Bud shrugged, as if to say, "Yeah, I guess you're right."

"Look, Pete," McIntosh said, concern in his voice. "Pretty soon, we'll be off killing Krauts. We've got jobs to do. You don't want to mess things up for yourself. This is what we've been training for."

Bud nodded. He understood. He still could not recall the name of the general in whose honor the parade was held, but McIntosh's words rang true: Bud needed to approach the Army with a more serious attitude.

·   ·   ·

In the early days of the war, the leaders of Boise, Idaho, had enticed the federal government to make Gowen Field a key site for pilot training. From 1943 through 1945, 15,000 men trained there. Its open landscape gave pilots a perfect line of sight, the land outside of town provided plenty of space for bombing practice, it had the longest landing strip in the States, and a climate devoid of frequent rains made the location ideal. It offered the added feature of sitting too far inland to feel threatened by enemy attack.

With a population of only 27,000, Boise was large enough to support the influx of government visitors but small enough to not provide cover for prying eyes.

Named for the Great War flying ace Paul Gowen of Caldwell, Idaho, who was killed after take-off in his B-10 while on duty in Panama in 1938, Gowen Field lacked the appeal of

Miami Beach or a busy city like Chicago, but Bud and his military peers did not feel slighted: they had the opportunity to drop real bombs from their planes.

When Bud arrived in November of 1943, Gowen Field had already established itself as a key Air Corps stop in the training life of the soldiers. Gone were the B-17s; the B-24s dominated the skies.

.   .   .

The B-3 flight suit and accessories covered every inch of his body except his nose, mouth, and cheeks, which were covered by the oxygen mask. Donned in an oversized brown sheepskin flight jacket with a fleece collar which climbed to the bottom of his ears and covered his mouth and chin, Bud looked like a chocolate lump of humanity, particularly when wearing his flight goggles, which concealed his eyes. Matching pants kept him warm, at least up to a certain altitude. With temperatures reaching beyond –30 degrees, the suit and long underwear provided minimal warmth.

To add to the amusing look, he found himself curled up inside the ball turret at the rear of and underneath the B-24. The turret pivoted as Bud searched for incoming planes; although, in the skies above southern Idaho, his chances of spotting an incoming Messerschmitt remained low.

The fleece around the waist and wrists of the jacket added additional protection from the cold, while the pants offered the same buffer at the ankles. A flak jacket covering the front of his leather jacket provided limited protection.

Covered with sheepskin from neck to ankles, he looked as though the cold could never penetrate his body; unfortunately, that was not the case. The extra pairs of socks in his boots and the gloves made of the same materials as his jacket and pants also failed to keep him warm on many flights.

Even for a Minnesotan, 18,000 feet up could be a cold place.

"There's too much talking going on, gentlemen!" the pilot snapped, his voice biting into the ears of his crew by way of their headsets. Captain Robert Gast did not elaborate further — they knew the rules.

Within minutes, the plane dropped to 8,000 feet.

"Navigator to pilot, one degree to the left, IP in one minute." The announcement alerted the crew they would soon reach the Initial Point, where the bomb run would commence.

"Bombardier to pilot, target in sight," Goshtoian called out moments later.

"Pilot to bombardier, you have control," Captain Gast said as he set the controls which linked the bombsight to the autopilot. This allowed the bombardier to command the plane's path. Goshtoian peered through the top secret Norden bombsight, which was protected by armed guard when stored on the ground.

"Bombardier to pilot, I have control. Opening bomb bay doors." After allowing time for the doors to open, he continued. "Bombardier to radio operator, confirm doors are open."

"Bomb doors are open," Donald Holbert responded.

After a minute of silence, the interphone again came alive as Goshtoian focused on his task. "Stand by." Another pause, then the Detroit native announced, "Bombs away!"

"Roger," Captain Gast said. "Pilot to gunners, let us know what you see."

"Roger," Bud answered from his tiny, transparent round cave.

"Pilot to radio, did all the eggs drop?"

"Yes, sir. A dozen eggs on their way to the kitchen."

"Roger. Bombardier, close bomb doors."

"Closing bomb doors," Goshtoian responded. "Bombardier to pilot, you have control."

"Pilot to bombardier, I have control."

"Bomb doors are closed," Holbert reported.

The long wait ended with the announcement from Bud. "Ball turret to pilot. The eggs missed the plate."

"Short or long?" Gast asked.

"Short. Dropped too soon. But congratulations, Andy," Bud laughed. "You hit a big pile of hay. That hay is out of commission for the rest of the war."

"Pilot to bombardier, take a photo of the hit."

"Already done," Goshtoian announced. "And thanks for the description, Peterson."

"Any time," Bud said in mock seriousness.

"Gentlemen, we're headed back."

"Navigator to crew. No more oxygen checks are needed. We're below 10,000 feet."

"Affirmative," Gast responded.

The four-engine plane banked 30 degrees to port and flew back to the Gowen Field airstrip.

•   •   •

"I wonder what life will be like after the war?" McIntosh asked as he stared over the heads of the men around him.

In the mess hall, the entire crew sat together, regardless of rank. Captain Gast, a mustached native of Ohio, wanted to ensure the men bonded, even though the members of the team would change soon. His long eyebrows and sleepy eyes did not give him the appearance of an officer, but when needed, he commanded a room.

"When this war is over and we're on top again, I swear any man caught kicking on the U.S. isn't an American." Bud took another bite of his potatoes.

"Yeah, I get that," Goshtoian offered. "But I wonder if we'll all be hurting for work again."

"Look at all the skills we've gained," Savage chimed in.

"Yeah," Bud added. "Look at me. I can fix an airplane now. Hell, I'd never been in an airplane before joining."

"If we let those Nazis have their way," Gast joined the conversation. "There ain't gonna be an America — at least not France and England and a bunch of other countries, for sure."

"Don't forget the communists," Goshtoian added. "That Stalin gets some good press, but he's not good, ally or not."

"Boys, we lick these Germans and we'll never have to worry about fascism or communism in our country," Gast said with conviction. "That never comes from the people; it comes from tyrants, forced on the people."

Packed with men, the mess hall looked like a miniature hangar with its roomy eating area. The dull roar of male voices telling stories, laughing, and joking filled the hall up to the metal rafters.

"And we're all better shots now in case they try," Bud chuckled.

The men paused enough from devouring their food to laugh.

"This is the best food I've had in the Army," Bud said as he changed the subject.

"I agree."

"Same here."

The muffled responses ceased as the feast continued. Conversation gave way to individual thoughts and dreams as well as recollections of the day's bombing practice.

With good food and lots of work, Bud preferred to stay where he was, but the Army had other ideas. He had met part of his crew, although he did not know who would leave the group. After dinner, it was back to studying as he had a lot still to learn and military manuals to read. He did learn of a plot afoot by his superiors; the men were going home for Christmas before shipping off to their next locations. Bud was about to head back to Bemidji.

•   •   •

Gertrude Elizabeth Graham passed away on December 12, 1943. Born Gertrude Strand, she left behind a husband, two adult children, and a nine-year-old son.

Anne had resided in San Francisco for less than four months when her mother died of cancer. Anne's brother Norman was somewhere in the Pacific, so her half-brother, Leroy Graham, was Gertrude's only child at the funeral.

Three days prior, Gertie's mother, Anna Marie Strand, had died. In a brief span, Anne lost her mother and grandmother. It ate at her heart that she could not attend the funerals, but the die had been cast when she moved to California.

The ordinarily upbeat Anne fought her emotions and gave as much attention as possible to her two children in order to soften the blows. It did not work. No matter what she tried, the pain remained.

Chapter Twenty-Two

"This seems familiar, doesn't it?"

Hulda nodded while Thelma stood with a silent but sad smile.

"It's really a shame Connie couldn't come home," Bud said. He paused for the whistle of a train to complete its call. "We could've all been together. Well. Except Carl."

Hulda smiled and squeezed her son. "Are you going to see Conrad?"

"Yes," Bud said as he stepped back from the embrace. "Then I'll catch another troop train to Wendover."

Bud kissed his sister on the cheek, then hugged her. Fear prevented the ladies from speaking — fear of the tears which would roll down their faces.

"Give my love to all the Petersons and Gustafsons," Bud added as he turned to leave.

"I love you, Eugene," Hulda called out.

For just a moment, Bud froze. She frequently called him "Eugene," but in this moment he understood her enough to realize the casual "Bud" or "Buddy" would not suffice. The emotional moment ended when he answered before he turned toward the train. "I love you, Mother."

Hulda's eyes did not dry until she arrived back at Thelma's house. Her youngest child could not come home and the next youngest was only months away from war.

•   •   •

"I'm sorry, sir, but you can't see him."

"Of course I can. He's my little brother."

The nurse's rotation to front desk duty came at an inopportune time for her; she had to deal with an indignant Peterson. The white nurse's cap which rested on the top and back of her head matched her white uniform. Her reddish-brown hair seemed to turn another shade redder when she responded. Her young age of twenty-five did not chisel away her firm attitude. Her brown eyes transformed from sweet to intense.

"Young man, your brother is in quarantine." Her dark eyes flashed with an unexpected brightness as she squinted in controlled anger. "That means no one can visit him. Now, if you think you'd like to get scarlet fever, you may go ahead and visit with him, but you won't get out of this place anytime soon." She rose to her feet as she uttered the last several words.

Bud sighed and considered his response. Although she possessed an attractive face, at the moment he did not care. "Okay. I understand. Thank you."

Neither spoke again as Bud turned and walked through the doorway to leave. Once outdoors, he traveled the length of the building, found a side door, and turned the handle. Success. He entered the building, looked in both directions, saw no one, and checked for Conrad's room number. He went up a flight of stairs to the second floor and resumed his search. When he reached the correct room, he looked around, then opened the door with a slow, deliberate motion. No nurses inside.

Conrad looked up when he saw the door move, then was hit full force with astonishment. "Bud!"

Bud moved his forefinger to his mouth. "Shhh. Go to the porch." He pointed at the tiny balcony on the other side of Conrad's roommate. "I'll be out there in a minute."

233

Moments later, Bud stood in the courtyard, looking up at Conrad on his second-story balcony. "How ya feeling, brother?"

"You fat-head! What are you doing here?"

"I just got back from home and stopped by to see you."

"You're nuts!"

"Yeah. So."

"Look, Bud. If I don't get out of this place soon I'm gonna go bananas! I hate being cooped up all the time."

"When are you getting out?"

"Supposedly by New Year's Eve. I still haven't had three cultures in a row come back negative." Conrad's frustration caused him to speak louder. "I can get to two, but the third always comes back inconclusive." For Conrad, this was a lot of words to come out all at once, although he never struggled to converse with his brothers. "Then some chucklehead nurse made some mistake and wrote down I had a positive result. These people are nuts and they're making me nuts!"

"Connie, you need to talk quieter or we're going to get caught."

"Caught?! What can they do to me?! I'm already in jail! Or maybe it's Hell, I don't know for sure."

Bud could no longer hold back and let out a cackle.

"What?! What's so damned funny about this?!" Conrad demanded.

"You." Bud paused to laugh again. "You sound like you're trying to escape the looney bin."

A nurse with a mask covering her mouth and nose appeared behind Conrad. "Mr. Peterson! Mr. Peterson, you are supposed to be in bed!"

"But I couldn't see my brother from bed," he deadpanned.

"Your brother?" The golden-haired, green-eyed nurse walked to the balcony and looked down at Bud, who waved at her.

Her tense body relaxed. "Okay." Her eyes narrowed as she spoke and looked at Conrad. "But only for a few minutes. And keep your voices down. If the Head Nurse knew about this she'd be pretty bent." She instinctively adjusted her mask to ensure it rested properly on her face.

"You're a swell egg, Donna."

"Oh, hush up." She turned and crossed the room, only to pause at the door. She pointed for emphasis. "And remember what I said — only a few minutes."

Conrad cut loose with a warm, genuine smile.

"Oh, hush up!" She turned and left the room.

Conrad turned back to his brother, and in a much quieter voice said, "Okay, tell me about being home at Christmas."

•   •   •

Conrad's letters home sounded like a man at the edge of death — from boredom. His usual brief letters to loved ones managed to become mere notes, often of one page in length. At one point, he claimed to have sat for an hour, pen and paper in hand, without a single idea about which he could write.

His furlough — thus his trip home — disappeared in early December. Once he left the ward, furlough would not be an option: studies and catching up in classes would be his focus. Meanwhile, as he lay in his bed with the mind-numbing monotony, other soldiers achieved the required three consecutive "negative" results and found themselves liberated from medical isolation. Somebody, somewhere, had acquired scarlet fever, but Conrad only knew of those who left, healthy the entire quarantine time.

The one piece of news he conveyed did not concern the family or himself, but it managed to amuse everyone, nonetheless. One of the young men working at the hospital had difficulties with authority:

> *One of the ward boys was a PFC until the other day. The major came in the kitchen and started snooping around the garbage so the ward boy got mad and dumped the garbage all over him 'so he could get a better look at it.' Now he's just a Private.*

He spent his days working crossword puzzles from two different newspapers and responding to the letters he received. At first, he enjoyed "the soft life" and having food served to him, but that enjoyment gave way to boredom, which ushered in frustration. Next came feelings of madness — not the literal insanity requiring medication, but the kind of madness which made him *wish* he would go insane, just to relieve the frustration.

Christmas had come and gone, but Bud's visit before New Year's came at a time of promise, with New Year's Eve as a release date. However, when the third "negative" did not materialize, the consecutive culture count began anew.

Conrad did not get out of quarantine before the New Year; in fact, he remained "stuck," as he called it repeatedly, in the hospital until the end of the first week of January. Forty-four days of nails on a chalkboard, at least in his mind. When he finally returned to his classes, he found himself far behind his peers. Prior dreams of transfer into the Air Corps gave way to the need to learn and pass his classes.

The calendar turned to 1944. Instead of Texas, the brothers found themselves at different locations in Utah, closer to the inevitable overseas deployment. Conrad no longer thought about going to Europe with his brother, but instead, worked toward the day he would become a full-fledged medic and a surgical technician. The events of 1943 would stay in his mind for the rest of his life; however, the last year had merely set the table for the year to come.

Chapter Twenty-Three

The four-engine, twin-tailed B-24 Liberator flew higher, faster, and farther than the B-17. The B-24's bomb load was greater and the plane was more versatile than the B-17. Consolidated Aircraft had designed the B-24 as an upgrade from the Boeing B-17. Unfortunately, with its "slab-sided" fuselage, the B-24 earned the unofficial nickname of the "Flying Boxcar," while the B-17 was known as the "Flying Fortress." The B-24 lacked not only the appearance of grace, but evidence of any intention by the designers to make it attractive. The choice was simple when choosing between a Flying Fortress or a Boxcar, and the public and media looked to the B-17 to win the air war, despite the better capabilities of the Liberator.

The aircrews took to calling the Liberator the "flying coffin." With only one exit, through the bomb bay, a B-24 about to crash afforded the crew little opportunity for escape.

B-24s were manufactured in San Diego, Fort Worth, Dallas, Tulsa, and Willow Run, Michigan, with the most coming from San Diego. The famed moniker for women working jobs which had been traditionally reserved for men, "Rosie the Riveter," took its name from Rose Will Monroe, who riveted her way to fame on B-24s in Willow Run. Over 18,500 B-24s had been produced when production ceased in June of 1945; more than any other aircraft during the war.

Four Pratt & Whitney engines, long, high-lift "Davis" wings, and three-bladed propellers with variable-pitch technology made the plane a powerful, high-flying, efficient air machine. The R-1830 turbo-supercharged radial engines mustered 1,200 horsepower each, allowing the plane to reach speeds of 290 miles per hour, if necessary. The 110-feet wingspan, along with the powerful engines, gave the aircraft the ability to reach 28,000 feet, which made it less vulnerable to enemy anti-aircraft artillery.

The 67-feet long, 18-ton aircraft was designed to be a flying bomb bay, with an 8,000-pound ordnance capacity. Instead of two large bomb bay doors that opened to each side, as on the B-17 and most other bombers, the B-24 had roll-top-desk-like tambour doors which retracted up along the outside of the fuselage. This reduced drag that would otherwise slow down the aircraft on a bombing run.   Browning M2 .50 caliber machine guns in the nose, sides, top, and tail gave the Liberator adequate defense against incoming fighter planes.

The "tricycle" landing gear configuration was an American first for bombers, though it had been utilized by other countries. A circular hole with a channel leading to the base of the landing gear was underneath each wing, between the engines. It allowed the wheels to fold up and away from the fuselage, into the wings, where they were uncovered yet flush to avoid drag. The nose landing gear, with its single wheel, disappeared into the fuselage underneath the cockpit and was protected by two doors which opened outward, like curved metal French doors.

Bud's plane, a B-24H-20 built in Willow Run, Michigan, carried the tail number 42-94932, with the first two digits representing the fiscal year in which the plane was ordered. An olive drab paint scheme with gray meanderings across the fuselage, wings, and tail gave the aircraft an Army look. The military insignia of the United States, known as a "roundel," which was a white star sandwiched by white horizontal stripes, was on each side of the fuselage behind the wings.

The B-24 would not win any aircraft beauty contests, but to Bud and his crew, the boxy, unattractive plane was the Taj Mahal with wings — a beautiful but complicated woman. It may have been ugly, but it was *their* ugly bomber. The ground crew and enlisted aircrew worked with feverish anticipation on exterior and interior parts, learning the importance of every system and every piece of the plane to understand how it worked and the best method to replace it should the need arise. Meanwhile, the officers checked every dial, light, alarm, and operation which could fail, suffer damage, or provide warnings of mechanical breakdown during flight.

"It seems that everything is wrong with it and we have to fix it," Bud later wrote. They did not inherit a bomber straight off the assembly line; rather, a craft which had been used in countless practice runs.

They flew their unnamed warship on occasion, up to seven hours at a time, on training missions which included dropping dummy bombs and occasionally live ordnance. At first, not every day saw time in the air; however, that changed as the need for in-flight training outweighed the need for ground training. The men still had parts, plans, and procedures to learn, but the more they learned, the more they needed to fly.

Bud saw the Grand Canyon for the first time in his life aboard their plane. Flying over the Rocky Mountains contrasted to trips over the western deserts. The beauty of Zion National Monument proved elusive at 20,000 feet, but Bud viewed the topography when he had the opportunity; he could not help but stare at terrain so different from the Land of Ten Thousand

Lakes. When over Oregon, he realized he was nearer to Chrissy, who was residing in Washington on a temporary basis, working as a welder.

Another aspect which would never leave Bud's memory was the lack of electrically heated flight suits. The Army had delivered many promises but not the suits themselves. The issued gloves proved ineffective, as did his standard flight suit and layers of underclothes. He only knew the temperature others told him but would believe any number: -30 degrees; -60 degrees. He only knew it was colder than the journey he took from Bemidji to check on Anne.

Once the E-1 suits arrived, his life would be warmer — much warmer.

Checking on Anne; how long ago that seemed. Life had become nothing but a blur — a low-level plane flight through his adventures and memories. Life in Bemidji felt so distant, and not just physical distance. Williston was a foggy memory, and even recollections of Puposky maintained an ethereal glow in his mind's eye.

When he had worked the grain fields or dug up potatoes in North Dakota or cleared the forest near Cass Lake, the idea of flying at 20,000 feet in a state-of-the-art bomber never crossed his mind.

The men now became a permanent team. Gone were the days of flying with different people at different times. Once in battle, when casualties occurred, changes would be made out of necessity, but injury — or worse — did not enter their minds at this point.

They cared for the aircraft with the understanding it would be their lives — their shelter — but it could also be responsible for their deaths if not maintained with proper attentiveness. The tradition of referring to planes and ships in the feminine reflected the fond attention the B-24 received. She was a lady, and they treated her as such.

•   •   •

Surrounded by distant mountain ranges and desert everywhere else, Wendover Army Air Field, Utah, rested at the state line with Nevada on Highway 40, close to 120 miles west of Salt Lake City, nearly equidistant between Utah's capital and Elko, Nevada.

Isolated and on the salt flats, the base was more of a recluse's paradise or a scorpion's playground than a military training center. For good measure, in case loneliness got the best of anyone who decided the world needed to know what was happening in desolate Wendover, the government had every phone line tapped. The men of the 489th Bombardment Group had no way of knowing of work taking place elsewhere and about to move to Wendover. The soon-to-be famous B-29s *Enola Gay* and *Bock's Car*, along with their pilots, Paul Tibbets and Charles Sweeney, would have an extended stop at Wendover on their way to flying into the history books.

Phone taps and signs designed to remind future warriors of the need for secrecy started early, even though the nuclear group would not arrive until after Bud and the many Air Corps Bomb Groups left.

Rows of five barracks for the airmen — buildings as plain as the ground around them — ran east to west. Next to them were more comfortable quarters for the officers.

Additional barracks stood on a hill within the confines of the base. Across the vast range, the buildings and hangars littered the brown soil like warts on a witch's face. Wendover was not a pretty place, especially for someone who hailed from the Land of Lakes.

The headquarters building stood out because of its size, its long, gabled roof and six-feet-tall windows peppering its sides. One door on each end allowed entrance. In the absence of grass, round stones lined the driveway to the building. Beyond the stones, dirt resided where grass should be.

A sign at the entrance read:

> *"What you hear here —*
> *What you see here —*
> *When you leave here —*
> *Let it stay here —"*

Wendover was lonely no more: the 1940 population of 100 ballooned to a fantastical 19,500 by the time Bud and his coalescing crew reached the 3.5-million-acre facility.

At the end of the war, when the third atomic bomb was not needed, the military stored it at Wendover.

•   •   •

"Where's Sund?" Savage called out.

"He's not coming," another member of the crew yelled from inside the barracks.

"Ann again?" Savage shouted his question.

"Yeah," the voice answered.

243

Savage turned to Bud. "Sund's wife's a nice gal."

Bud nodded.

"Can't believe we've actually gotten to meet one of the boys' wives." Savage, a native of San Bernardino County, California, like the other officers on their still-unnamed plane, never found a reason to be inaccessible or stodgy toward the enlisted men.

"Well," Bud said as they waited for the others so they could all leave the base together. "When you live in Boise, Gowen and Wendover are great places to be stationed."

"Ain't that the truth," Savage nodded.

"Poor guy's the only one who doesn't get to have a good time," Bud added with a straight face.

•　　•　　•

Glasses clinked, men shouted and laughed; young women blushed and giggled. The music of Glenn Miller, Rudy Vallee, and Harry James alternately filled the air of the large bar. A military hang-out teeming with soldiers, the longer the nights the bigger the fights. Captain Gast and his crew decided early in the evening they would not allow the bar to wear out its welcome.

A three-hour trip ahead of them — the 120 miles back to base on 40 Highway was not a fast drive.

Around the large table in the spacious, crowded bar, the eight men engaged in conversations, most about the women they left behind in order to fight for Uncle Sam.

"Things are heating back up," Bud told radio operator Donald Holbert. "We're writing each other more. I guess she's finding more time despite her welding job."

"I'll get a girl when I get back to Staten Island. I figure I won't have time after we go over." Holbert's curly, thick dark hair moved as he chuckled and instinctively stroked his mustache. "Unless we land long enough in Germany to pick up a few *Fräuleins*."

"Fat chance of that," Bud said with a laugh.

"We could also — " Holbert found himself interrupted by their captain.

"Gentlemen, are we ready to start heading back? It's not often we all get out of the zoo at the same time; we wouldn't want to blow it."

"Well, let's see," Gast's co-pilot, Robert Savage, offered. "We've drank a lot of beer."

"And whiskey!" gunner Lige McIntosh interjected with a shout.

Savage laughed. "Yes, you have!" He paused while the men all laughed. "We failed to agree on a plane name, and we flirted with the barmaid. It's been an evening of mixed results."

"That's a 'yes, he's ready to head back,'" McIntosh declared, his deep-set eyes and large smile contradicting each other.

"I still like 'Tiger Shark,'" Holbert shouted.

Alfred Lane, of Wichita Falls, Texas, slapped him on the back as they rose from their chairs in near-unison and began their meander around tables and chairs, squeezing by patrons and barmaids.

"It's two tough animals," Holbert pleaded in a voice loud enough to be heard over the dull roar of the patrons.

"Hey!" McIntosh called to the others. "Where the hell's Stodtmeister?!"

"How many times did I tell you?!" Lane maintained enough composure to explain. "He went home; he lives in Ogden."

"Ogden? Who's that?" McIntosh again yelled.

Lane looked at Gast and announced, "We're ready."

•   •   •

"Another bathroom stop?!" Captain Gast moaned with humor in his voice. "Who is it this time?"

"McIntosh," someone called out.

Gast looked around, baffled. "Where did he go?"

Savage pointed to the hotel they had just passed. "There."

The men did an about-face and headed to the spacious hotel lobby. Chit chat dominated the moment as two discussed the need to find their "taxi" — the truck which had brought them to Salt Lake City.

"Hey, look at this," Goshtoian called out to the others. He walked over to a life-sized cardboard cutout of a smiling, pretty brunette holding a placard which read, "Utah Bell Telephone Company." Western Electric's 396A Switchboard Operator's breastplate microphone, or a "chest microphone," adorned her clavicle, below her mouth, so she could speak into the device yet keep her hands free. The small device featured a triangular metal plate which rested on the young lady's chest,

246

over her clothing. From the base emerged a funnel-shaped microphone, similar to what early record players used to amplify sound, although in this case, the sound traveled in the opposite direction, to transmit the woman's words. Her curly hair hid most of the headset, and her two-piece attire — a suit jacket and long skirt — presented a professional appearance. A switchboard operator was considered a woman's job, and many young women around the country earned their living assisting people as they made phone calls, whether across town or around the world.

"Look at that doll!" Goshtoian marveled. "She looks real."

"It's a photo of a real dame," Bud responded.

"I think we need to keep her," Goshtoian said as his serious delivery caused several guffaws.

"What do we need with a paper doll?" Gast asked.

"Our mascot, or whatever you want to call it," Goshtoian responded.

Before the conversation could continue, Lane and McIntosh emerged from the restroom.

"We ready to go?" McIntosh asked.

"Yeah, let's get going and we can get back to base at a decent time," Gast half-ordered.

The group poured out of the hotel and onto the sidewalk. One called out, "He brought the girl!"

Gast looked, laughed, and shook his head as he and the group continued along the sidewalk. The others laughed and mocked Goshtoian. Eight men and one switchboard operator — at least a cardboard representation of such a woman — made their way through Salt Lake City, on their way to the rendezvous point.

•   •   •

With the vote completed, the men visited their plane to admire ground crew chief Lionel Bousquet's artwork. The always happy, coveralls-clad mechanic stood smiling in front of the plane as the others stepped up to view his work. His mop-like brown hair, parted down the middle, bobbed along with him as he expressed his excitement. Painted below the cockpit and above the nose wheel, the fuselage displayed the words "Paper Doll," with the first word painted above the second, the letters arced to give a football-shaped appearance. A small, yellow haystack separated the words. The bright blue, billowy letters stood out on the olive drab fuselage. The over-sized, puffy script gave each letter a rounded appearance, void of straight lines.

Laughter and cheers mixed with more mocking of their bombardier. Someone had pulled out a camera, so they posed for photos next to the paint job and with the cardboard girl.

"Hey, what's that small blob in the middle?" Bud asked.

"Well," Bousquet answered. "Gosh is the one who grabbed the dame, and he's the one who blew up the haystack at Gowen, so I figured, why not?"

The amused men peppered Goshtoian with more jokes, with him as the butt every time.

"I hope nobody thinks we named it after that song," Savage said, referring to the number one hit of 1943 with the same name, the ballad which reestablished the Mills Brothers as a popular group after a brief loss of popularity.

"I wouldn't worry about it," Bud said. "We know. Plus, we've got the doll." He laughed, as did several of the others.

"Yeah, maybe we can get Bous to paint a dame on there, too," Gast said while he laughed. He observed the men and was happy they could let off steam in a positive way, minus the theft of the cardboard cut-out, of course.

"I've decided," Bousquet added. "That I'll make the letters different colors the first time I have to touch it up."

"Why would you touch it up?" Bud asked.

"Well," Bousquet responded with a sheepish look, "When it gets shot up."

"Oh. Nuts. I forgot about that," Bud shook his head. "Those damned Krauts shoot back."

The sudden realization of the risks of war could not damper spirits, as the men continued to laugh and pose for photos with the plane's new paint job and the paper doll.

The ugly aircraft which they had treated like a beautiful woman now had a pretty young woman as its mascot. *Paper Doll* sat outside the hangar, ready for a date in Europe.

Chapter Twenty-Four

The boys started a comeback, although they would never catch the girls in number. In January, Thelma gave birth to her third child, a boy, Delbert Arlyn Beckstrand, on her way to five kids. Hulda and the family celebrated again. The first five grandchildren were all girls, while the last three, including Elsie's child who died after ten hours, were all boys.

Hulda bounced around in her thoughts just as she bounced around in her living arrangements. At the moment, she found herself at the house she rented on Irvine Avenue; she had spent considerable time at Thelma's, helping her through her pregnancy, and before that with Elsie, assisting her with the kids and housework.

Her thoughts turned to money, the one subject which had seen improvement over the last year. Bud's promotion to sergeant and Carl getting the foreman job he sought at the shipyard allowed their contributions to make an immense impact. Carl had his own family now, and his contributions were understandably irregular and waning. Conrad tried to help, but with a private's pay, he endured his own struggles.

Thelma's various health problems meant her mother and sister, Elsie, played important roles during the pregnancy. Hulda felt happy about being able to assist, but the Depression and the war had turned her into a worrier.

Hulda and her mother, Grandma Thompson, struggled to see eye-to-eye, leading to tension. Additionally, sadness continued to hold on to Hulda after the loss of her longtime friend, Gertie; Anne's mother had been more than just her son's mother-in-law.

She continued her letters to her sons, but at some point in each letter, her fears seeped out of her heart and through the pen and poured onto the paper. As time passed and the inevitable transfers neared for Bud and Conrad to ship out of the country and into harm's way, the weight of the world at war pressed on her shoulders and held her down in an attempt to suffocate her spirit. Her siblings struggled to recognize the happy-go-lucky, fun-loving girl and woman she had been for so long. However, since 1929, the moments to celebrate, laugh, or enjoy grew rarer and rarer — other than the births of grandchildren.

She read with a warm heart that her military sons had visited one another in late January one more time, with Bud doubtful they would again stumble onto such an opportunity because of the orders he expected each to receive in the near future.

She would not admit it in so many words, but Hulda felt old and tired. Worry burdened her.

She found an outlet with her grandchildren, however, and they became an escape from the troubles of life, at least when they were well. The most recent illness had seen Valrae and Bev battle the measles. The children nearly brought out the fun-loving and mischievous young girl trapped inside Hulda. While missing Carla and Jim, who now resided in California, she still had Valrae, Beverly, Joanne, and Judy, along with new arrival Delbert.

Carl had been in California for over a year, which gave a reprieve to their occasionally difficult relationship. Hulda loved her son, but since his father died, Carl had become aloof, particularly toward his mother. Carl's detached attitude in a family already stoic in their emotions could not be missed;

however, she reveled in the knowledge he was a good man with good character who worked hard and loved his family. No one in her entire brood displayed great outpourings of emotion, but Carl's taciturn demeanor took the expression "holding his cards close to his vest" to a new level in the context of emotions.

She thought her relationship with Carl in some ways mirrored her relationship with her own mother: they loved each other, they wanted the best for each other, but they struggled with each other at times.

Bud, the biggest personality of her boys, would adapt to any situation and find a way to succeed. Her worries about Conrad eased somewhat because she knew he would grow out of his intense shyness around women and overall diffidence.

While Hulda held to her habit of not speaking ill of family members, even to other family members, she did voice a bit of her frustrations toward her own mother, and her attempts to help others patch up their differences. She confided in Bud, who responded with advice, which could be summarized as, "Ignore the people who bother you, including Grandma Thompson, and let people solve their own problems; you have enough of your own." The sound advice served as a reminder Bud had been growing in wisdom during his time in the Army Air Corps.

Hulda continued to write letters to her three boys and to help care for her two daughters and their families. Approaching her fiftieth birthday, Hulda felt old — older than she should feel.

She felt confident that, when the war ended and her two youngest sons returned home, and perhaps Carl could bring his family back to Bemidji, life could return to normal, perhaps without the difficult financial situation.

When not working — for pay or for her family — Hulda spent part of her relaxation time praying. Her fervent prayers and strong faith helped sustain her and gave her more strength. The widow held hope the world, and her family's lives, could return to a semblance of normalcy.

•   •   •

On multiple occasions, Conrad had the opportunity, usually through people he met in public, to eat at the homes of local Mormon families. Bud encountered the same experience during his brief stay in Salt Lake City. One evening, after he had such a satisfying experience, with amazement at the American people's willingness to take in soldiers for meals and stuffed to his ribs with delicious food cooked by the lady of the house, Conrad left the Latter-Day Saints family and joined his friends at a roller skating rink hosted by the USO.

Perhaps somewhere, somehow, Conrad received credit for trying. He went to the rink in uniform and, in a repeat of his experience at the dance in Texas, found himself uncomfortable.

Conrad arrived just as a competition had ended and general skating resumed. He struggled for several minutes as he determined ice skating was completely different than roller skating.

"Pete!" His friend Mac skated up to Conrad. "Pete, how are ya?"

"I think I'm gonna wind up breaking bones I didn't know I have," Conrad said with a straight face. Before the conversation could continue, the lanky lad, who had recently turned twenty, found himself on his derriere. "Aaaa. That didn't feel good!" He climbed to his feet looking like a ten-minute-old fawn. "This is a tough way to end up in the hospital, eh?"

"The guys are over there," Mac pointed to the young men congregated by the half-wall on the opposite end from them. "We've already met several girls."

"Girls?!"

Mac's laugh could be heard over the Benny Goodman music blaring from the public address system. They both began to skate in the same counter-clockwise direction as the scores of others did. "Yeah, girls. You do know what they are, right?"

"Yes. I do!" Conrad's indignation did not run deep. "But they all want to talk my ear off or tell me how handsome I look in a uniform or just giggle at me."

Mac spun his head with a slow roll of his neck before returning his eyes to his friend. "What a terrible problem to have, Pete! Women think you're handsome. That must be horrible for you!"

Before he could respond, Conrad found himself on the hardwood floor again, and another groan of pain preceded his response. "Yes. It is horrible."

With a smile, Mac shook his head and stuck out a hand to help up his bashful friend.

•   •   •

After thirty minutes of general skating, the music changed and many of the soldiers found themselves on the floor, dancing with their partners as they skated to the strains of the horns and clarinet of Tommy Dorsey's "Boogie Woogie." All the men wanted to be out there with a young lady. All except one, that is.

As Conrad sat at a table in the spacious area for those wishing to rest or sip a soda, a long-legged strawberry blonde skated up to Conrad.

"Hello, soldier. Would you like to skate with me?" She looked at him with a sweet smile, her hazel eyes beckoning.

Without a word, the seated Conrad bent down, unlaced his skates, and with impressive alacrity replaced his skates with street shoes. As he later wrote to his mother, when a "sweet young thing" asked him to skate, "Right then and there I took off my skates and hit for the door."

Conrad was indeed a unique young man. The private first class referred to himself as "a P.F.E. That means, Private For Ever." Somehow, though, his complaints were always comical, his observations amusing. He signed a letter to Thelma as "Your beaten, blistered brother, Connie." He made pain sound hilarious and conflict entertaining in his letters. He wrote the family often, but his letters, just like his spoken words, were concise.

Before he had much time to complain about being shipped from the University of Utah back to Texas, at Camp Barkeley ("Beautiful Texas — Phooey!"), the surgical technician-in-training found himself headed to Camp Beale, in northern California, staying in the state he learned to hate — Texas — long enough to pull guard duty once every four days and to not enjoy long march after long march.

On his way to Beale, Conrad's path swung far to the north, and Hulda took the opportunity to catch the train and ride a portion of the trip with him, to Grand Forks, North Dakota, on the Minnesota border seventy-five miles north of Fargo. After

255

departing the train in Grand Forks, she took a bus back to Bemidji.

Excitement filled Conrad's quiet existence as he once again escaped Texas and now found himself but 130 miles from Carl. He began to see his path and understood the next step before it happened. He was destined to become an Army medic and surgical technician, and he accepted that destiny.

In the meantime, the Peterson civilians in Minnesota and California read the newspapers with great attentiveness, with an eye on the war's progress, and understood the sands of time were about to run out on stateside training for their two family members.

Chapter Twenty-Five

James Harold Doolittle did not become a "hero" because of the damage he and his men exacted on the Japanese in the early days of the conflict, for it was minimal. Instead, the daring raid made him an instant hero because of the bravery displayed and the way he lifted up the nation. Although Doolittle and his raiders hit the Japanese with bombs, the propaganda and psychological values far exceeded the physical damage. Americans felt happiness over any retaliatory attack on Japan, and the people of Japan did not feel as safe — their supposed impregnable defenses proved insufficient.

When sixteen B-25s leaped off the deck of the *USS Hornet (CV-8)*, few felt confident they could even take flight while loaded down with extra fuel and four bombs each. Instead, they not only survived takeoff, they dropped their bombs on Tokyo and dashed to China, where they crashed for lack of fuel in their attempt to make it to land occupied by Chiang Kai-Shek's forces. Eventually, 73 of the 80 men made it home to the States.

A two-step promotion and a couple of military jobs later, Brigadier General Doolittle gained command of the Eighth Army Air Force, which at the time was anything but "Mighty," the nickname it would later earn.

The Eighth was initially established as the VIII Bomber Command in Savannah, Georgia, forty-three days after Pearl Harbor. Headquarters were established in England soon afterward.

The Eighth inflicted heavy damage on German targets as well as its own men. Unprotected bomber squadrons presented easy targets to German fighters, including the Messerschmitt Bf 109 and the Focke-Wulf Fw 190. By October of 1943, the Eighth's darkest days arrived, with some missions enduring the loss of 30 of 36 bombers. One mission saw the loss of 77 of 291 bombers, or over 26% of the attacking force. The Germans had found they could face less resistance by flying straight at the B-17 Flying Fortress, where they encountered fewer machine guns. They could then peel away after their attack, giving them a better chance of avoiding being shot down.

Bomber crew death tolls for daytime bombing raids remained high throughout the war, for obvious reasons, but 1943 had been a year to forget.

In January 1944, Doolittle took over the Eighth. Doolittle put his fingerprints on the organization by allowing fighter escorts to chase down German fighters. This change, combined with the effectiveness of targeting the manufacturing plants the Germans badly needed to feed their war machine, turned the tide in the favor of the Allies. Over the course of 1944, the Allies gained control of the skies, which would be a key factor on D-Day.

General Doolittle standardized bomber formations, whether B-17s or B-24s, to consist of four squadrons, nine aircraft each and fighter formations of three squadrons divided into either three or four flights of four planes each, providing from thirty-six to forty-eight fighters to protect the heavy bombers.

Doolittle's tactics proved to be the impetus for turning the Eighth from a demoralized group with low survivor rates to an effective force from the air for which Hermann Göring and the Luftwaffe had no answer.

During the war, the Eighth deployed 42,000 combat aircraft, with many more support craft. By war's end, out of 350,000 men, 26,000 had lost their lives.

• • •

Bud sat cramped inside the contraption which gave many people queasy stomachs: the ball turret. Many professed fear of the position, some from experience flying in the bubble during training, while others grew weak at just the thought of being trapped inside the three-feet diameter compartment with a panoramic view of the world 20,000 feet below. Crews were training to complete missions while being shot at by anti-aircraft artillery and facing attack from Luftwaffe fighter planes, but a position on the plane scared them. This was the reputation of one of Bud's duties. When not acting as a gunner in other parts of the plane or filling in as engineer, Bud poured himself inside the insane bubble underneath the rear of the plane.

Every ball turret gunner understood if a malfunction occurred during flight and the ball could not be raised, then the gunner could not exit the dangling bubble; the gunner would be obliterated upon landing. The plane did not have to suffer battle damage to pose a risk to one's life. Over the course of the war, modifications were made, including a manual backup to retract the turret.

Finished with the cleaning of the .50 caliber Browning M2, Bud climbed out, backward, through the turret door and onto the ground.

"Good thing I'm not as tall as my brothers," Bud laughed.

"You gotta be out of your mind to crawl inside that thing," Holbert said with a serious tone. "I'll stick with my radios."

"Aaaa. You get used to it. It's a little cramped, no question."

Holbert referenced Bud's hands. "You got the longest fingers I've ever seen."

Bud held up his hands and wiggled his extra-long fingers. "Yeah, I don't know how that happened. My oldest brother has normal fingers. My other brother's fingers are a little long, but not much. Mine," he stretched his back as he recovered from being wadded like a piece of paper in the tiny turret. "They're just weird."

The New Yorker shook his head. "You're an interesting dude, Bud."

"I think I'm kinda boring, especially compared to the rest of my family."

Will Plate, a pilot from the 847th Squadron, strode by *Paper Doll*, headed to *Plate's Date*. "Hello, boys," he said with a pleasant voice. He carried a friendlier demeanor than a lot of pilots. As trained leaders, they often possessed strong personalities which did not lend well to making friends with others, especially non-officers. Plate however, as well as Bud's pilot, Gast, shunned the aura of superiority. "Peterson, I want you to know I've flown in every position on my plane. There is no way in hell I will ever get in that ball turret again."

The three looked in the direction of the turret. "It's no big deal," Bud answered.

"Well, you can have it. Never again for me. It scared the piss out of me, it's colder than Hell froze over, and you don't get

260

a parachute. That's just too much for me!" With that, the pilot shook his head in recollection of his experience and continued toward *Plate's Date*.

Before Bud and Holbert could continue their conversation, they reacted to a whistle from a distant figure. Near the barracks, Andy Goshtoian struggled to gain the attention of the two crew members.

"Apparently, we're wanted," Bud stated the obvious.

•   •   •

Colonel Ezekiel W. Napier, commander of the 489th Bombardment Group, which was recently determined to be composed of the 844th, 845th, 846th, and 847th Squadrons, led the meeting. He spoke without notes, charts, or other visual aids. He delivered his message with a brief but serious announcement.

"Gentlemen," the man who was destined to become a brigadier general began as he eyed every man in the room, including ground crewmen. "We ship out in ten days. No additional three-day passes will be granted, so if you have one, count yourself lucky."

Bud looked at Holbert and gave the "thumbs up" sign.

"For now, I cannot give you much information. The less you know the less you can accidentally tell others." He allowed a slow gaze around the room add effect to his words. "I can tell you that you're about to become the enemy's worst nightmare." He paused while a number of men hooted with joy at the news. "We're going to bomb the hell out of them, whether it's the Japs or the Krauts, and we're going to bomb them into submission." He eyed the men with another careful, deliberate sweep of his head. "Mark my words. We have some crack crews who work together well, and we have some who haven't gelled yet. Those who are not up to snuff need to get there or the enemy will blow you out of the sky."

Every man stared at their commander. All the training mixed with fun took on greater importance, although the fun was about to become a memory.

"Some of the Eighth will have their groups fly out tomorrow, then the 489th and a couple other groups will fly in ten days. Ground crews will take a ship to friendly ground, then will be flown to the base where you will report." With each sentence his voice deepened and every word gained a new level of drama. "Once we arrive in theater, we will have time to acclimate, get used to our base's facilities, and drill. We will test every plane, every crew, and every grounds crewman. We will push you to the limit, then expect more."

A mild rumble of excited exclamations filled the room, but only for a few brief seconds. Colonel Napier did not find the need to ask for silence, he merely spoke and the group quieted.

"We are going to be in a foreign country, and you will represent the United States with perfection and without incident. You will be the men we trained you to be — of that I have no doubt." After a delay to allow his words to sink in, he continued. "At oh-700, we will meet with your pilots and give additional details. They will not provide you with information, so don't bother to ask."

With the words of encouragement and the lecture out of the way, he closed his speech. "We have a job to do. You do your job and trust the man next to you will do his. We've worked on teamwork, and now you are ready to go win a war for the United States of America. Thank you, gentlemen."

The airmen applauded, ready to fight the enemy at that moment.

Bud looked at a couple of his crewmates and quipped, "I'm just happy we got the electric flight suits. We get to be warm when we bomb those Krauts or Japs."

With the men on their feet, they mingled, discussing plans for their evenings. "Bud," Goshtoian approached him. "Are we still on for Salt Lake?"

"Of course. And I was thinking about seeing *The Sullivans*," Bud answered.

"Sounds good to me."

"Are you ready to go over?"

"Oh yeah," the first lieutenant answered the E-5 sergeant. "How long have we been training now? You bet I'm ready."

"Tired of blowing up hay bales, eh?"

"I'm tired of the anticipation. We've been keyed up forever."

"Well, let's go see some Navy guys drown in a ship."

"Leave tomorrow morning?"

"Sounds good."

•　　•　　•

Camp Beale lay 150 miles from San Francisco, a trek which took over three hours due to narrow and winding roads intermittently spread out on the path into the Bay Area. Once in "The City," as residents referred to their home metropolis, the

263

bus driver had to negotiate traffic — foot, automobile, and trolley. The City by the Bay, with its famous hills and beautiful views of the water, bustled with business and leisurely activity every day, with only Sundays witnessing a slowdown of the frenzied action.

A few blocks from the harbor, on a late Saturday morning, Conrad knocked on the door to a small apartment. A young girl opened it before shouting with joy. "Uncle Connie!" Carla shouted, her little red dress bouncing along with her. "Uncle Connie's here! Uncle Connie's here!" Her glee overtook her as she ran into the kitchen to alert her mother. "It's Uncle Connie."

Three-and-a-half-year-old Carla, her brown hair thrown to and fro from the animated head movements, ran to her brother, who lay asleep in a handmade crib. "Uncle Connie's here."

"Conrad!" Anne shouted with almost the same excitement as Carla. "You made it." The brother- and sister-in-law embraced before she motioned for him to sit on the small couch. "Carl will be here in a few minutes. He had to buy some part for his car or something." She flashed a look of bewilderment. "I don't remember what it was."

"It's good to see you again." Conrad's shy habits did not manifest in such a severe manner with family. "Where's your little one?"

"Oh!" Anne jumped up as though bitten by a spider. "Come see my handsome little devil."

Before Conrad could speak again, he was holding his extra-small-sized nephew. "Boy, he really looks like your family," Conrad remarked at the puffy cheeks and deep eyes. "I bet he's going to grow up to be an angel."

Anne laughed. "Not if he takes after my family and our orneriness."

Conrad laughed. "Yeah, your family has its share of pranksters, but that's just like Mother, too." When a brief pause filled the air, Conrad continued. "He's a little chunk for his age."

"Oh, yeah!" Anne smiled with her broad, Danish face. "Ten months old. He's cute as a button."

"A fat button," Conrad added.

"Uncle Connie." Little Carla in her flowery dress tugged on Conrad's sleeve. "Uncle Connie. I'm going to have another brother or sister."

Conrad's eyes widened on cue.

Anne smiled. "That's right. We're gonna have another one."

After overcoming his shock, Conrad blurted out, "Well, congratulations!" He did not know whether a hug was in order, so he remained fixed in his place, standing in the middle of the room. He returned Jimmy to his crib and then offered a gentle hug to his sister-in-law.

"I want another sister!" Carla demanded while looking at her uncle.

"Is that so?" Conrad asked with a serious face. "Not another brother?"

"No. One is enough! Brothers cry too much."

The adults laughed as they made their way to the couch.

"Oh, they do, do they?"

"I'm due in November," Anne added.

"Well, that'll be interesting. Three little ones running around."

"Yeah," Anne beamed. "Three little ones." She sighed.

Before the conversation could spiral too deeply into small talk, the door opened to allow Carl's entrance.

"Conrad!" Carl, a little more than three months from his twenty-ninth birthday, set down a paper bag which concealed car parts. His tall, angular frame was now packed with a little more meat, a little more muscle, than it had been during those lean years in Minnesota. He stepped forward and gave his youngest brother a hearty handshake and squeeze of the shoulder with his left hand. "Glad you made it in one piece!"

"I had my doubts a few times on those roads. That bus driver made it interesting," Conrad chuckled.

"I'll show you my Chevy later. It's a beaut!" He motioned toward the same couch on which Conrad had rested only a minute earlier. "Have a seat. I'll grab you a beer." Before Conrad could respond, Carl had completed three strides toward the kitchen.

"How long are you here?" Anne asked.

"I'm not a big beer drinker, Carl," Conrad protested.

"Sure you are," Carl retorted. "You're in the Army now."

Conrad turned to look at Anne. "I have a three-day pass, so I'll leave Sunday evening, when Carl goes to work."

Carl walked into the room and held out an open bottle of Lucky Lager. "Here ya go."

"Oh. Thank you, Carl." Conrad grabbed the bottle and took a small sip.

Carl sat in his chair and took a big swig. "I'll show you around and you can tell me how the Army's treating you. I see you've added some meat to your bones."

"Oh, yeah," Conrad said, a big smile crossed his face. "Bud and I both. It's not Mother's cooking, but there's lots of food in the Army."

· · ·

"I'm surprised you even have an automobile, Carl."

"Yeah, well. In this crazy place, it don't get to stretch its legs much," Carl said, chuckling at the thought of driving in San Francisco. "You know Anne doesn't drive, and I don't drive to work most days."

"You walk to work?"

"I walk to the ferry," Carl said as he pointed across the bay to Richmond Shipyard No. 3. "I work right there." He drove north on The Embarcadero, an avenue which hugged the edge of the bay on the city's east side before turning west with the land to reach its end at Aquatic Cove, just past Fisherman's Wharf. He stuck his right arm in front of his brother's chest and pointed over the narrow channel across from their location.

"That's Oakland." He then pointed straight ahead. "Across the water over there is Richmond. See the cranes?"

"Yeah."

"That's Shipyard Number Three, where I work."

"Oh, yeah," Conrad admired the sight. "Are you gonna take me there?"

"Nah. Can't." He shook his head. "Off-limits. They get all in a snit at the thought of spies and saboteurs."

"A 'snit'?" Conrad's eyebrows popped up in a state of confusion combined with amusement.

"A tizzy. They get all in a tizzy about strangers."

"Ah," Conrad nodded.

"There's people from all over the country. You can't help but pick up words. You can see a couple of ships we just finished. I gave one of those dolls a test run on Thursday."

"Jeepers! I forgot about that." Conrad was impressed by his brother's words. "You get to ride in them!"

"I just got that foreman job I wanted, so I'm going to be living fat."

The car turned north into what appeared to be a turnout but was a wide entrance into a construction area. The car came to a stop and the two got out and made their way toward the north end of the spit.

"There's the Golden Gate." No additional words were needed to describe the incredible feat of architecture.

"That's a killer-diller bridge!" Conrad exclaimed, the quiet young man unable to contain himself.

"They say that sucker's almost two miles long," Carl reported. "It's only seven years old and it's the longest suspension bridge in the world."

Conrad shook his head in wonder.

"Tallest, too."

"In the world?!"

"In the world."

Conrad continued to gawk until Carl steered his view to various points of interest, until he finally settled on Shipyard No. 3.

"I take a ferry over. I could drive it, but I'd have to drive that damned Bay Bridge. It's a bear getting across that in traffic."

"How far's the ferry ride."

"I think it's about six miles."

As he looked out at the water, the younger brother exclaimed, "This bay is bigger than a lot of our lakes!"

Carl smiled. "All I care about is it never freezes here."

"That's the most impressive part of this whole place."

"I plan on moving the family to Richmond or San Pablo or somewhere over there," Carl pointed in the same direction for both towns.

"Where's San Pablo?"

"Just on the other side of Richmond. They have some war housing over there that would put me closer to work."

"Makes sense."

The two looked around for a couple of minutes, with Carl answering Conrad's occasional questions.

"So, this is your contribution to the war effort," Conrad said with pride in his eldest brother. "That is quite an outfit over there."

"Yeah, but I expect my '1-A' pretty soon."

"What? How can that be?"

"They didn't let me in the first time because of my knees," Carl said with disappointment. "I think they'll take me this time."

"You got two kids and a wife."

"I know, but I'll just move them back to Bemidji."

Conrad sighed as he summed up his brother, at least in this context. "You always like a fight."

"It's in our blood."

Conrad nodded, unable to argue the point.

The clouds lifted just enough for the pair to see the top of the nearest tower of the Golden Gate Bridge. The morning rain had given way to fog, and now the Sun fought a losing battle against the low clouds. Conrad stared at the international-orange suspension bridge until his brother urged him to head back to the Chevy.

As they climbed in and prepared to drive off, an idea struck Carl. "Let's go find Hap."

"Yeah, and Vernon's here, eh?" Conrad asked, referring to Hap's seventeen-year-old and eldest son.

"Hap has been really swell to me, in Puposky and now here. I owe him a lot." Carl paused, remembering how good his mother's brother had been to him. "He'll be happy to see you."

• • •

The brothers failed to find their uncle and cousin, but Carl promised to try again during Conrad's next visit.

"I think I can be back in a couple of weeks," Conrad reassured Carl.

"I got that bottle of liquor I told you about. I don't even remember now what it is, I've had it so long."

Conrad laughed as he responded. "Your letters are a hoot. You can't spell liquor! It's not 'l-i-k-k-e-r,' it's 'l-i-q-u-o-r.' Bud and I get a laugh out of some of the stuff you say in your letters, especially when you were mad Anne wasn't coming out."

"I guess I was pretty fired up — at least that's what Hap tells me."

Conrad laughed again as the car rolled through the crowded streets of San Francisco.

In fact, Conrad did return two weeks later, but the timing never worked out to see Hap. With a little less to do because they missed their uncle, the brothers did drink the bottle of "likker" Carl had saved for Conrad's visit.

•   •   •

Paper Doll's first stop was Herington, Kansas, where the heavy bombers received an inspection and repairs as needed. But the inspections were not just for equipment: men underwent physicals; clothing endured Army scrutiny; the men sat through a class about appropriate behavior in England and surviving capture by the enemy; briefings were given about their destination and route; and schedules were revealed.

In an area of the state which did not see many civilian travelers passing through, the airfield sat alone, in the middle of nowhere. In reality, the small town with the large airstrip eight miles outside of town lay halfway between Manhattan and Newton in east-central Kansas. Three large hangars and numerous barracks made up only part of the 1,700-acre facility, which had become an important launch point for war-bound heavy bombers.

The B-24s of the 489th Bomb Group now sported twin tails of Army green, with the outsides of the tails, port and starboard, displaying a single vertical white stripe splitting the green. On *Paper Doll* and several other aircraft, "+C" adorned the center of the white stripe, signifying their squadron: the 846th.

"You guys know where Culkin and Tankersley are?" Will Plate asked as he entered the barracks. "Colonel Napier is furious."

"No, what's up?" Goshtoian asked.

"Haven't seen them," Bud added.

"Keep your eyes open, boys," Plate responded. "They're in big trouble. If the colonel's mad, they're in trouble."

Bud shrugged and returned to the letter he was writing.

"I wonder what that's about," Lane half-asked. "What do ya think, Gosh? You're an officer."

"Like officers know anything," Bud chided.

Goshtoian responded by throwing a pillow.

• • •

The Sun rose over Kansas to reveal unhappy and nervous airmen.

"What the hell's going on?!" Mickey Baskin demanded, as he burst into the barracks. "Why are there gonna be new guys on my crew?!"

"What are you talking about?" a voice from the back of the barracks called out. "They're not gonna make a change this late."

"The hell they ain't. They just said they were, when we get to England." Baskin's displeasure could not be missed.

Paper Doll's co-pilot, Bob Savage, entered the barracks. "*Paper Doll* boys, gather around, please."

As he made the request, Baskin left the barracks.

"You guys probably know Larry Culkin and Tank are buddies. Well," Savage hesitated. "No one knew where they were last night, and it turns out they were back in town, sitting on the ground in a parking lot, leaning up against the outside of a bar."

"Oh, boy." Bud saw it coming.

"That means several planes are going to be affected."

Bud looked at Savage, concerned. "So, which one of us is going to *Special Delivery*?"

"Nobody from *Paper Doll*."

The only *Paper Doll* men present — Lane, Goshtoian, Holbert, and Bud — felt relief.

"Then why are you telling us? Is there more?" Holbert asked. Nervous, he ran his hand through his curly hair.

"No. No. Nothing else. Just wanted you to know."

"Okay. Sounds good," Lane said.

"They're switching up the crews of the *Lynda Lee* and *Special Delivery*. They're splitting up Culkin and Tank. It sounds like at least one other plane may be involved. I'll know more later."

"Oh, that'll help them make new friends," Bud laughed, his words dripping with sarcasm.

"Oh, yeah. The boys are gonna be pissed at them," Goshtoian chimed in. "Mickey already is and he don't know why."

"They're letting them fly together to England," Savage continued. "They said they'll give the details of the reshuffle at our destination. They're going to move more than just two pairings. It'll be other crew members moved, too."

•   •   •

After three days in Kansas, they flew to Florida, then Brazil. After fifteen months in the military, Eugene Peterson was, at last, on his way overseas. What began as job training, at least in Bud's mind, had grown into an urge, like an itch which

273

defied relief, to serve; to fight the enemy and to experience combat firsthand. As the warplanes traveled toward South America, every mile revealed a new place he had never before found himself.

Bud felt confident. He did not give frequent thought to the hazards, but the idea of bombing the Germans excited him. He was being handed the opportunity to play his part in defending his country — and Europe — from the evil personified by the little man with a loud mouth and funny mustache.

Before departing Florida, Bud wrote his mother:

I am on my way to distant lands, I don't think it makes any diff where but I'm on some coast of the U.S. and ready to leave for a place I don't know.

Included with the letter was a $10 money order. His reason given for the money was cut out by a censor — his first letter which had to pass military muster.

Chapter Twenty-Six

The men held their near-perfect lines as they marched along a road which seemed to have had gravel applied on the hour, so numerous were the rocks. Conrad could not hide his grimaces when he stepped on particularly large rocks, which cut through the worn soles of his boots.

East of a little town called Browns Valley and north of a village known as Smartville, the troop paraded along a trail just beyond the Yuba River which, to Conrad, looked more like a creek. A smattering of live oak and digger pine trees dotted the landscape. Just as the unit reached a flat area, of which there were not many in the area, an airplane could be heard approaching.

At first, no one looked up, but before they realized a second plane trailed the first, the bombardment began. Tear gas.

Without the proper equipment — the men wore t-shirts and long pants in the warm countryside — the chemicals burned their skin and left burning sensations in their eyes and lungs. Formation broke. Men scurried like cats fleeing a dog which had entered the alley. The second wave hit, but few had managed to run far enough to avoid the falling gas. Cries, gasps, and shouts overcame the peaceful sunny day.

The Army simply wanted the men to experience the hardship of a gas attack. Officers, who had not accompanied the men on the march, appeared from the woods and began barking commands. Order must be restored. Lines must be reestablished. The march must continue.

As with every other group which had endured the noxious assault, the establishment of order did not come quickly and tranquility was harder yet to find.

Back at the camp, no soldier skipped the showers.

•   •   •

"That was dirty," one of the medics-in-training griped when safely back in the barracks, his face red and swollen, his eyes barely visible. "Just rotten!"

"I guess they want us to experience it now," another man chimed in, his arms matching his face in a swollen, plum glow.

"Some way to treat a medic," Conrad complained. "I'd like to dunk whoever thought that up in a tank of that juice."

"Tear gas," the first man said, pain lacing his words.

"We all teared up and were crying," Conrad shook his head. "So, I guess it's tear gas."

After another soldier added to the complaint, a conversation broke out about which was worse: crawling through the pit with machine gun bullets flying overhead or the tear gas.

"I don't understand something," Conrad said as he stared toward the ceiling. "My brother is in the Air Corps and he did the whole machine gun pit thing, but he never told me about no tear gas."

"That's because no one gets tear-gassed in airplanes, Yankee," a southerner stretched out on his back called from his bed.

"I feel like I'm back in Texas," Conrad answered the comment without a smile on his face.

"Well, it's hot," one soldier laughed.

Conrad did not laugh. He looked in the mirror for a moment and realized he would not be able to shave in the morning.

Despite his sore condition, Conrad slept in his bunk all through the night, the morning, and into the afternoon. He later told his friends he would sleep late every day if he could get away with it. The twenty-year-old maintained his boyhood innocence, even if he could not see it in his swollen face.

• • •

"Hey, Bud! Are you starting yours?"

"Heck, I don't know. I guess."

"Well grab a dollar."

"A silver certificate right here," he said as he held it for the others to see.

"Everyone's going to do it," Holbert added.

Bud examined the silver certificate dollar bill, dated 1935 and carrying the signature of Henry Morgentheau, Jr., Roosevelt's Treasury Secretary. He turned the bill over, to its backside, as he saw others do, and wrote "SHORT SNORTER E.M. PETERSON" along the white border at the extreme right end, perpendicular to the bill's design. He wrote on the bottom white strip, upside down to the bill's design, "4-30-44 FORTALEZA, BRAZIL".

"Let me see that, Peterson." Goshtoian grabbed the dollar bill from him and signed it "F.O. Andy Goshtoian".

"Even though I'm not part of the crew, do you mind?" It was Joe Parker, an Intelligence man for the Army Air Corps.

"Sure. Of course," Bud allowed.

"You're up, Fred," Parker said as he handed the bill and pen to gunner Fred Stodtmeister, who proceeded to sign "Sgt. W.H. Stodtmeister." The native of Ogden, Utah, wanted it to be official.

Sergeants Alfred Lane, Lige McIntosh, William "W. E." Lowther, and Thomas O'Brien finished up the honors. O'Brien and Lowther were gunners on Edwin Florcyk's as-yet unnamed bomber.

"Hey, where's Trowbridge?" Lowther asked O'Brien as he looked around. "I saw him a minute ago."

"I don't know. He can sign it later," came O'Brien's response.

Bud looked around the hut but did not see anyone else. "So, I fill this up with names, then tape another bill on?"

"Yes, sir," Goshtoian answered. "Now that you've crossed the equator, you're all right to start one. Then, when we're sitting in a bar in London with a couple of sweet English ladies beside us, whoever has the biggest bulge gets free drinks."

The others laughed.

"So, I'm gonna use my own money to make a big wad of cash that I can't spend, just so someone else will buy me drinks?" Bud mixed incredulity with an honest search for the truth.

"Yes, sir," Goshtoian answered again.

Bud shook his head before answering, "Okay."

O'Brien enjoyed the experience. "Well, we've got everyone's names on these, with your own name at the top. This is fun." He paused before adding, "Hell, I didn't even know we crossed the equator until you knuckleheads told me."

Bud rolled his eyes as several men agreed with O'Brien's assessment of fun. "Short Snorter? What kind of name is that? Sounds like a tool for nasal ingestion."

"Oh, Peterson," Holbert teased. "Leave it to you to be skeptical about a proud military tradition."

"I'm only planning on establishing one tradition: that I come home in one piece." A sudden solemnity overcame the men as they all agreed with Bud's sentiment.

The 845th and 846th Squadrons waited two days before the weather cleared for them to fly to Dakar.

•   •   •

Conrad used every opportunity in letters to urge his mother to visit Carl in San Francisco. Hulda wanted to do so, but she resisted until she ran out of personal and family matters which required her attention. Unfortunately, by the time she arrived in California, Conrad had shipped out of Beale. As she set foot in the Bay Area for the first time in her life, her youngest son was seeing Pearl Harbor from an airplane, on his way to Hickam Air Base following a ride in one of Carl's Liberty Ships — at least one just like Carl's. Conrad had made the journey from San Francisco to Honolulu without incident.

Carrying a small light-blue bag and a medium-sized dark-blue bag, Hulda knocked on the door, confident she had reached the correct address. After a ten-second pause, she knocked again. Another ten second delay saw a more vigorous rap on the wooden door. Out of curiosity, she turned the door handle but it stubbornly remained in place.

A woman in a neighboring apartment stuck her head out of her doorway and watched the confused Minnesotan. "They moved," were the only words she offered before shutting her door. A thought struck Hulda: perhaps Conrad was correct and she should have let Carl know of her impending visit.

In the tradition of her mother and other family members, Hulda had a tendency of "just going," as Conrad had so adeptly put it. "Just going" led her to San Francisco and an empty apartment.

With information from Carl's prior landlord followed by a ferry ride across San Francisco Bay, then asking questions of strangers in Richmond, Hulda at long last arrived at 5330 Carlos Avenue, Apartment 1-E.

The "war housing" sprang up due to the lack of adequate accommodations. By May of 1944, only a smattering of people called the parks and empty lots "home." The same sudden overcrowding which had forced Carl to live with Uncle Hap resulted in government housing to provide roofs not only for factory workers like Carl, but for families who had followed their soldiers to California.

The housing was not built to last for years, and the quality was merely adequate, but the shortcomings were not a focus of many who still had traces of the Great Depression flowing through their blood.

Within three miles of Shipyard No. 3, Carl found himself closer to work and away from the crowded west bay. While he did not mind the ferry rides, the cost was adding up and the rides took too much time.

The Richmond area possessed a different feel: more blue collar, more reasonably paced, and less congestion. He held no feelings of loss for living without the traffic across the Bay Bridge, either.

Once Carl and Anne recovered from the brief shock of seeing Hulda in their doorway, they all attempted to settle in for a nice visit.

•   •   •

"I can tell you're your mother's daughter," Carl chuckled.

"I guess I should've listened to your brother," a rueful Hulda responded. "He said I should let you know I was coming."

"It's fine, Hulda," Anne said in her sweetest tone.

"I know," Hulda looked at son and daughter-in-law before laughing. "But I'm tired now."

The three sat around the wood table Carl purchased just before Anne and the kids arrived from Puposky.

"Well, you don't worry about a thing," Anne averred. "Now that you're here, only the kids will wear you out." With that, Anne left the room to check on Carla and Jim.

"How do you like that swing shift?"

"I'm used to it," Carl said without emotion. "I don't mind either way. Fortunately, they've been good enough to keep me on the same shift most of the time." He paused before adding, "They still have me work days occasionally, especially when I'm giving a new ship its shakedown run. I really enjoy those."

"I understood why you left Puposky the way you did. I'm just happy it worked out."

"Yeah, I was unhappy here for a while."

"I know. I was with Anne a lot, especially when Gertie was dying."

Carl detected a rare display of emotion in her voice.

"She wanted you around then," Hulda continued, referring to Anne. "But I'd remind her there'd be better days ahead."

"Thank you. I appreciate that." Carl said with sincere gratitude.

"I talked to Hap when he visited after Christmas," Hulda added. "He told me how well you were doing and it really made me proud."

Carl pursed his lips as if to hold back a barrage of emotions.

"You didn't need me the way your brothers and sisters did. You were always the strongest one. They're all four strong, but you're the strongest."

"I guess that's what ends up happening when a fifteen-year-old boy leaves home. He grows up pretty fast." Carl's face could not hide he had just broached a taboo subject — a subject which had put an invisible wedge between mother and son for well over ten years.

"I did what I thought was right." Hulda paused, but Carl did not fill the void. Hulda continued after ten seconds of silence which felt like ten minutes. "I didn't marry him like he wanted." She referred to a man for whom she had cared since her youthful days; however, the Peterson and Gustafson families had molded a destiny for William and Hulda which ensured the two would marry. While Hulda loved her husband, her heart held a soft spot for another man throughout the early years of the 20th century, as well, until she finally hardened it.

After marriage, children, and years gone by, the disappointment of a relationship not meant to be had long-since burned out. When William died of cancer in 1929, the former suitor saw his opportunity. Hulda hesitated. She compromised by allowing him to move into a small house on the farm a year after William's death, which angered fifteen-year-old Carl. Carl packed up a few belongings and left.

With nowhere to go as an economy shattered in front of everyone's eyes, he moved in with Uncle Hap, who at the time had only three children. Carl's nearly three years with Hap proved life-changing. For the rest of his life, Carl would credit his uncle for teaching him the skills he needed to become a home builder. Young men needed mechanical skills, and after Carl left Hap's house, he spent time as a lumberjack and at a sawmill. With the Civilian Conservation Corps, he worked on numerous projects, using the skills learned from his mother's brother. His family could take pride in Carl's work on a project which went on to symbolize the little town of Bemidji and has weathered time: statues of Paul Bunyan and Babe the Blue Ox, which resided at a park at Lake Bemidji.

Carl was hard-headed like his mother, and their relationship had never completely recovered, but now, they both saw their opportunity to close that gap.

"You know why I never married him," Hulda continued as she shifted in her chair. "I kept thinking back to Oscar and how he treated us kids." Grandma Thompson's second husband had a cruel streak which manifested when interacting with Hulda and her siblings. "Emil, Ragna, and Olga were fortunate enough to have been gone already or able to leave. Me and Hap and Lillian weren't so lucky."

"Did he beat you up a lot?"

"Not a lot. He did his physical damage, but he was mostly just mean." Hulda stared over Carl's shoulder, casting a blank stare at a kitchen cabinet. "It was no way to treat children, and I wasn't gonna give you kids a stepfather, too. I didn't want you to have to deal with what I did."

"I would've just whipped his ass," Carl said with an even voice.

"Well, that's true." Hulda did not laugh; she understood humor had not been her son's intent.

Carl's assessment hung in the air until he finally continued the mother/son healing. "Mother, what's done is done. You've got a bucket-full of grandkids now, including two here."

"And one on the way," Hulda added with a smile.

"Since we can't change the past, let's play the cards we got."

Hulda nodded as she stared at her eldest son. Her intense expression reflected sincerity, pain, and a touch of relief.

"That's all we can do," Carl added. "Play the cards we got."

Chapter Twenty-Seven

When the Eighth Air Force's 56th Fighter Group vacated Halesworth Airfield in April of 1944, the 489th Bombardment Group wasted little time moving into their new home. The base could house 3,000 men, and with its two large hangars and three runways, the 489th possessed the space to work on and fly their Liberators without stepping over one another. The first contingent of B-24s to arrive received a "circle W" on their tails — just as it sounded, the letter "W" with a circle around it. Not long after the first came the second group of squadrons, with their "+C" tails, including *Paper Doll* and crew.

All the ground crews had arrived earlier, regardless of when their aircraft had flown over. They set up their tools, organized the spaces for each aircraft, patrolled the runways looking for debris and other runway hazards, and molded the base into a home away from home.

Ninety miles northeast of London and due west, across the North Sea, from German-held Amsterdam, the airfield sat seven miles from the coast. The River Blyth flowed in an easterly direction not far south of Halesworth on its continuous journey to the North Sea, surrendering to the larger body at the little town of Walberswick. At one point, near the town of Blythburgh, the river became engrossed with a swampy lowland. Farms and truncated forests littered the land, the fecund soil hidden by the multiple shades of lush green crops and trees.

At the easternmost point of the British Isles, Halesworth Airfield provided an ideal location for launching airstrikes against the Third Reich.

"Hey, Pete!" Mickey Baskin called out as he hustled across a tarmac to catch Bud. "All of us were right — we're gonna bomb the Krauts all to hell." He caught up to Bud as he finished his comment.

"About time, ain't it?" Bud said with firmness despite ending his words as a question.

Baskin eyed Bud's swinging arm and looked at his wrist. "Hey, that's some watch!"

Bud smiled with a touch of pride. Possessing such a luxurious item was foreign to him. "Yeah, got it in a market in Fortaleza," he said, referring to their stopover in the Brazilian port city. "Twenty-one dollars."

"Twenty-one bucks?! You've gone uptown, Peterson!" Baskin teased. "I can tell you're on a sergeant's salary now."

Bud's sheepish grin reflected the austere life he had known; in his younger days, buying a twenty-one-dollar watch would have seemed not just an impossibility, but a waste of money. Now, living on $117 a month and having just sent $100 to his mother, Bud felt good about his finances. He also did what he could to help out Conrad.

"Have you heard training's about to end?" Baskin asked with excitement flooding his eyes and voice.

"Yeah. No more dummy bombs or real bombs blowing up fields." Bud smiled at a sudden thought. "I'd like to see Herr Göring's face when we start dropping our eggs on the Fatherland."

Bud did not write home much in his early days at Halesworth; Colonel Napier kept the men busy. The importance of strict discipline would not be enforced to the same degree

286

once they entered the fray, so this was a good time to get the men into good habits.

An excitement filled the air above and throughout the base. Everyone knew what was coming. They were now a full three months past their first fatality, when Lieutenant Daniel Blessington of the 845th, the co-pilot on Lieutenant Roy Anderson's crew, perished at Wendover in a crash landing as they attempted to bring a crippled bird down while short an engine. Pilots had shared stories about the B-24 morphing into a beast when it lost an engine, and the men never forgot the shock of the loss of life — and the pilots remembered the lessons of the struggles at the controls of a three-engine Liberator. The manual stated the Liberator could be flown with two engines, but the pilots had the attitude of "to hell with the manual."

On the day before they went operational, two of the bombers collided during a training exercise at a cost of twenty men. The flyers of the 489th were anxious to get training out of the way.

Then, on May 30, 1944, the day finally arrived. While some felt trepidation as the date approached, most did not consider friends and acquaintances would be lost. "Bombing Hitler" sounded exhilarating, but the reality of war could not be properly anticipated. The difference between the men on the evening of May 29 versus the evening of May 30 could not be missed by any observer. The war, at long last to Bud and his peers, had arrived. Lives would be changed, and lives would be lost. Hell had opened its doors.

•　　•　　•

The early morning Sun found itself obscured by the low, dense clouds. As the Liberators rolled off the tarmac and rumbled down the runways, the 0530 sky should have allowed a greater amount of light to penetrate to the ground. Instead, the murky darkness added additional weight onto the men's nerves.

The locals understood the significance of the never-ending roar of engines. This was not a few Liberators here and there on practice runs. Townspeople who braved the early morning only saw the aircraft for mere seconds until the low clouds swallowed up the bombers one by one.

To Bud and his friends, the realization of striking at Germany itself brought quiet glee. Though they did not care what the target was, they were just happy with a mission over enemy territory. The assignment was a Focke-Wulf factory airfield which was used for testing new fighter planes.

What the enlisted men were not allowed to know was the purpose of the attack: D-Day — the long-awaited Allied land invasion of Europe — lay only days away.

Soviet Premier Josef Stalin had begged and shouted and pushed in every way he knew for the invasion. He wanted it to happen long before now, but Roosevelt and Churchill were not about to commit until every piece of the puzzle could be removed from the box and readied to be put together in a swift assault.

Because of their crew's successes at Wendover, and the flying and leadership abilities of Captain Gast, *Paper Doll* had been designated to fly as "Lead" or "Deputy Lead" and thus guaranteed to be one of the first planes on every mission it flew. As such, they only flew about one-fourth of the missions compared to most other crews. Gast's job was to participate in strategies and airborne logistical planning.

As one of the leads, *Paper Doll* also carried an extra navigator, who served as a back-up to Sund, and manned the opposite waist gun from Bud. In their case, they lacked an assigned second navigator, so they were given a different "extra" on each flight.

The planes began their evasive actions, changing course and altitude every thirty seconds. Once the anti-aircraft artillery fired as they passed over land, they flew higher than the Germans expected and the flak exploded at a lower altitude than needed, allowing safe passage for the bombers. The next time through this area, other tactics would be necessary.

Just a reference to flak — an acronym for the German *Fliegerabwehrkanonen*, which roughly translates as "aircraft defense cannon" — resulted in lumps in the throats of the fliers. While the size of the shells varied, flak was essentially German high-powered grenades which exploded in attempts to bring down enemy aircraft. The detonation altitude was set by a timer in the shell's fuse which was adjusted to allow the projectile to explode at a different delay.

The flak did not necessarily have to cause damage to be effective. Its presence forced the alteration of altitude and speed by Allied pilots, which many times diminished bombing accuracy and could mean the difference between mission success or failure.

"Navigator to pilot, IP in one minute," Sund called over the interphone. "Heading looks good."

"Target in sight, ready for control," Andy Goshtoian called out from his bombardier's pit, located below and forward of the navigator, who himself was stationed between the nose turret and the cockpit.

"Pilot to bombardier, you have control," Gast offered.

"Bombardier to pilot, I have control."

Bud could not see the men on the ground, up ahead, scrambling to their planes, but he felt them. He knew they were there, preparing to shoot them from the sky. He rotated his turret in slow increments as he scanned the skies and ground, watching and waiting for the inevitable.

As ordered by their superiors and enforced by Gast, only limited, necessary interphone traffic was acceptable.

"Bombardier opening bomb bay doors," Goshtoian announced.

After several seconds of pause, Holbert confirmed. "Roger. Bomb bay doors are open."

"Fighters! Two o'clock low and climbing!" Bud's excited exclamation did not impress Gast, who recognized his gunner's voice.

"Pilot to gunner, easy. No need to worry about it."

"Co-pilot to gunners, fire when they're in range."

An explosion underneath the formation rocked *Paper Doll* — flak, close enough to be considered "accurate."

"Flak. Looks like Eighty-eights," Bud announced, referring to the common and much-feared 88-millimeter German shells.

"Roger," Lane barked.

"Pilot to crew. Stay calm."

The sphincter muscles of each man tightened even as Gast gave the order to maintain lower blood pressure. At the same moment, another burst of flak exploded 200 hundred yards below and behind them. Bud saw one of the three other planes in their separate formation rock. Within seconds, the dozens of other four-ship formations watched as the flak grew closer yet.

"Bombardier to pilot, bombs away."

"Roger, bombardier."

"Radio to bombardier, all bombs away."

"One-oh-nines coming in from two different points, port-side, low." It was the Utah native, Stodtmeister, itching for action. "Ten o'clock low," he corrected himself.

"Savage, let's get the hell outta here," Gast said in an even tone, despite the urgency of his words.

"Fighters at ten o'clock and closing!" McIntosh tried not to shout lest he draw the ire of their captain. The flak had stopped, clearing the way for the fighters.

"Don't worry, gunner," Gast said, his voice as smooth as velvet. "The escorts will take care of them."

"Ball to bombardier, nice eggs," Bud called out.

"More incoming!" McIntosh shouted from his top-turret position. He had no patience for the American fighters to engage. A direct hit from McIntosh eased his tension. Smoke puffed from the Messerschmitt Bf 109 as it fought to descend at a survivable rate. McIntosh followed his training and avoided the urge to watch or continue firing at an enemy out of action. Instead, he scanned for additional threats. Unfortunately for him, most of the fighters attacked bombers behind him and out of range.

"Bombardier to crew, we put several holes in the tarmac — took some planes with it, too!"

"Congratulations!" someone shouted without identifying himself.

Bud had begun firing when the first enemy fighters came into range. He watched as one of the B-24s rocked hard from a hit from a fighter, dropped 100 feet, then fought to regain its proper placement in the formation.

"Dammit!" Bud stopped shooting at a German plane when it flew too close to the bomber formation. He did not wish to down one of his own.

As Bud and company watched, a rising 109 raced through the formation. They wanted to fire, but could not risk hitting friendlies. He could not be sure where the German 13mm machine gun rounds ended up, but he had no indication *Paper Doll* absorbed any hits.

Bud lost sight of the rising German plane for a few seconds before it pitched downward and through the formation again, firing its machine guns. Bud could not get a shot until it passed below the formations to allow for a clean line of fire.

"That pilot's crazy," Bud called out in an even voice.

"He's not going to survive the war," Lane agreed.

As the formation flew toward the Netherlands, the German fighters peeled off. Additional flak began over the Netherlands, but quickly died out.

"Pilot to radio, what did you learn about our escorts? Why the no-shows?"

"Radio here, there was confusion among the fighter groups. Less than half made it to us."

"Navigator to pilot, oxygen check."

"Pilot to navigator, oxygen good."

"Navigator to co-pilot, oxygen check."

"Co-pilot to navigator, I'm still here."

"Roger that. Navigator to bombardier, oxygen check."

This went on through the entire crew, in a specific order, every fifteen minutes, until they passed below 10,000 feet. Until Bud's name was called, he drifted away mentally, thinking about his situation. Four thousand miles from home, dropping bombs and firing guns, visiting foreign lands but rarely a tourist, Life had taken a turn he had not foreseen while living a great life in Puposky as an innocent kid, or hauling grain in North Dakota, or even yelling at the Army recruiter in Bemidji.

The killing did not bother him, which to his knowledge, the crew of *Paper Doll* had yet to do, but the odd thought of having visited multiple countries, flying over two more today, and seeing the world under unfathomable circumstances caused him to pause and observe his surroundings.

He knew the formation had entered the airspace of Holland — the northern part of the country of the Netherlands where the term actually applied — but he did not know anything about her people or her history. He could not see their art or architecture or scenery from the air, even though the first two topics did not ordinarily concern him at any other time.

His first experience in battle saw bombs drop, fighters attack, anti-aircraft artillery explode, and tensions rise. But he survived. He looked down at the Netherlands and the approaching North Sea — a body of water he could not recall even knowing about until recently — and ended his ruminations with an overwhelming urge. "Ball to pilot, I'm getting out of this contraption!"

"Radio to Pete, I hear we get a shot of whiskey after every mission," Holbert teased Bud. "You're gonna need a double shot."

"Whiskey? No kidding?" Bud asked as he climbed out of the ball turret and grabbed a walk-around oxygen bottle.

"No kidding, Peterson," Holbert laughed.

•   •   •

"Will," Bud called out to a friend a few feet away in the mess hall.

"Hey, Pete," Will Plate answered. The pilot in the 847th, he had a wife back home in Crane, Texas.

"Did you fly today?"

"Yes, sir," Plate said. "We dropped our eggs and had a direct hit on some Nazi birds on the tarmac!"

Smiling, Bud added to the story. "Same here. We were near the front — deputy lead plane — and it was a helluva view from the ball turret, I'll tell ya that."

Plate shook his head at the little ball of death at the back of the planes.

"I heard we lost somebody," Bud said with a slow, pained voice.

"Yeah. I didn't hear which squadron," Plate said as he stepped up to request food from the servers. "I'll take one of those."

"I just know it was a 'Circle-W'. I don't know who." Bud looked at a man holding a large ladle, ready to dip it into a vat of dark soup when requested. "What's that, pal?" Bud inquired.

"Look, mister," the corporal snarled. "If everybody asked what everything is, it'd take all day for the line to go through. We ain't got all day. You want it or not?" The northeastern accent made the experience worse for Bud.

"Might as well," Bud sneered. "If the Germans don't kill me, a smartass corporal from New York will."

"New Jersey!" the man snapped.

"New Jersey," Bud repeated. "Hey, we don't need to drop bombs, we can just drop knuckleheads from New Jersey. The Krauts will kill themselves."

The corporal sloshed the soup into a bowl and thrust it over the counter at Bud.

"I know somebody else got killed on a plane, but I don't think it was anyone we knew," Plate added as he slid down the line and motioned for a piece of pie.

"What got 'em? Flak?"

"Yeah, that's some nasty stuff, that flak. It looked like flies on rotten meat," Plate added.   "When I'd spin and look backward, it was a sea of black puffs everywhere, until the fighters came, of course. Well, half the fighters."

"How nervous were you in the ball turret?"

"Not too bad. It was a view like no other, I can tell you that." Bud smiled. "I could see the whole show."

Emotionally, the day's events did not take a toll on Sergeant Peterson, but when he returned to barracks he did not feel the urge to write family members. Instead, he lay on his bed, on top of the blanket, leaned his head against the wall, and listened to his friends tell their tales.

At this point, successful missions and returning to base safely were all that mattered. After listening to others for a while, Bud finally relaxed enough to undress, crawl under the covers, and sleep. As anticipated, he dreamed about the day's mission.

Chapter Twenty-Eight

The warm waves crashed into Conrad's legs and lower torso as he struggled to maintain his footing. Once the wave passed, he again dropped underwater and felt with his hands to find the object he had stepped on. When he popped up for the second time, he held the prize in his hands. He examined the seashell for two seconds before passing judgment. "Aaaa. Broken." He tossed the shell away, into deeper water, with a flick of his wrist.

After the next wave passed, he struggled back to the sandy shore.

"Peterson, your collection ain't gettin' it done." Fellow private and good acquaintance Gerald, in his red swim trunks, looked at Conrad's blanket. "That's not many seashells."

"Yeah, I keep finding all the broken ones," he said with frustration as he walked to his towel, which he had previously spread flat on the sand.

"You're not very good at this, especially for a guy who comes out here every day."

"Hey, you're dripping on my towel."

"Oh. Sorry." Gerald stepped backward.

Conrad reached down and grabbed a few of the objects. "But look at how many sharks' teeth I've got."

He held out what looked to be ten to a dozen thin, black teeth, each from half-an-inch to an inch long.

"I never thought I'd be searching for shark teeth someday," Gerald chuckled. "We didn't have many sharks in Tennessee."

"Same with Minnesota," Conrad smiled as he bent over and dropped them the final six inches onto the towel. He took a seat as Gerald sat next to him, on his own towel.

"After the war, I've got to come back here," Gerald exclaimed, excited as a child on Halloween after an evening of trick-or-treating.

"I don't know," Conrad said as he gazed out to sea. "This place ain't like the movies."

"You just say that because we work so much."

"Probably."

"Hey, if I'm gonna dig ditches, it might as well be in Hawaii."

"Yeah, that's just it," Conrad explained as he continued his stare, watching birds he could not identify dive into the water as they fished for lunch. "You, dig a ditch. You, put up that tent. You, clear that brush. I don't think Hawaii was meant to be a place where I'm tired all the time because I'm doing busy work." Conrad shook his head as he watched a bird emerge from the ocean water with a wriggling fish in its mouth. "All we've done is work since we landed on this rock."

"Well, they can't have a crew of people who don't do any work," Gerald reasoned. "That's for doctors."

Instead of laughing at the joke, Conrad pursed his lips and nodded. "Something tells me those dudes are going to drive me crazy. Instead of dig here, clear there, it's gonna be, 'Hand me that. Wash this. Go bury the dead guy.' Stuff like that."

"Well, that's something I haven't done," Gerald said as he joined in the bird watching.

•　　•　　•

The tents to which Conrad had referred were not the basic portable versions, which children would use in the backyard or hunters would pack for a multi-day excursion. Instead, each tent measured sixteen-feet long by twelve-feet, was built on a wooden base, and contained wooden floors. Three-step stairs climbed to the front of the lone entrance. The tent's weight was distributed on stilts evenly spaced to provide the appropriate amount of support. The Army olive drab canvas tops rose to form "teepee" peaks, which presented the appearance of a military circus come to town.

The fifteen-feet-tall pole in the center pushed the height of the tent upward in the middle, making the chore of erecting such a tent a team effort.

Before the afternoon rains hit, the walls of the tent would be opened to allow in air through the sheer mesh. Once the daily rain made its appearance, rolled-up canvas on each side would be untied to cover the mesh walls and allow the canvas to provide the soldiers a degree of protection from the elements.

The wood floors made the tents seem a little more tolerable and gave a feel of living a step up from ground sleepers. Life in these tents did not feel like tent living, at least until high winds, usually accompanied by rain, hit the encampment.

Conrad and Gerald continued their conversation as they approached the tents

"I've been in the sterilization tent so much I'm beginning to wonder whether that's where I'll end up permanently," Conrad half-asked, half-stated.

"Nah, they're keeping everyone in place to get experience before mixing it up," Gerald said with enough authority to convince Conrad.

"Well, I guess you can't kick on playing in the ocean every day," Conrad said with a smile. He held out his bare forearms in front of him as they walked. "Look at this. I'm getting as brown as a roasted nut in this place."

"Can't beat that," Gerald responded.

"Yeah, except I'm Norwegian. That's not supposed to happen."

•   •   •

Conrad had learned upon his return from the beach he had been given the afternoon off. He did not know the reason for the respite, but arguing about it was last on his short list of things to do. He sat on the edge of his bed as he wrote letters home. Before the afternoon rains hit, he received mail, including from his mother. Excited he no longer had to worry about V-mail, which he called "dehydrated letters" due to their slow movement through the postal system, he wrote until the rainy time arrived and he needed to help lower the canvas "walls."

Victory Mail, or "V-mail," was correspondence that went through mail censors before being photographed and transported as a thumbnail-sized image in microfilm, saving weight and bulk for other war materiel. Upon arrival to their destination, the negatives would be printed at 60% of the original document's size, creating a sheet four-by-five inches. The processed delayed delivery of mail, provoking frustrations for both sender and recipient.

Medic and surgical technician training continued. Conrad remained comfortable with his beach schedule and did not make visiting Honolulu a priority, only making the short trek on rare occasions.

•   •   •

Besides her trip across San Francisco Bay in a ferry and time spent with her loved ones, Hulda did not care for California. Her biggest complaint was the crowds of people every place she ventured. The country girl lived strong within her, and her California experience lacked the rural living and quiet life she preferred.

While waiting at the Richmond apartment for Carl to return from his shift and take her to the train depot, Hulda wrote a V-mail to Bud. Despite her best efforts, she had lost the ability to hide her worries. With two young men overseas — she had no idea where Conrad's adventure had led him — and both in, or soon to be in, harm's way, the calm, serene, stoic Hulda became more and more difficult to find; by the day she became more and more of a worrier.

I miss you boys so much and pray for this terrible war to be over soon. We will all have to have stronger faith and try and keep cheerful as possible... God bless you and keep   you safe. Our prayers go with you and your crew wherever you are.

Worries never ceased, and the reason for worry had just increased. The thought of both Bud and Conrad overseas gnawed at her spirit. Before, it had been only a fear of the inevitable; now, the inevitable proved real.

The matriarch could not control the situation, as she usually succeeded in doing, and it bothered her. She wanted to steer her sons safely back home. She did not wish to be in control out of ego or a sense of superiority, but like every mother, she wanted what was best for her family. "We will all have to have stronger faith..." applied to her as well, and she understood that. Although she possessed strong faith in God, as a mere human she worried. She felt — she knew — events could unfold in a way which could result in multiple tragedies, and if that happened, it would destroy her. So, she prayed more. Fervently. Frequently. She was too proud to tell anyone she was scared, but indeed, she trembled at what could be. Only her faith and time spent with her family sustained her.

Her trip west ended successfully. She spent time with her two grandchildren, spent a lot of time with Anne while Carl worked, and made progress in her relationship with her eldest son. With a long train ride remaining, the only disappointment she felt centered around missing Conrad at Camp Beale. After struggling to gain information from tight-lipped Uncle Sam, she only knew he had shipped out.

Chapter Twenty-Nine

The term "Normandy" finds its roots in the "Normans," or "North men." Vikings raided the area on multiple occasions during the eighth century, conquered the land, and spread their roots. By the early tenth century, the great Viking leader Rollo ruled the area, ostensibly while under the French King Charles III the Simple's domain. Rollo had left Norway because he did not wish to be of service to Norway's King Harald I, so he conquered and inhabited areas free from the Norwegian monarch.

Out of sheer convenience, having no intention of serving King Charles III the Simple, Rollo possessed the ability to rule his portion of northern France while placating the French King. At the ceremony for both parties to demonstrate their acceptance of the treaty, Rollo was ordered to kiss the foot of King Charles III as a sign of fealty — something Rollo would not show to any man.

After hesitating, Rollo turned to his top lieutenant and ordered him to kiss the King's foot. The lieutenant paused, then approached the King, grabbed him by an ankle, pulled the royal foot up to his mouth, and kissed the foot. While lying on his back, King Charles III the Simple received the foot kiss he demanded.

Over a thousand years later, French Normandy became German-held territory after its subjugation of France. Now, Eisenhower and the Allies were ready to take back Rollo's land as a launching point to reclaim the continent.

Planning proceeded and anticipation skyrocketed as the invasion day approached, but weather delayed Operation

Overlord by one day. When the sun rose on the Norman coast on June 6, an avalanche of men and equipment flooded ashore and engaged German forces.

Hitler believed the build-up in the area to be an Allied feint. He considered General George S. Patton to be the best Allied general, and could not fathom the invasion of the Continent could take place without him.

The Germans would not recover from their strategic loss of June 6. Once again, Hitler the charismatic leader was once again undercut by Hitler the military strategist; he was his own worst enemy. Fierce fighting marked the famous day, but had Hitler exhibited better military strategy, or better yet, allowed his generals to run the war, the outcome of Operation Overlord would have been in doubt much longer than history records.

The bravery displayed on D-Day is legendary, with entire books devoted to heroics of just that single day. The Allies, with the bravery of Rollo, attacked in numbers which would have dwarfed a fearsome Viking raid. Although the land's history held no meaning for Eisenhower and the Allies, it did seem fitting to hit the believers in Aryan superiority in a former Norse stronghold.

Bud and his Peterson line did not descend from Rollo, but that bold, strong mentality seemed to have reached across all the Viking bloodlines. Now Bud found himself flying toward the land of his Norse cousins.

"Socked in? What do you mean?" one of the gunners asked over the interphone.

"It means we can't drop our eggs," Gast responded to Scofield. The gunner knew what the term meant, but disappointment enveloped him. Rumors had spread this day would bring an important mission, though the enlisted men knew only bits and pieces.

"Yeah, I won't be able see anything to hit," Goshtoian added. If off by even a short distance, they could kill their own men with their bombs.

With radio calls between the planes flooding the air, the mission to hit targets in St. Lo, inland from the famed beaches, was officially scrubbed. Their mission to soften German positions inland from Utah and Omaha beaches could not be fulfilled. With Allied forces flooding inland, they could not chance a blind drop, which was something they never wanted to do anyway. Lead pilot Robert Gast knew enough of the details of the large-scale operation, thus he understood the need for precision, at least as much precision as was possible with their unguided 500-pound bombs.

Bombs still unarmed, the dozens of aircraft in the attack force drew a large semi-circle in the sky and headed back to base. As the day progressed, news would leak out about a tremendous assault onto the European continent. The countdown clock for days Hitler had remaining on this Earth began to tick.

•   •   •

"Well, that was a lost opportunity," Bud lamented as the pair strode from *Paper Doll*.

"I think you're missing the bright side," fellow gunner Scofield answered. "No one shot at us, and we got credit for a mission."

Bud smiled. "I like that. It was only our second mission, so we got a ways to go. The magic number is twenty-five, unless they up it."

"Well," Scofield said with bounding energy. "That was my third mission." The Iowan-turned-Angeleno's emphasis on "third" displayed the giddiness at being one step closer to going home. The sooner he hit his number of missions, the sooner he could see his wife in Los Angeles.

"Oh, that's right," Bud recalled as he heard Scofield's glee. "You got that ride yesterday."

"Sure did — two days ago." His elation climbed still. "The *Lynda Lee* was short a gunner. Some knucklehead on their crew got a cold or something. I found out later we hit artillery batteries at some place called Le Touquet." He ran his thoughts together, excited at the strategy he had hit upon to get out of the war sooner. Scofield's mission included linking up with the 384th Bomb Group in dropping a huge number of bombs in a brief period.

"If you hit German AA batteries, you were obviously helping to prepare for today," Bud reasoned.

"I guess so." Scofield paused when a thought hit him. "Hey, if you promise not to drag in any other guys, we should work together on this, catching other rides."

"I don't know," Bud started, hesitating as he considered the plan. "I'm kinda enjoying this once-every-several-days bit." Bud paused again to consider the idea as they neared their barracks. "I mean, we hit 'em on May 30th. Today's the sixth. Sure, I'd like to go a little more often, but I'm sure I'm gonna appreciate some breaks."

"Suit yourself, Peterson. I'm going home early. I'm grabbing every mission I can." With that, Scofield patted Bud on the back as he entered the barracks. Bud paused to have a smoke.

•   •   •

Over the past fifteen months, Bud had evolved from a young man focused on getting a job and finding a way to obtain the skills which would allow him to earn a reasonable living, to a patriotic, dedicated soldier who felt a desire to defeat the enemies of liberty. He was not shy about his patriotism. When he finally joined the military, he felt patriotic, though the thought did not enter his mind often. Had he taken the time to think about it, he still harbored concerns about employment upon return to Bemidji, but such thoughts escaped his mind when in the middle of a war.

His personality was such he would never be the guy in front of a group, waving the 48-starred Red, White, and Blue; nevertheless, during his final training days and subsequent deployment overseas, the reality of what needed to be accomplished took center stage in his thoughts and life.

When he entered the Army, he needed a job. He was broke. The Civilian Conservation Corps only allowed him to keep one-sixth of his pay. The arrangement of the remaining twenty-five dollars going to his mother was a blessing for the family, but as he liked to say, it was "pinching his jeans." He saw Uncle Sam as an employment agency.

Thoughts of employment wandered far from his mind with the daily missions. Though no soldier flew every day and the men rotated in and out of assignments, the morning thunder of engines occurred almost daily. The ground crews, stuck in limbo as they "sweated out the mission," as they called waiting for the aircraft to return from their bombing runs, became the epitome of the low-keyed, quiet worrying that occurred when the bombers were away. The airmen themselves, when off duty, sweated out the missions in the same way. They did not want their friends to know they worried, but indeed they did just that.

Planes returned shot up, struggling to fly, or with dead or injured aboard. And every day, others did not return at all.

Bud no longer saw Uncle Sam as an employment agency, rather as a symbol of why he had to perform his duty. Now twenty-one, Eugene Peterson had grown up — rapidly.

"You coming?" Holbert interrupted Bud's thoughts as the former walked out of the barracks.

Bud glanced as his $21 watch. "Oh. Yeah." It was a small ceremony, but he could not afford to be late in front of the visiting colonel. He straightened his clothing as he stood, then remained next to his bed to check his face and Army-regulation haircut in a palm-sized mirror.

Now confident he appeared presentable, Bud left the barracks and fell in line.

After a few instructions and congratulations from one of the majors and the visiting colonel, the small group of fifteen men remained silent as their commanding officer approached the formation.

The ceremony was a brief affair, with Colonel Napier pausing to salute each soldier, shake his hand, and move to the next man. No pins, no cloth stripe — that was each man's responsibility to sew on — and no pomp. With a salute and handshake, Bud found himself promoted to staff sergeant. He only cared about the extra money he could send home and the extra cash he desired when, at last, he received a weekend pass to London.

• • •

Part of the pre-flight ritual included receipt of a survival kit, the "Escape Packet," as it was known. The packet contained multiple maps, a small compass, anti-malarial tablets known as "atabrine," energy pills, a small amount of currency, a quality photo of oneself so the Underground could make a fake passport, a pair of black, European-styled shoes, and a Hershey bar. Many ate the Hershey bar immediately.

One other dividend of mission day was real eggs for breakfast rather than the powdered variety.

• • •

The Sun peeked through the morning clouds as Bud poured himself into the tiny ball turret, memories of the prior day's textbook bombing outside of Domleger, France — his fifth mission — fresh in his mind. The 489th had obliterated railroad targets, emasculated Germany's ability to ship material to build the weapons, and damaged their ability to deliver needed weaponry and supplies to the troops.

Paper Doll rested in a location away from the runways reserved for parked bombers not on the verge of a mission. The ground crew worked on various parts of the plane, while the air crew — the enlisted men — repaired shrapnel damage to keep the flying lady looking pretty. The officers were scheduled to complete their post-flight checks, but a planning meeting had demanded their presence instead.

"How many holes were there?" Lane yelled from inside the airplane.

"Not many," Crew Chief Bousquet answered with a shout of his own. He stood on a step ladder positioned underneath the open bomb bay. As he craned his neck to see the bomb racks, he finished his answer. "I think there were sixteen."

"That's too many for me!" Lane's serious tone made the other men, scattered around the inside of the bomber, laugh at the show of concern. "Well!" he continued. "It didn't look like the Krauts were getting close to us. But they hit us."

"One of the no-named birds took a bunch. The crew chief stopped counting after one-hundred. Another got over three hundred holes," Bousquet responded.

"And yet those bastards didn't even have us dialed in!" Lane marveled, even though his assessment was incorrect; several B-24 crews had perished due to flak.

Bud had lowered the ball turret from inside the fuselage, opened the now-accessible turret door from outside *Paper Doll*, and wormed his way into the ball.

Rumors abounded the ball turret would be removed any day now in order to save weight for extra bombs and reduce drag. Many assumed the real reason lay with the fear a majority of the operators felt, which cut into their effectiveness. The Army's selling point of the position fell on deaf ears: statistically, based on losses recorded, the ball turret provided the safest position on the plane. Fewer ball turret gunners were killed than any other place on Liberators.

Bud pulled one of the twin M2 Browning .50 caliber gun's charging levers back to ensure it did not harbor a round, which would then clear the way for disassembling the weapon. He had cleaned these weapons dozens of times and Uncle Sam considered him an expert.

Bud pulled the lever back on the second gun to check whether a round was chambered just as he adjusted his body for comfort inside the confining space. His hand slipped off the lever at the same moment he saw the live round. In that split second, horror filled his mind and a burning sensation cut through his chest. He could not, in the quarter of a second, stop the inadvertent firing.

As he prayed the area in front of the M2 was clear, his eyes darted upward as the explosion of the single shot sounded louder than normal in the peaceful setting on the base, with men tending to their aircraft.

What he saw through the turret window caused Bud to feel simultaneously sick and hollow. A knot the size of a baseball squeezed at his stomach. He wanted to vomit. He wanted to cry. He wanted to slit his own wrists.

Screaming emanated from multiple points in the area. A man ran to tend to a fallen soldier. Shouts continued. In a blur, Bud found himself outside the turret and on the ground.

Concerned men around the bomber asked questions and expressed their horror in different ways — some by shouting, others with excited exclamations, and still others by sitting in quiet solitude.

"Is everyone okay?" Stodtmeister asked, not fully aware of what had just occurred.

"Peterson's okay," McIntosh said as he looked at his sullen friend with the ashen face.

Bousquet poked his head around the aircraft to deliver the news Bud already knew. "Somebody's been hit."

"Hit?" Lane sounded shocked. "You don't just get hit. That round will cut you in two!"

Holbert and Stodtmeister quickly jogged the three hundred yards to check on the situation. A crowd of perhaps a dozen men gathered around the corpse. The pair tried to catch their breaths as they arrived.

"What the hell happened over there, Holbert?!" Marlin Gehrke, a radio operator on one of the unnamed planes in the 846th demanded.

"We don't know," Holbert answered as his breathing returned to normal. "Our ball turret gunner was cleaning his weapon and…" Anything further would have been redundant as he saw the blood and a chunk of the torso ripped from the rest of the corpse.

"Who is he?" Stodtmeister asked.

"He was our ground crew chief," Gehrke answered, his emphasis on "was" serving to correct Stodtmeister's question.

The small gathering stood in silence; some looked away while others stared at the gory mess of humanity. Each time another soldier arrived, the same question was repeated: "What happened?"

•   •   •

The thrill of flying his first missions eluded Bud, as did every other feeling of the last few days and weeks, and even

311

months. He only felt the sickness in his stomach and a hollowness which caused him to move as though his muscles did not exist. He wanted to crawl inside a plane, curl up, and die alone.

Nothing usually bothered Bud, but this was nothing "usual." The deep, immense sadness for what he had done grated on his innards as though they were being fed through a large cheese shredder.

All through his training — even before, when his desperation to enter the Army peaked — he never blinked at the consideration of killing enemy soldiers. Despite being only twenty-one years old, his views of life and death and survival were simple: "Don't think about it too much because you can't do nothing about it." He did not waste time with philosophical discussions or challenging analysis of the various facets of life and death. The man who knew him best, Conrad, understood all the thinking Bud did in his quiet moments was private and not open for discussion.

Growing up as they did, struggling through the Depression and poverty, they understood death happened. The inevitability of death caused Bud to live his life as he saw fit, unconcerned about the opinions of others, besides family — at least until he had to care what his Uncle Sam thought.

He had contemplated his own death and that of loved ones, but he never considered the possibility of inadvertently killing one of his Brothers in Arms.

The memory haunted him from the moment he saw the body fall. Sleep eluded him on occasion, and usually for the same reason. Rest proved difficult to achieve. But now, at this moment, as he lay on his back in his bunk, Bud could not shake the urge to curl up and die. A strong, resilient, and tough man, Bud felt weak — a feeling he could not remember experiencing. Ever.

On the first day after the accident, he skipped meals, roll call, and all human interaction besides the one he could not avoid: the inquiry.

The inquiry into the accidental shooting of the crew chief — Bud knew the man's name but wished to not repeat it — did not attain the level of a Hollywood military movie or a Washington, D.C., dog-and-pony show put on by Congress. Instead, Colonel Napier asked a couple of questions, Bud answered in a weak, flat voice, then returned to his barracks.

The Army ruled the incident an accident and did not dole out punishment. The man's family would be informed their loved one died in service to his country.

The lack of punishment, the encouragement from his crewmates, and the preparations for the next mission failed to lift his spirits. Bud could not remember feeling so low at any point in his life.

Once an emotional rock; now crumbled into a pile of gravel.

In his letters home and to Conrad and Carl, Bud neither mentioned the incident nor gave any hint of such a gut-wrenching, horrific experience. Because of how he felt and his wish to not come across as feeling sorry for himself, he took a twelve-day break from writing family members. His sorrow was for what he had done and because he had taken an innocent — American — life. He did not want others to show sympathy toward him, rather for the crew chief who died without warning, without knowing what hit him, on the tarmac that June morning at Halesworth Airfield.

Chapter Thirty

Conrad's skin continued to darken and his features roughened. The tropical Sun soaked into his Scandinavian skin with ease. His mother even commented about his changing appearance after receiving a photo of him standing in front of a few of the raised tents. Learning to swim, searching for shells and shark teeth, and, oh, yes, working and sharpening his medical skills kept him busy. He always felt tired, he confessed.

Twenty years old and in the midst of a transformation from a lazy complainer, who came across as an old boy, to a young man who worked hard as he matured yet kept his ironic sense of humor. His pithy observations kept friend and family alike laughing or just shaking their heads as they chuckled.

His primary purpose in the Army — combat medic — found little mention in his letters. One had to assume he looked at it as too uninteresting to mention. The oddity of Conrad, even as he matured into an exceptionally likeable man, revolved around his reserved nature. Much of his family shared the "reserved" gene, but Conrad took that characteristic to a higher level of language efficiency. However, as he made friends, he opened up when around them. Life in the Army helped him develop his interpersonal skills.

After failing to get into the Army Air Corps and lying down for over a month of quarantine, Conrad had become itchy — ready to get his war underway. To his disdain, deployment remained elusive, but he did see his orders to a specific detachment as a promising sign for the months to come.

•   •   •

"It's not because of me, is it?"

The lanky, cheery ground crew chief let out a low chortle. "No, Pete. It's not because of you." Lionel Bousquet's brown mop of a hairdo bounced as he laughed, as it often did. He and one other ground crew member worked on removing the ball turret from just behind *Paper Doll's* bomb bay. Afterward, another crew would weld a metal plate over the hole.

The area inside the bomber felt crowded, so Bud stayed back several feet, in the waist gunner's position.

"They say it's because they want the weight to go for bombs," Bousquet explained. "My theory is they've scraped too many boys off the runway when they couldn't get the ball back up before landing."

"Yeah, I'd prefer not to go that way," Bud responded with a straight face.

"This has been in the works for a while now."

"Okay." Sullen and emotionally depleted, Bud wandered aft from his former position and climbed out through the belly hatch.

"Peterson!" Captain Gast jogged up to Bud as the latter stood after ducking the fuselage. "I've been meaning to tell you. You're now my waist gunner."

Bud nodded.

"Since you're no longer in the ball, you'll get to rotate in as my lead engineer occasionally. We usually put back-up engineers at waist gunner, so this is perfect."

"It just means I'll have air conditioning when I shoot at the Krauts."

"Attaboy," Gast laughed and slapped Bud on the shoulder before disappearing into the plane.

•   •   •

Captain Gast felt certain keeping Bud involved would benefit the young gunner. Three days after the shooting incident, Bud found himself looking out the port side of *Paper Doll*, holding onto the mounted M2. Unlike the twin guns mounted in the ball turret, Bud only had one gun to serve as his new weapon.

Many flying soldiers claimed they felt "exposed" at the waist gunner position. To Bud, he had been exposed as ball turret gunner but was now free to move, so any exposure was not noticeable.

He also felt relief. He knew he lacked the ability to undo his mistake, but he also knew dwelling on the subject would not help the matter. His first five missions had been as ball turret gunner; those days were over. The flight proceeded without digging a deep groove into Bud's memory. They went up; they faced flak; they did not see German fighters; they dropped their bombs; they returned safely. It was a four-hour, forty-five-minute blur.

The next time Bud cleaned his gun, he took more care than he had since his first days around the weapon in gunnery school in Florida. Pensacola felt so far away in distance and time.

In fact, so did Puposky.

•   •   •

His enjoyment increased as he lay on top of his groomed bed for the fourth reading of Chrissy's most recent letter. He needed her friendly, loving words.

Chapter Thirty-One

With seven missions under his belt, Bud's mind had adapted to the carnage and forced out thoughts about the accidental killing of the ground crewman. At Don Holbert's request, fellow radio operator Marlin Gehrke, who was part of the crew which suffered the loss of their crew chief, chatted with Bud. The occasion was less psychological help and more a demonstration Gehrke's crew, while saddened, held no ill will against Bud.

To the delight of George Scofield, *Paper Doll* participated in two assaults over France on June 24. Eighteen days after D-Day, Operation Overlord remained in full swing and the Liberators continued to supply air support in various ways. While most of the missions targeted German manufacturing plants, the occasional troop support sortie occurred, as well.

Unfortunately for the Allies and the individual bombardiers, the crew dropped "dumb bombs." That term would not be invented for many years, but the unguided bombs dropped subject to the errors induced by both man and nature when attacking from 22,000 feet at 275 miles per hour. Misses happened. On the first mission of the day, with cloud cover playing havoc on visibility, the target remained untouched by the bombs dropped five miles away. The military made it a habit to not notify the men of what they hit; they did not want the crews to know if they had bombed civilians.

When civilians did become targets, the military explained it was to keep factory workers from completing their missions of assembling war materiel which would kill Americans and other allies.

The men hated to miss, but such a result was not uncommon.

After the two missions in one day, Bud could count eight missions in his drive to twenty-five. It was the only time *Paper Doll* undertook such a busy day.

Bud secured time off. He even secured a pass to London.

•   •   •

She was in love with a heavy bomber crewman; going to see the movie "The Purple Heart" was not her wisest move. Back from time in Seattle as one of the numerous women to take on "men's jobs," Chrissy Anderson awakened from her nightmare — screaming. Seeing the Dana Andrews propaganda movie about the crew of one of Doolittle's Raiders did not produce a positive reaction.

The movie depicted the torture the downed Americans suffered, including execution. Although her boyfriend served thousands of miles away, in a different theater, she nonetheless could not shake the images of the movie.

She feared for Bud's safety. Attempts at concealing those fears were unsuccessful.

The usually cheery Chrissy had taken Bud's situation in stride, but when she received a photo of Bud in front of *Paper Doll*, the reality of his new life sunk in.

And then she saw the movie.

Chrissy had nowhere to release her nervous energy. The pent-up fear manifested itself in her dreams.

She remained confident Bud would return and their love life would proceed as planned. Until then, she resolved to stop seeing war movies. She could not truly keep that promise, but she tried, nonetheless.

For his part, Bud felt relief their love continued, although it seemed to cough and sputter like a Liberator returning on three engines — a successful landing was possible, but at best, the odds were daunting.

•   •   •

Carl preferred to stay on a consistent shift, but July 1 was not a day to ignore. On this day, an era came to a close. The average citizen could not feel the impact; the average soldier had no way of knowing, but on July 1, 1944, the last Liberty ship splashed into the water at Kaiser Shipyard No. 3.

Foreman Carl Peterson's tenure guiding Liberty ships from blueprints to first sail came to an end. The moment the celebration ended for the Liberty ship, the focus shifted to Victory ships, which were already in production.

To truly possess a "Victory" ship, a nation should first attain victory. For the Allies, the end of the war held no mystery. The only open questions were the number of dead they would bear and the date of complete and total victory. The Allies made it clear Germany would not be allowed to surrender with conditions. As Japanese atrocities came to light, the same dedication to clear-cut victory was true for the Orient.

The Victory ship was already a year old by the time Liberty ships ceased production. Carl, with a growing family and excellent pay, did not care at all what the name of the ship class was so long as it was built with outstanding quality, served the war cause, and he helped build it.

He now found himself a foreman over the production of Victory ships.

•   •   •

"I don't understand. What's the problem?"

"Ray thought he was going into the military, but he thinks his boss blocked it."

Hulda tried to stay out of Thelma and Ray's arguments, but this sounded less an argument and more a rant by someone who did not wish to be consoled. She set her crochet materials onto her lap and looked at her daughter, who stood at the edge of the kitchen floor, and remarked, "Sounds like a good thing to me. Two in the family is enough to be off to war."

Ray's brother, Caleb, had shipped out, and Ray looked forward to going overseas to fight for his country. His boss had indeed been able to convince the government Ray's job with the railroad was essential to them.

Ray emerged from around the corner to express his disagreement with his mother-in-law.

"Harding had no right to get me a deferment!" The forcefulness of Ray's voice put the impassioned statement just shy of being a shout.

"It sounds like it's over and done with," Hulda responded in an even tone.

"It's just ridiculous!" Ray slammed his hand down onto the kitchen counter.

The Beckstrands had only been in this house for a few weeks; Ray was comfortable it would serve as a good place for Thelma while he went off to war.

"Ray!" Thelma took a couple of steps to reach her husband. "I've already got two brothers and a brother-in-law in the military. I don't need to be worrying about my husband, too."

The approach did not work well with Ray, who did not wish to be the man left out. "Yeah. Wonderful! But I don't deserve to defend my country?!" For many, going to war presented a test of manhood. To stay home was to show weakness or — God forbid — cowardice. In fact, many stateside jobs proved essential to the war effort, but with more and more women entering the workforce, doing "a man's job," many men felt even more pressure to serve.

Going to war provided an outlet for other men to express true and fervent patriotism. It was a man's duty to protect family and country, and duty called. Either way, Ray did not want to miss out on what he should, or wanted, to do.

Hulda rolled her eyes and shook her head. He could not see her reaction, but her presence during one of his tantrums made him even more tense.

"What right does my boss have to do this to me?!" Though stated as a question, Ray believed he knew the answer. "None! I'll tell ya. None!"

Hulda continued crocheting, but much of her focus flowed to her efforts not to speak.

"The kids and I will be happy you're still here." Thelma attempted to counterbalance the tone and decibels emanating from her husband.

Ray gritted his teeth and shook his head as he looked through Thelma.

"Thelma, have you read Bud and Connie's latest letters?" Hulda called out, as though Thelma stood farther away than just the fifteen feet to the kitchen.

"As far as I know," Thelma answered. "Bud got promoted — that's the last thing I've read."

"Oh. There's one more," Hulda said as she moved toward a handbag on the other end of the couch. "Let me see if I brought it."

Ray plopped down at the kitchen table, landing with a thud on a wooden chair.

"Here, honey. Look at this." Hulda handed a letter to the approaching Thelma. A smile broke out over the face of the mother, which caused the daughter to do likewise.

She was kind and gentle, but she was also smart, and she knew how to shut someone up.

Chapter Thirty-Two

Because of the launch of Operation Overlord on D-Day, June 1944 became the most influential month in the European Theater of Operations. Many Allied activities, by way of air or ground, were to support the goals of Operation Overlord; but, Overlord was more than assaulting the northern France beaches — it was a full-scale invasion of Europe. To rid the continent of the scourge of Hitler and his henchmen, every rock had to be turned over, figuratively speaking, and every door had to be opened to ensure German soldiers were not lurking.

Over 50,000 Allies hit the beaches. Two million more followed. Many were fresh faces to war, which had both negative and positive aspects. True, many of these men had not faced incoming fire, but they were also not exhausted from years of fighting.

The Germans felt the Allied pressure, to the point they took their frustrations out on the little town of Oradour-sur-Glane. In retaliation for French Resistance attacks and the turning tide of the war, German soldiers rounded up the townsmen and put them into barns. They did the same with the women and children and jammed them into a church. They then set fire to the town, burning 642 people alive.

But not all signs pointed toward a victorious Allied result. In June 1944, the Luftwaffe assembled a unit of Messerschmitt Me 262 fighters, the world's first operational jet-powered fighter. The V-1 rocket, an early cruise missile, continued to create fear in the hearts of Londoners. The futuristic technology of the long-range, guided ballistic V-2 missile remained three months away. Without the Allied bombing of

German facilities, weapons such as the deadly and unstoppable V-2 would have been more common.

Western leaders and many citizens believed the war would be won, but predictions of victory by Christmas proved optimistic. The German soldiers, most of whom were non-fascists with no connection to the Aryan superiority "religion" which had sprung up among the SS and other Nazi operations, were smart and tough. German equipment, as demonstrated by the jets, exhibited cutting-edge technology. The Germans were not whipped yet.

The Germans fended off defeat by moving forward when possible, retreating when necessary. The Red Army continued doling out defeats to the Germans the old-fashioned way: they threw more bodies at the enemy than their enemy could send the other way. Death tolls were horrific. The American and British forces captured the German-held areas of Italy. The European map did not lie; German influence shrank as the "thousand-year Reich" appeared set to fall short by close to 990 years.

When the calendar turned to July, a plot — one of many — was coming together, with its culmination only three weeks away. A suitcase bomb planted underneath a heavy wooden table should have put an end to the Führer. Instead, he saw his survival as proof he was favored by God, even though his pantheistic view of God happened to be that He resided in everything and was not a literal being. Nevertheless, that which did not kill Hitler made him more fanatical in the belief of his own god-like status.

Confidence rose with every triumphant military operation the Allies planned, and success bred success. Usually a worrier, Roosevelt felt confident enough to announce his bid for an unprecedented fourth term as president. Physically, Roosevelt had no business running again, but with the war tide flowing his way and still popular with the people, he ran again because he could.

American and British forces fought their way through France and found great help from the French Resistance. The war in Europe progressed remarkably well for the Allies. The key to victory now was to not let up. Men were still dying, but the head of the serpent had to be crushed.

•　　•　　•

"Hey, guys," Goshtoian shouted as Bud, Holbert, Lane, and Scofield entered the barracks.

"What's up?" Bud asked as he walked to his bunk and set on it a small bag of presents for family members.

"How was London?"

"Got any gum, chum?" Lane snickered as he spoke. The men all understood the humorous reference to the British children and their oft-repeated question to American servicemen.

"Interesting. Quite an interesting place," Bud dropped onto the foot of his bed. "No buzz bombs while we were there, and people went about their business, like there wasn't a war on."

"Yeah," Holbert interjected. "But signs of war was everywhere."

Bud nodded in agreement. "Yeah, the people just didn't act like it."

327

Before Holbert could add to their story, Goshtoian got to his point. "You had a visitor, Peterson. A guy named Bob 'Hover,' something like that."

Bud snapped out of his slouching position and looked alert. "I missed Bob?!"

"Yeah, he scribbled a note." Goshtoian pointed at Bud's bed, where on top of the pillow sat a small piece of paper with a handwritten note scrawled on it.

"Son of a gun! Bob Hovde was here!" The excitement turned to instant disappointment. "When was this?"

"Yesterday. He said something about he had just enough time on his pass to see you."

Bud frowned and slapped the paper on the bed.

The Hovde family were longtime friends of the Petersons, Gustafsons, and Strands — the latter being Anne's family. They were also charter members of the Our Redeemer's Lutheran Church in Puposky, and like Bud and his extended family, buried many of their dead in the tiny cemetery behind the church. Bud and Bob had been friends for as long as they could remember.

"Well, I gotta go see the lady who washes my clothes." With that, Bud pulled out a bag of dirty laundry and headed out the door, intent on bumming a ride from someone on his way into Halesworth.

Bud's friends saw the signs he was emerging from the dark world he had been thrown into after the accidental killing. He had fallen back on his reserved nature and still spoke less than normal, but that finally began to change, gradually, after a few weeks. The disappointment of missing Hovde did not help, but in perspective, Bud knew he could not let the lack of a reunion drag him down.

•   •   •

The target was Saarbrucken, Germany, and the primary target was a marshalling yard. At yards such as this, the enemy loaded train cars with equipment and supplies and sent the iron wagon along their tracks to keep the war machine whirring. Due to clear skies, the *Paper Doll* crew approached their target with great confidence.

"Pilot to bombardier, she's all yours."

"Roger, Captain. Opening bomb bay doors."

"Doors are open," Holbert added after a brief wait.

"Stand by," Goshtoian announced.

In the moments before the bombs fell, Bud allowed his mind to wander along with his eyes as he scanned the sky for enemy aircraft. He had not fired his weapon on the prior two missions because German fighter resistance had grown less frequent — the result of Allied air support and diminishing war-making capabilities by the Germans. The Allies had bombed countless factories to the great detriment of the German war machine.

He thought about what he would do when he returned home. He would see the family in Bemidji, then see Chrissy and begin working on uniting the couple permanently, and then would take a trip to see Carl in California.

His flights increased at a slow pace. Instead of the current mission being his tenth, on a non-lead aircraft he would probably be closer to thirty by now, almost to the coveted thirty-one he needed to go home; the magic number of twenty-five was now but a memory.

Excited shouts nudged Bud out of his thoughts. He had missed the "bombs away" call and the considerable time for the bombs to fall.

"Do you see that?!" Lane shouted into the interphone as they watched the direct hits annihilate train cars and equipment. Though people could not be seen from their altitude, they knew German workers had paid with their lives, as well, but no one worried — friends of the airmen were dying, too.

"Beautiful!" Sund, the native of Westby, Wisconsin and 1943 graduate of the University of Wisconsin, shouted. He would have rather been in Boise, Idaho, with his wife, but this sort of "beauty" would have to do for the moment.

"Pilot to crew, keep calm. Nice shootin', Gosh."

"Thank you, sir," Goshtoian responded.

On the ground, they would have congratulatory drinks, but for now they could celebrate from their positions in the bomber, in the cold, thin air.

Before the congratulations could continue, Bud's eyes widened. "Nine o'clock low and rising fast. Messerschmitts."

"Well, I'll be. Haven't seen any of those lately."

Before Bud could consider identifying who uttered that last comment, he opened up with the M2.

"Radio to crew, there are a bunch."

"Pilot to crew, hold on tight. Our fighter escort is switching out. They're a couple of minutes late. There's a squadron of Krauts coming right at us, dead on."

The pulsating vibrations from machine guns reverberated through the plane. Gast made a sharp turn and climbed as they headed off in the general direction of Halesworth, both taking evasive action and attempting to get them back to base as quickly as possible. Within seconds, two targets beckoned and Bud again opened up with the Browning.

A rapid series of small *thuds* vibrated through the Liberator and the bodies of the men as lead punctured aluminum. It occurred to Bud that, even as he fired his weapon, he could still feel the plane take the punishment from the 7.9 mm rounds, which translated into approximately .31 caliber.

Paper Doll endured a beating. With German fighters slicing through the bomber formations and the B-24 pilots taking evasive action, the sky felt and looked like a crowded parking lot before a sporting event, only deadlier.

"Got one!" Lane shouted. Static replaced voices as several men attempted to congratulate him at the same time.

"No!" Scofield shouted. "Sorry, Captain, but this one Kraut got two of our planes within just a few seconds. Two -24s got it."

On many missions, the P-51 Mustangs turned back the German attackers, forcing the enemy to rely on flak. In this case, however, the Messerschmitts rallied with significant numbers and created confusion for the Allied force.

Bud and company had to stop firing as P-51 Mustangs and P-47 Thunderbolts raced in. The Army preferred the bomber gunners not take any chances around fighter support unless the aircraft's safety demanded immediate action. With squinted eyes and intense focus, Bud saw his moment with a German fighter which had shed its Allied pursuer. He squeezed the trigger long enough to fire twenty rounds. He could see the German plane erupt in black smoke.

He did not have the luxury of watching to ensure the plane would leave the battle, but he felt confident it would. Instead of watching, he took aim at another Messerschmitt and opened fire. Bud glanced at the first plane and saw it plummeting, out of control, toward the Earth. Eyes back to the second plane revealed another dive toward the Earth, but a lack of smoke puzzled him for a moment, until he realized his rounds most certainly struck the pilot or his controls.

Calls over the radio quieted as the remaining Messerschmitts bugged out.

"How many did you get, Peterson?" Lane asked.

"Two."

"What about you, Scofield?" Lane's curiosity continued.

"One."

"McIntosh, did you down any?"

"Not that I know of," came the response.

"Stodder, how did you do," Lane asked of Stodtmeister.

"None."

"Pilot to tail, what about you, Al?" Gast asked.

"I got two." The crew could hear Lane beaming as he spoke.

"Alright, boys. We got some work to do on this old girl when we get home," Gast announced, stating the obvious. Before he could continue, the flak resumed as they flew over a cluster of German artillery. Bud and crew shook their heads and prepared for a bumpy ride.

• • •

Upon arrival at Halesworth, the crew learned that one of the Liberators crashed on take-off, with only one survivor. Holbert had informed the crew early in the mission a plane had crashed, but no one knew its status. With so many unnamed planes, it was difficult for the men to quickly learn about the identities of their injured or dead friends.

The ground crew had all the information and the aircrew listened to the details about the crash as they stood and stared at their plane. *Paper Doll* had weathered the metallic storm, but between patching and replacing portions of the outer skin, the bomber would receive a face lift. Captain Gast, stating the obvious, reminded the men they had a long couple of days ahead. "We have to be back up in four days. In meetings, we planned out the next week, and we're going up the 17th." They usually did not have such advanced notice, so they appreciated the information.

As they walked to their barracks, Holbert changed the subject away from the just-completed mission. "Well, hell. I was hoping to go into town tomorrow."

"You've been gone a lot," Bud noted. "What do you got going on?"

"I got a girl in town. Sweet young thing," Holbert smiled as though he might start radiating light from his face.

"Son of a gun, Holb," Bud laughed. "You said you'd get a girl when you got home. I guess you can't wait."

"No." The oversized smile continued. "Didn't wait at all."

•   •   •

That night, the men hung out together as a team and drank and laughed and laughed and drank. Bud had taken his frustrations and anger out on the enemy and felt better.

With their previous mission to Munich taking just under nine hours, then a rough day on the Saarbrucken mission, they felt tired but satisfied. They had survived; at least today they knew with certainty they hit their targets and the plane could be repaired. The damage from flak and a Messerschmitt's cannon fell far short of what Bud had imagined. They likely would have the plane fixed in twenty-four hours.

At their table in the crowded base bar, pilot Will Plate walked by. Seeing Bud, he stopped.

"Hey, Peterson. How are things?" He looked up and saw Captain Gast. "Hey, Captain."

"Plate! It's good to see you!" Gast responded.

Bud pursed his lips and smiled. "Doing well."

"Good. Good. Good to hear."

"You?"

"I'm still pretty pissed."

Surprise enveloped Bud. "What? What are you talking about?"

"*Plate's Date*. Didn't you hear?"

"No."

"We flew it once, on our first mission, but a couple days later another pilot took it out and got it shot up bad."

"Yeah, I heard about that."

"Yeah," Plate continued, "Well they couldn't repair it. They scrapped it. We flew a dump truck for a month," he said, referring to a plane which did not respond well to controls. "We kept trying to get them to get my plane back, but it was too far gone!"

Bud laughed and scrunched his face into a tight, pain-laden expression. "Oh, man! I did not know that. That's rotten."

"I mean, the pilot didn't do anything wrong. It wasn't his fault, but that flak took care of the plane."

"So, did you call your next plane, '*Plate's Date II*'?"

"Yeah," Plate laughed and nodded his head. "But that got tore up with me in the seat, so that one was ditched, too. I hated that damned plane! We just figured we're gonna quit naming them. They don't live long enough."

Bud chuckled. "So, I guess you just call it 'the plane.'"

"Yeah. That's about right." He extended his hand to Bud. "I'll see ya sometime soon."

"Okay." Bud nodded, then turned his attention back to his shipmates.

"Who was that?" Lane asked after Plate was out of earshot.

"A good guy in the 847th. A pilot. Will Plate."

"He sounded like a Texan," Lane added.

"Yeah, he said he was from Iowa but moved to Texas as a kid, so he sounds like them yokels down there."

"So, you didn't like all that time we spent in Texas?"

"No, but I didn't hate it as much as my brother did," Bud said. "He'll be fine if he never steps foot in the state again."

"You just remember, son," Lane said. "There's no place like Texas." A fat smile covered his face.

"We can agree on that," Bud laughed.

The two got caught up in the group's conversation about the day's events and forgot about Texas. The tales of metal zipping two feet from one's head and shooting down German fighters mixed with the beer and whiskey.

"Well," Bud said in a wistful tone. "Helluva way to spend your birthday."

"What?!" Several of the men shouted at once. "It's your birthday?!" Gast asked in shock.

Bud nodded. That called for another round, and at the end of the night, they picked up his portion of the tab. What was going to be *a bit* of a late night now became destined to be a *very* late night.

Indeed, dropping bombs and getting shot at *was* a hell of a way to spend one's twenty-second birthday.

Chapter Thirty-Three

Bob Hope: (to the audience) I'd like to be one of you.

Frances Langford: You couldn't cut it being one of them.

Hope: You don't think so?

Langford: No, you have to forget all about beer.

Hope: That's for me.

Langford: You have to forget all about comfort.

Hope: That's for me.

Langford: You have to forget all about women.

Hope: That's for them.

The crowd, including Private First Class Conrad Peterson, roared with approval. The sun-tanned young man had made the short trek to join in the fun and found the diversion as entertaining as intended.

The tour began on July 10, 1944; five days later, Conrad joined thousands of men who gathered at the Schofield Barracks to witness the comedy and entertainment routines which would soon be famous. Bob Hope launched what would become a lifetime commitment to entertaining American troops, putting on 150 shows throughout the summer. The troupe began their island-hopping in Hawaii before traveling to numerous dangerous areas in the South Pacific.

Hope had fun at the expense of his great friend Bing Crosby, as well as Frank Sinatra and others. He announced that he had just finished his last "Road" movie, with the next series of films dubbed as "Detour" films.

Singer and actress Frances Langford, dressed in a two-piece outfit with a bare midriff and a skirt down to her knees, sang "Thanks For The Memory" and added the line "I wish I could kiss each and every one of you" to the crowds' exuberant approval. During the pause created by the reaction of the men, Hope leaned into the microphone and told her, "Be careful or we'll get trampled to death." The alto also sang "I'll be Seeing You."

Conrad and company hooted and hollered when twenty-two-year-old Patty Thomas strutted onto the stage. Had the Army commissioned a poll, the odds of any in attendance knowing the identity of the young tap dancer would rest at or close to zero, yet no one cared about her profession. With light brown hair to her shoulders and donning a dancer's outfit, catcalls abounded for the young beauty. The black outfit, bare at her shoulders and across the top of her chest, immediately caught the soldiers' eyes. She sported black sleeves, from biceps to wrists. The bottom of the one-piece outfit clung to her derriere and barely covered it completely; she accented her legs with high heels. The men loved her from Moment One. During the catcalls Hope took the microphone, looked out at the audience, and deadpanned, "I just want you boys to see what you're fighting for."

The men approved. Even detached Conrad admired the young woman who was only one year his senior.

Trombonist and comedian Jerry Colonna, with his thick mustache darkened by his Italian roots, entertained the crowd, as did Fresno, California, guitarist Tony Romano.

Those in attendance had no way of knowing they were witnessing the origins of a phenomenon which would last for decades. Conrad left the concert with a smile, as did the other men. Humor, song and dance, and, of course, two beautiful women did the trick.

• • •

Bud rested in his bunk, writing letters. He admitted in a letter home he struggled to find things to write. He failed to inform her of what troubled him — no need to worry her or delve into that matter. Instead, his normal four-page letters had shortened a bit and only provided snippets of his life. He could not write about his job. In fact, not long after his birthday he had written to Hulda:

I've tried to give you all the answers to the questions you ask. What I did on my birthday is one I can't answer directly but you can guess. That's life in the E.T.O. (European Theatre of Operations).

Scofield entered the barracks, saw Bud, and approached him. "Hey, are you writing your mother?"

"Yeah."

"Tell her 'thank you' for the cookies. They were great."

McIntosh overheard the conversation and piped up. "Yeah, tell her 'thank you.' She can send all she wants."

Bud smiled. "I'll tell her."

"Guess what?" Scofield offered nothing more than the question.

"What?" Bud took the bait.

"I'm going up tomorrow," he said with a trace of excitement in his voice. "I'm piling up those numbers. I'm getting out early."

Bud nodded. "You're gonna get back to your wife sooner. Who are ya flying with?"

"Ed Florcyk's bunch. The plane Bill Lowther's on," Scofield said. "Tom O'Brien is sick, so they needed another gunner." Lowther and O'Brien had been friends with several of the *Paper Doll* men going back to Wendover. The pilot, twenty-four-year-old Lieutenant Edwin Florcyk, had a good reputation. While reputation was not on Scofield's mind, as with Captain Gast, Scofield knew he would be in good hands.

"I gotta get up at oh-two-hundred and my briefing's at oh-four-hundred, so I gotta hit the hay," Scofield added.

"All right," Bud said. "I'll see you tomorrow afternoon."

With that, the native of Los Angeles headed to his bed and Bud resumed writing his mother.

•   •   •

Bud and McIntosh played catch with borrowed gloves and baseball. The cloudy day needed to be livened up, so the two had decided they had laid around and done nothing for long enough.

"What are you gonna do when you get home?" McIntosh asked the question they had all asked or been asked a thousand times.

"Sleep," Bud responded.

"Yeah, but after that," McIntosh said while laughing, which caused him to make an errant throw.

Bud returned to their fifty-feet distance, ball in hand. "I don't know, Lige. I try not to think about it too much." Bud hurled the baseball back to his friend. "I mean, I get homesick occasionally. Nothing bad, just a little. So, I don't see any sense in dwelling on it." Bud stabbed at the next wild throw and caught

340

it, thus avoiding another chase. He returned the ball to McIntosh as he continued. "No offense meant, but besides marrying Chrissy, I'm trying not to think about it."

"Don't be sore."

"I'm not — not at all." Bud caught the return throw and stood still for a moment. "I used to answer that question and think about going home, but I'm trying not to think about anything that will drag me down. If I'm planning for when I get home, then I'm gonna get down because I'm not there."

"We all write a lot of letters home, but you seem to write more than most." The ball arrived in McIntosh's glove as he continued speaking. "No wonder your mother sends us cookies all the time."

"You guys should fly my missions for me," Bud joked as McIntosh threw the baseball back to him. "So I can write more letters. Maybe I'll write my sisters more and they'll send food, too."

"Fine with me," McIntosh responded. As Bud looked the baseball over, a new thought struck the crew's lead engineer. "Your girlfriend writes a lot. Get her to send cookies, too."

Bud's laugh filled the outdoor air and, for a brief moment, blocked out the sound of a distant Liberator taxiing down the runway over a quarter-of-a-mile away. "I've got a good system with her," he said as he fired a strike back to his friend.

"Oh, this I've gotta hear."

"She writes to me every day, and then she sends what she has when she receives a letter from me." Bud took off his glove and re-tied one of the laces. "So, if I don't want one of them big long letters, I write more often. If I don't have time to write, then

I know the next time I do she'll send a long letter." Bud grinned at his supposed control over Chrissy until McIntosh took away the smile.

"Seems to me," McIntosh said as he waited for Bud to finish his repair work. "She's controlling you."

"How so?"

McIntosh threw the baseball back to Bud. "She makes sure you keep writing. She's not going to keep feeding you unless you feed her."

"Hmm," was all Bud could manage. He looked at the ground and moved his head several times. He looked up at McIntosh and frowned. "You may have a point."

Bud brought his arm back as he started to throw the ball again when Bob Savage ran up. "Lige, Pete!" He huffed numerous times and struggled to catch his breath. After a couple of seconds, he resumed speaking. "Did you guys hear the news? Florcyk's plane didn't come back."

As Savage brought his breathing to a normal pattern, McIntosh reached Bud and Savage. Bud spoke up, alarm in his voice. "Scofield was filling in. Lowther was on that plane, too."

"Yeah, O'Brien is pretty broken up," Savage told them. "If he hadn't been sick, he'd be dead, too."

"Wait a minute," McIntosh interjected. "You said it didn't come back. Do they know what happened?"

"Guys on Shroyer's crew told me it was hit by flak over St. Lo. They had dropped to 12,000 feet for their run. It happened right in front of them. It just blew up in midair. They told me they saw one parachute, that's it."

"I think John Rainey's on Shroyer's crew," Bud offered.

"Yeah, he's one of the guys who told me. They fly *Little Iodine*," Savage answered, referring to the name of the Liberator.

"So, somebody lived then," McIntosh half asked, half stated.

"Well, somebody made it out, but that's all we know."

With his shoulders slumped, Bud turned and, without a word, headed to his barracks. Watching him go, the other two deflated soldiers decided to do the same. They had lost a member of their crew — someone who, like the rest of the *Paper Doll* team, had become like a member of the family. They knew Scofield well enough to know he would not be wearing his parachute. Without a doubt, their good friend, Private George A. Scofield, was dead.

• • •

Officially, the men aboard the plane with the nickname of *Censored* were listed as "Missing in Action." On occasion, bombers would crash land and the crew would find themselves prisoners of war; less often, they would find their way back to their bases of origin.

Nevertheless, the *Paper Doll* crew did not hold out hope. One man may have survived, but they knew Scofield was not that man.

Only later would the men learn that, after the plane exploded, Technical Sergeant Frank Trowbridge, the plane's radio operator, found himself hurtling through the air, blown out of the aircraft. The Virginian dropped safely in Occupied France. The mission had been to provide air support for the First

343

Army, which found itself in a protracted battle near the town of St. Lo; but, over 1,000 of the planes had their mission aborted because of weather. Florcyk's craft was one that did not abort and thus able to drop its bombs. Furious German flak hit their Liberator, which started a fire. The fire led to an explosion which doomed the crew, except Trowbridge, who through no action of his own, other than having already donned a parachute, survived the calamity.

• • •

Captain Gast wanted Bud back up in the air. Because they were a lead plane, *Paper Doll* did not fly as often, so Bud found himself on *Tiger's Revenge* of the 845th squadron.

The B-24 was named for pilot Bob Mitchell's brother, who went by the nickname of "Tiger" and lost his life in a fighter. This mission, Bud's first not aboard *Paper Doll*, was his twelfth.

Located halfway between the wing and tail, the opening for the waist gunner in the side of the fuselage extended from Bud's waist to above his head. The four feet wide and three feet high opening allowed adequate self-protection for the plane — not the operator. Despite having the weapon in front of him, the waist gunner felt exposed to the world. Unlike in the B-17, Liberator waist gunners did not have to slouch to fire at targets.

Consolidated's design mounted the gun on a modified tripod, with two legs extending to the floor of the fuselage and the remaining section bolted to the fuselage, against the bottom of the opening. The squared-off, U-shaped tripod mount attached to the tripod allowed the gun to swivel side to side or pivot up and down to facilitate the tracking and downing of German fighters.

The disintegrating metallic link-belts of ammo allowed the large rounds to feed into the machine with ease; 105 rounds could be fired before having to set up the next can. The gun's positioning allowed it to have a respectable range of motion, though gunners would have preferred to shoot downward farther than what the design would allow. The 65-inch-long, 83-pound machine gun was no stranger to Bud.

While technically the weapon could spit out over 450 rounds per minute, the barrel could not survive such a barrage and the gun was modified for the B-24s to keep it at a more survivable forty rounds a minute.

Bud felt a little more comfortable operating the single gun after the accidental firing and could not help but feel amazement the gun could bring down an airplane.

As the squadrons neared their target, Bud felt as nervous as he had on his second mission — not as bad as his first, but not as good as he should feel. The first call of "fighters, port side," snapped Bud out of his doldrums and his military-trained mind responded.

"Nose gunner to crew, they're climbing rapidly but out of my range."

"Pilot to crew, they appear to be headed toward us, so stand by."

"Roger that. Waist will have a bead on them in a few seconds," Bud said as he leaned closer to the opening and attempted to calculate how long before they were in range of his M2.

The diamond formations, spread out over many miles, began with Tiger's Revenge and thus became the Messerschmitt pilot's focus.

"Nose gunner to crew, they're 109s. I can't see port side but I can see what's coming up from one o'clock low."

"I thought we haven't been getting the fighters until after the flak," the co-pilot half-asked.

"Evidently, we're passing near an airfield we didn't know about," Mitchell responded as he scanned outside the aircraft but frequently readjusted his eyes to monitor the instruments. "Or more likely, they just added an airstrip somewhere."

"Roger," the co-pilot responded.

Bud and the tail gunner opened fire.

"Starboard waist to pilot, they're coming into range on my side."

As the bomber armada faced Messerschmitt 109s racing toward them from two directions, Bud let out a shout. "Got the bastard!" No one could hear Bud growl over the cacophony of machine gun fire. "I'm taking ten Krauts for my mistake," Bud snarled, as he squeezed off a few extra rounds.

"Pilot to crew, I didn't hear that last comment. How are we looking?"

Bud decided not to take credit for the unnecessary chatter.

"Tail to crew, got one!"

"Nose to crew, several more coming, one o'clock low."

"No!" The shout from the tail gunner caused everyone to check their surroundings in and outside the bomber. "They got one in the formation behind us!" he shouted.

"Focus," Mitchell announced with a calm voice.

"I think it's the *Mary Lou*," the tail gunner said.

Bud shook his head, then quieted his movements as he prepared to squeeze the trigger again.

"Bombardier to radio operator, confirm bomb bay doors are open."

"Doors are open."

Bud realized he was so focused he did not even notice the interphone exchange for the bombardier to take control of the aircraft.

"Got one!" the starboard waist gunner shouted.

Tiger's Revenge jolted as four quick rounds punctured the fuselage with powerful *thuds*, but the Liberator kept flying forward.

"Get him, Al, get him!" Bud shouted to Alfred Lane, even though the latter was not the tail gunner, or even on the plane.

"Missed him!" the tail gunner shouted.

"Pilot to crew, easy."

"Bombs away." Despite all the excitement, the bombardier made it sound like they were dropping water balloons on Wendover's hot desert floor.

"Roger." With that, Mitchell jerked the plane to eventually head 210 degrees from their previous course.

"Incoming at — wait." the co-pilot cut himself off.

"Waist to pilot." Bud tried to maintain the level of calmness the military expected. "They're bugging out. I'd say we're in for some flak."

"Pilot to crew, to hell with flak. We're bugging out ourselves."

"No!" the tail gunner barked into his microphone. The crew understood what that single word meant. In this case, it was *Yankee Rebel* which took a hit from the first volleys of flak and fought its rapid descent toward the small town. The men who had accessible views watched until they saw it explode just outside of the town, somehow missing the populated area.

"*Flak Magnet* just took a hit!" the tail gunner said with a calm voice. "It looks like she'll stay airborne. They're still flying true."

"Slein's crew is going down! Watch for chutes, gunners," the co-pilot announced.

"One chute!" Bud called out.

"That's it?" Mitchell asked in disbelief.

As Mitchell brought the plane out of its steep turn, he took it into a slow dive to pick up speed.

On the way back to base, and after the final oxygen check was completed, Mitchell allowed the men to chat about what they saw, as long as they did not tie up the interphone for long periods.

"How many did you get, Peterson?" a gunner asked.

"One," Bud replied. "How about you?"

"Two," came the response.

"Good egg drops," another gunner said to the bombardier.

"Scratch that V-1 plant," the bombardier joked.

"Tail gunner here. I can tell you there were several other good hits I could see."

"Maybe the Brits will sleep easier tonight," Mitchell laughed.

• • •

An explosion filled the air as the men exited *Tiger's Revenge*. Liberators continued to flow in, so they understood without thought what had happened. Out of curiosity and concern, they ran to see, although they did not really wish to know. A column of black smoke rose up above a short-lived fire. The lack of survivors was obvious.

As the men exchanged concerns, they agreed they were too far away to assist, even though such attempts would have proven futile, anyway. Others were closer and running to the scene.

They were about to depart when Mitchell shouted. "Look!" They looked up in time to see another Liberator on approach, the pilot obviously struggling with the controls. With its nose too high and tail dangerously close to the ground, the sight was a bad omen.

"Full throttle!" Mitchell shouted, as though the pilot could hear. The moment he shouted the order, the pilot of the struggling plane had the same thought. The bomber's nose dropped toward the ground. Liberators were not built to respond like fighters, but the rate of descent slowed just enough.

The sight of the large plane's fuselage crashing into the ground, its wheels crushed, frightened all who saw it. The aircraft skidded only a short distance on the runway before plowing through earth and grass and coming to a metal-bending halt.

The men of *Tiger's Revenge*, as well as another crew, raced toward the crashed bomber. As they arrived, all ten crewmen emerged from waist gunners' windows, in pain, but not seriously hurt. The aircraft had been reduced to metallic debris, but the men were alive and well. The same could not be said for the crew of the other Liberator, whose flames had nearly burned out.

The day after returning from St. Lo with *Tiger's Revenge*, Bud and the crew of *Paper Doll* were removed from the "fly list" — the entire crew because of Scofield's death and Bud a week longer as a precaution for what the Army feared could be going through his mind.

•   •   •

Bud continued to think about the irony of Scofield's wish and how he died in pursuit of that same wish.

The loss of Scofield meant the addition of another man: Lieutenant Robert Clendinning, who became the second navigator, a preferred arrangement for a deputy lead plane. With dark brown hair, dark eyes, and a neatly trimmed mustache, the native of Passaic, New Jersey, looked like an actor playing a military officer.

The impact of Operation Overlord paid dividends to the bombers. They still dealt with the deadly flak and continued to deal with fighters on occasion, but the skies now felt at least a little safer. Since D-Day, the bombing missions targeting manufacturing plants, bridges, and railroad marshalling yards made a tremendous impact on German capabilities.

Bud wanted to see enemy fighters. He wanted to down Germans on Scofield's behalf. He wanted a fight. The thought did not enter his mind flak had brought down *Censored*, not fighters. He would have found such a thought irrelevant had he taken the time to pursue the line of reasoning.

• • •

On a chilly, rainy English day, nearly the entire complement of the base jammed into a large hangar for the memorial services. With few exceptions, the only men to not attend were those away, on missions.

This was one of many losses of a 489th Bombardment Group aircraft and crew, but each one felt personal to the men. For a year — longer, in some cases — these men had been together. As with any gathering of people, not everyone liked every person; however, the crew of *Paper Doll* had terrific harmony as a group. Now, one of their own had been taken from them. Scofield also left a wife in Los Angeles.

Florcyk, too, left a wife, in New Jersey. He had lost his first wife in 1939 and remarried after he enlisted. His second wife was now a widow.

The deceased crew's Liberator was known around the base for its depiction of a curly haired young lady clad only in a short skirt, the word "censored" plastered across her bosom, a beer bottle in one hand, and in the act of rolling dice with the other. The aircraft now only existed in their memories.

Eventually, having evaded capture by the enemy, the lone survivor of the crash, Technical Sergeant Frank Trowbridge, returned to the base. The airman became a bit of a celebrity upon his return. The men wanted to hear the stories of the lucky man, then envied him when he was allowed to go home.

Chapter Thirty-Four

New energy swept through the airfield and gave new life to many of the men. The repetition, humdrum, deaths, and dangers all felt secondary to the big news, and now the day had arrived. On August 6, the Glenn Miller Orchestra arrived at Halesworth Airfield. That afternoon, hours before the concert, one of the Liberators did not return from a mission. The men at the base had no way of knowing the bomber had crash-landed and the entire crew became prisoners of the Germans. Even with the excitement of Glenn Miller's visit, death lingered nearby.

"We're on the map, boys," Holbert declared.

"I love that guy!" Lane blurted. "I love his music."

"Hey, Holbert," Bud asked. "Are you going to bring your girl?"

"Yes!" Holbert's excitement could not be concealed. "She worked out her schedule with the hospital. She got another nurse to cover for her. I gotta go to the gate and get her in."

"Do you think we can meet him?" Lane asked, an excitement in his voice underscored the seriousness of his question.

"My girlfriend is a girl!" Holbert responded with mock seriousness as he headed out the door.

"I'm talking about Glenn Miller, knucklehead!" Lane shot back, his Texas attitude coming to the fore. He then laughed as he finally understood the humor in Holbert's response.

"Nah, there's too many people here." McIntosh shook his head as he spoke. "Lots of the boys want to meet him."

"Why do you guys want to meet him?" Bud asked, amused by their enthusiasm.

"Are you kidding, Pete? He's a legend," Lane answered. His voice climbed an octave in amazement.

"He's a musician," Bud chuckled. "He's good. I like him, but he puts his britches on just like you do."

"Let's go," McIntosh called, and the group followed him out the door.

Miller's packed schedule did not diminish the lively show. After visiting places with names like Thurleigh, Newbury, Polebrook, and Kimbolton, Halesworth was the band's twelfth concert on a thirty-seven-stop tour, spanning from July 14 until October 3, 1944. Like so many celebrities of the time, they wanted to play a part in the war effort, even if that part amounted to only a temporary respite from battle for the men.

Bud and his crew joined the late-afternoon crowd gathered in the large hangar. They were amused to see men on top of the wings of a Liberator at one end of the hangar, while hundreds more sat on the facility's concrete floor.

The framing for the hangar walls allowed a man to climb up the wall using the braces as steps. Over a dozen did just that, making perches of the hangar wall and its metal supports, behind and above the band.

The entire band put on a memorable performance. With their backs to one side of the hangar, a temporary bandstand held the musicians and their trombones, saxophones, piano, base viola, drums, and other instruments. The bespectacled Miller brought entertainment the men enjoyed with immense pleasure.

•　　•　　•

When the show ended, as the men flowed out of the hangar, Bud and McIntosh stumbled across a group of friends — the flight crew from another plane. The *Paper Doll* sergeants paused, surprised at the angry tones and words, especially after such an uplifting show.

While all five of the other men vented their anger, the most frustrated, at least the loudest, was Oklahoman Homer Haile, a flight engineer on one of the Liberators.

"What's wrong, fellas?" McIntosh asked while looking at Haile.

"I'll tell you what's wrong!" The engineer made no effort to hold back his vitriol. "We ain't flying with Fulks!" The longer he spoke the higher his rage soared. "I told Major Harper, to his face, that he can court martial me but I'm not getting on another airplane that bastard's flying!" The madder he got, the more his Oklahoma drawl thickened.

Bud and McIntosh exchanged glances. Men filed by and scattered across the tarmac, most headed toward their barracks.

Lieutenant Allan Newman, the navigator, nodded in agreement as he looked at Haile. "That's right. We're sick of it! The man's dangerous!"

Bombardier Lieutenant Fred Erwin, who did not look old enough to be an officer, spoke with equal ferocity. "Damn right! We may spend some time in the stockade, but we're not flying with that lunatic again! He's liable to get us all killed!"

"You bet your ass!" Haile seconded. "The whole crew's together on this."

"And they're not going to make us," Staff Sergeant Burke Anderson added.

"Wow." Bud did not know what to say, but after a pause continued. "I hope you boys stay out of trouble."

"We don't care!" Haile snarled.

McIntosh looked at the fifth man, whom neither he nor Bud knew. "You're an officer, too? Damn, that's something when officers are this pissed off."

"I'm Lieutenant Kell. Norman Kell. I'm the co-pilot." He extended his hand first to McIntosh, then to Bud.

After the handshakes, Bud and McIntosh exchanged glances. Every man stood in opposition to the pilot and risked their careers by complaining to the major. Perhaps the most shocking aspect was the co-pilot had joined the mini-rebellion.

"The whole crew's with us," Haile repeated his earlier statement.

"You think they'll get you a new pilot?" Bud asked.

All five men answered Bud at the same time. They repeated the same statements about their distrust of the outrageous pilot, but their answers jumbled together as they spoke over one another. Nevertheless, one message remained clear: they would not fly with that pilot, Frank Fulks, again. They understood the possible repercussions and did not care. To a man, they had reasoned it was better to be thrown into the stockade than to die a senseless death due to someone's stupidity.

Bud patted Haile on the shoulder and turned to leave. As he did, Haile offered a final comment. "You boys be glad you've got such a good pilot like Gast."

The *Paper Doll* men nodded as they departed. McIntosh looked at Bud and could only react with, "Yikes." Like the others departing the concert, Bud and McIntosh disappeared into the darkness as they headed for their barracks.

·   ·   ·

When *Paper Doll* lifted off without Bud, the sinking feeling had the opposite effect the Army had hoped. Nevertheless, the break was an important one for him, whether he understood it or not. The Army did not believe Bud had progressed psychologically as fast as they had wished. Grounding men was common in the 489th Bomb Group; Colonel Napier believed with certitude that mandatory breaks helped men recover from their missions and the loss of friends. Bud did not require a break because of the missions; rather, because of the accidental shooting. The rest of the crew had been cleared after a brief break due to losing Scofield.

Whether Bud needed the time off was a subject for debate, at least in Bud's mind. The truth was, even had he saved the lives of everyone at the base, outwardly he would have acted much the same. In most circumstances, unless he lost his temper, he reacted in a calm, methodical, reserved manner with a paucity of words, unless someone wanted to chat about banal topics. Nevertheless, the Army reacted to Bud's taciturn response to the incident by attempting to act in his best interest. Bud was mentally tough, but Colonel Napier read Bud's aloof nature differently.

·   ·   ·

A week had passed since the Glenn Miller show. The crew found themselves in a small room reconfigured to act as a conference room. Major Curly Harper, commander of the 846th, hosted the crew of *Paper Doll*. Seated along the long, rectangular table, all eyes focused on the major.

"First off, I want to announce to you a well-earned promotion." Harper turned his head to the man to his right. "Captain Bob Gast has shown us a lot during the planning of our missions, and effective today he is the new Operations Officer for the 845th."

The men waited in quiet as they looked at their captain.

"Well," Major Harper sounded almost indignant. "I believe congratulations are in order."

Forced smiles populated the room. Feeble statements of "Congratulations, Captain" and "That's good news, Captain" littered the tense air.

"Now I know you don't want to lose him," Major Harper offered. "But this is a great opportunity for your captain to do some good work and rise in rank, as well. It's good for all of us, really."

Bud's smile looked more like a man grimacing with pain yet attempting to look cheery about his situation.

"He'll be planning more missions," Harper offered. "And those missions affect us all."

The men admired and cared for their captain. Losing him was not want they wanted.

"You're gonna need another pilot." The major stated the obvious. "So, there are several moves happening for various reasons." He looked at the men around the table as he spoke. "You may remember Colonel Napier broke up the crew of

357

Special Delivery. Well, he's decided to reunite Lieutenants Culkin and Tankersley, so that's causing a few changes in the 844th."

Lieutenant Lawrence Culkin and Lieutenant John Tankersley, who were good friends, had paid a price for missing muster when in Kansas, which cost them months of flying together. Even though the interim pilot could not be faulted, Culkin nonetheless felt a touch of bitterness when *Special Delivery* sustained serious enough hits on a mission to warrant the scrapping of the Liberator. When the crew received their replacement plane, they dubbed it *Special Delivery II.*

"And I'm sure you're wondering who your new pilot will be," the major again stated the obvious. "You're getting Lieutenant Frank Fulks, who has decided to leave his current crew in order to fly with a top-rated crew such as yourselves."

Bud and McIntosh, at opposing ends of the table, flashed wide-eyed glances at each other.

"There's been a little scuttlebutt about Lieutenant Fulks out there," the major applied spin to his explanation. "But just disregard petty personality conflicts. He'll be just fine and he'll fit in with such a fine crew."

Bud knew what his facial expression was and fought to alter it, but failed. He could neither hide his disdain for the choice of pilot nor Major Harper's choice of words. "Personality conflicts" were not the issue. Holbert had later chatted with Fulks' radio operator and then told Bud details of the pilot's actions.

•   •   •

The men knew they would see Captain Gast around the base and have the opportunity to interact with him, but they agreed, to a man, life would be different without their leader. Despite Major Harper's contortion of what led Fulks to change planes, many men on the base knew of the revolt by Fulks' entire crew.

In the meantime, Bud learned an acquaintance of his, Dallas native John Lamar, had transferred from *Special Delivery II* to join a lead crew in the 847th. The two men joked about the "musical chairs" being played at the base, but again Bud forced himself to hide his true thoughts; he hid emotions well.

•   •   •

The "hut," as the men called the barracks, sat empty except for the man perched on his bed, back against the wall, as he read the most recent letter from Chrissy. She had written a question mark for the date; she was working twelve hours a day painting a farm house with her father and siblings as they scraped by; although, under the law, she was only permitted to work forty-eight hours a week due to her age.

A line in the letter struck Bud: "Do you realize I've never even seen what my guy looks like in a uniform?" He had sent her a photo of himself in front of *Paper Doll*, but apparently a more close-up photo in uniform was in order. He chuckled at Chrissy's mother, who had put a photo of Bud in a prominent position for when visitors graced the Anderson house.

Bud smiled when Chrissy joked she might end up in the coal mines and breathed a quiet sigh of relief when she admitted such a job would be too rough for her. She referred to him as

"Pete" and "Honey," but he wondered what she would call him after they married.

He shook his head when she considered obtaining her pilot's license because her brother-in-law was in the midst of lessons, at $10 an hour, and "you only need 10 lessons." He fretted when she described yet another incident of falling off scaffolding, and he laughed again when imagining her covered with white splotches of paint.

The word in North Dakota, she said, was the war was approaching its end. Indeed, the status of the war remained the hot topic in Minnesota, as well, and soldiers mentioned it but avoided speaking on the subject for long.

He felt sadness when she wrote her desire for him to accompany her to "Zig Zags," where the couple had roller-skated. When not out of town on a painting job, Chrissy still spent her Saturday nights with friends and family at the hangout. She ended her letter with "Love & kisses, Chris." On the back of the envelope she wrote "S. W. A. S. K.," which Bud understood to mean "sealed with a sloppy kiss."

Bud's thoughts flitted between the woman he wanted to marry, the events which saw the pilot of *Paper Doll* change from a friend and mentor to a stranger with a bad reputation, and the length of time he had been away from home. He wanted to avoid dwelling on what could happen during the war, so his mind floated back to Chrissy. He knew what he could and could not change, so he forced worries away and thought about the young lady who made him happy.

Chapter Thirty-Five

Not much had changed for Conrad. He left the austere Army life behind in the States and learned to spend his free time enjoying his stay in the American territory — his first journey out of the States. As always, he entertained his family with his brief but humorous letters, although he once wrote a four-page letter, which Hulda found the length so shocking she told her daughters about it.

What he did bring himself to write contained snippets of his daily life accompanied by his sarcastic humor. After complaining about Hawaiian mosquitoes, he followed with "What the hell, someone's gotta feed 'em." He entertained loved ones with his stories about Army swimming classes in the ocean — "I'm so full of water I feel like a pickle barrel." When a general arrived to inspect the camp, the officer reported he was pleased with what he saw, causing Conrad to quip to his family, "Thank God he didn't see me."

On one occasion, when Conrad was given time off, he decided he needed to sleep. When explaining why he had not written anyone in a week, he explained, "I s'pose you have been wondering what happened to me. I'm still here but have been too lazy to write. I have an easy job this week so I get plenty of time to sleep — and I make use of it." True to form, he kept the letter brief.

While he did take a trip to Honolulu and Waikiki to search for Christmas gifts, he finally had the opportunity to see more of the island when he was put on "sanitation detail," which was a crew that picked up trash around the island. Conrad was perhaps the only visitor to Hawaii who had to be forced to see the sights — besides the beach; he loved the beach.

He did not enjoy when the Army forced him to swim 100 yards in the ocean while still wearing his clothes. While happy he was not in the Navy, Conrad still had to prepare for war on islands, so he took the experience in stride. He did not have to like it, but he understood the exercise.

Like the rest of the family, he frequently asked the whereabouts of Grandma Thompson, simply because no one ever seemed to know, and also like everyone else, he believed the war in Europe would end soon.

Despite living a good life for a man preparing for war, the twenty-year-old Army private understood change approached.

•   •   •

"Hey, Don, how's your girl doing?" Bud inquired of his friend.

"She's doing great!" Holbert's face lit up. "She's excited to be engaged."

Bud smiled. "So are you."

Holbert's smile grew even larger. "Yeah. I guess so."

"Got yourself a nurse!" Bud laughed at Holbert's expense.

"Sometimes I go to the Blythburg Hospital to see her," Holbert said with stars in his eyes. "Usually though, I just get a pass to see her when she's not working."

"Well, I met her that once, and she's a nice gal." Bud paused. "Except for she can't talk, with that terrible accent and all."

Holbert laughed and threw a pencil at Bud. Waiting for word of their next mission, they relaxed in the barracks and wrote letters home.

•   •   •

The second consecutive flight of *Paper Doll* without Bud was piloted by Lieutenant Fulks. The first flight with the new pilot proceeded without incident, other than the usual heavy flak. Besides a few post-flight comments about Fulks running a looser ship than Captain Gast, no complaints were raised.

When his time off ended, *Paper Doll* did not have a mission scheduled, so Bud flew his second consecutive mission with another crew, going up as a gunner in *the Betty-Jim*. The 847th squadron bomber sported paintings of a woman's face followed by a man's, just above the names of "Betty" and "Jim."

Bud barely knew anyone on the crew, did not speak much, and went along for the ride on a mission to Rostock, Germany. They dropped their bombs on an aircraft component plant, faced accurate flak, but did not see any fighters, to Bud's chagrin.

•   •   •

"Hey, Dortch. How are ya?" Frank Fulks strutted up to ground crew armorer Neville Dortch with a wide smile pushing his thin mustache wider. His brown hair lay hidden underneath

363

his pilot's hat. Born in Lorain County, Ohio, but now living in Kansas, Fulks also had a brother in the Merchant Marine.

"I can't complain, Lieutenant." Dortch stood to put the finishing touches on a patch job two feet from the top of the right wing. He and all the ground crew members worked long hours to ensure their aircraft could complete their missions and return in one piece. They, and crews like them in other branches of the military, were unsung heroes, making the equipment and vehicles safe and operational.

"I got to thinking," Fulks nodded his head as he spoke, as though impressed with his idea. "Dortch, can you put the ball turret back on this bird?"

"Damn right. Why?"

"Because," Fulks began nodding again. "When I get to my last mission, I'll jack that sucker down and make a pass across the field and plow a furrow, then swing around and make an 'x' out of it!" He let out a hearty laugh. "I'll show these hotdogs how to buzz a field."

"You're crazy, Sir." Dortch shook his head. "The Colonel," he referred to base commander Napier. "He'll have your ass in a sling."

Fulks began nodding his head again and beamed a smile. "Once I get my last mission in, I don't care what they do. So, I get fined twenty-bucks. Who cares?!"

"You'd do it, wouldn't ya?"

Fulks over-sized smile vanished. "Do it? Hell yeah! I'm gonna do it. No question." He punctuated his last sentence with a poke of his forefinger at the air in front of him. "And I'll tell ya what, Dortch. If they fine you, I'll pay your fine for you, got it?"

Dortch shook his head and fought off a smile. "You are serious." It was not a question.

"Damn right I am!"

"Whatever you want," Dortch responded. "You're the captain of the ship."

"I've only got a few missions left, so I'll hit you up when the time comes."

The pilot turned and marched toward the barracks without waiting for a response.

Crew chief Bousquet dropped out of the bomb bay and strolled to Dortch as the latter shook his head while watching Fulks walk away.

"I guess he's earned his reputation," Bousquet observed.

"I'll put that ball turret back on. I want to see him do it, and I know he's crazy enough to do it."

"I didn't hear that," Bousquet responded before walking a few feet and climbing back inside the plane.

. . .

Bud had flown with Captain Gast on eleven missions and countless training runs. The comfort level the men felt with Gast's leadership had proven a tremendous factor in the crew scoring so well at Wendover and becoming one of the top crews.

Bud's last two flights — one before his recent grounding and one after — were with other crews: first *Tiger's Revenge*, then *the Betty-Jim*. He only had thirteen missions under his belt in almost four months. During that timeframe, men on other crews had already gone home.

Bud informed his brother of the pilot change and his concern. Conrad never forgot Bud's description: "hotdog." The man seldom worried or showed concern but felt such emotions about his crew's new leader he put his unhappiness to paper. The lack of trust he communicated in his letter to Conrad underscored the types of problems which arose when a team did not trust its leader. Fulks had to earn that trust, yet he displayed no interest in doing so.

•　　•　　•

As the aerial armada approached its target, Bud took note of the three different types of fighters he had seen providing support: P-38s, P-47s, and P-51s. Even though the Messerschmitt Bf 109s and Focke-Wulf Fw 190s were not attacking with the same frequency as before D-Day, to turn back the clock to the early days of the European campaign, to the dark summer of 1943, which culminated in horrific losses in October of that year, would have been utter foolishness. The Germans searched out bombers which had broken away from their formations or did not have escorts at all.

Flak filled the sky all around them, which guaranteed the German fighters were not going to attack, at least at the moment.

Bud felt more tense than usual, and he felt the same tension from his crewmates. This, their second mission with their new pilot, Bud's first, carried a different feel. He pushed the thought from his mind and continued his search for enemy aircraft; he felt pleased to be flying on *Paper Doll* again with his pals.

"Pilot to bombardier, we're getting close to the IP. Are you ready down there."

"Bombardier to pilot, I'm ready." Goshtoian seemed to be ready at all times. Recognized as one of the best bombardiers in the 489th, the Michigander displayed an intense appreciation of that recognition. He wanted to be the best, and he took nothing for granted as they approached every target. His concentration skills were his secret weapon.

"So far, boys, this has been a boring ride," Fulks announced, referring to no close calls with flak. "Maybe we'll see some Messerschmitts yet."

Bud frowned. They had endured a few minutes of flak on three different occasions — enough excitement for a man standing at an opening in the fuselage, exposed to the world from 18,000 feet.

"Navigator to pilot, we've drifted one degree to port."

"Okay," came the response.

Bud realized what was wrong: the pilot operated in a manner which was too casual. Before he could think further, Fulks' voice invaded his ears.

"Here we go, boys. Pilot to bombardier, she's all yours."

"Bombardier to pilot, roger. Opening bomb bay doors."

Ahead in the formation, bombs poured out of Liberators, then the formation wheeled to take a circuitous, unpredictable path home. Flak exploded at various altitudes as the German anti-aircraft gunners continued in their efforts to zero in on the bombers above.

"Bombardier to crew, we're a few seconds away."

A thought struck Bud. With his heart pounding to the point he could hear his pulse in his ears, he shouted into the interphone. "Gunner to Radio, did bomb bay doors open?"

"Affirmative, Pete."

Bud relaxed. He felt certain the standard confirmation had not been given.

"Bombs away," Goshtoian announced.

As *Paper Doll* and the other Liberators in their formation took a sharp starboard turn, Bud's view changed to the sky above them. The banking continued, keeping him from seeing the horizon, as the squadron raced away from the scene.

"Hit!" shouted Lane, who as rear gunner had the best view behind them. "I can see lots of explosions and fire at the railhead!"

"Gosh does it again!" Stodtmeister, the tallest member of the crew at six-feet, shouted before realizing the volume of his voice. "Nice job, Gosh!" he said, this time quieter.

"Blew us up some more Krauts and their supplies," Fulks laughed. "That's why we're here."

• • •

The flight back to base proceeded as planned. Bud tried to determine whether the tension was real or just in his own mind. With oxygen checks completed and the English coast in sight ahead, the crew felt the plane accelerate.

"Hang on, boys!" Fulks called out.

"What the hell you doin', Frank?!" Savage asked, the annoyance in his voice unmistakable.

"Watch this," had to suffice as the only explanation he received.

Savage, always calm under pressure, growled into the interphone again. "Lieutenant Fulks! We're too close to the plane in front of us."

The B-24 climbed and accelerated further. After fifteen seconds, the plane leveled off, then rocketed downward at a 30-degree angle, thus gaining additional speed.

"Whoa!" Lane attempted to not yell. "Rear gunner to pilot, we dropped in only 100 yards directly in front of that -24!"

"Don't worry, gunner," the pilot said while laughing. "He'll have to back off because of our propeller wash."

To the relief of the other nine men, they touched down without further incident.

As they walked from the parked *Paper Doll*, Bud looked at Lane and muttered, "I feel like kissing the ground."

• • •

Inside the large hangar, workers repaired Liberators which had returned with battle damage. Welders and riveters replaced plates of steel and aluminum. Men crawled around and inside the bombers, working with furious dedication. Inside the hangars was where the worst of the worst wound up — at least those aircraft deemed repairable.

Off in a corner, not terribly far from the crashing and clanking, stood ten men, all well-acquainted with each other. If an observer had drawn conclusions by sight only, it would be easy to determine nine men were requesting, with one sympathizing yet rejecting.

"I'm sorry, boys. You know I didn't want to leave *Paper Doll*."

"Captain, I understand you — "

"Sergeant," Gast returned McIntosh's declaration of rank. "If I could, I would. But this is good for me and good for our operation. I'm good at this."

"He's going to get somebody killed!" McIntosh attempted to remain respectful as his frustrations grew.

Gast turned to Sund, Clendinning, Goshtoian and Savage, who stood near each other. "I'm a little surprised by you officers, though."

"We listened to the boys and agree," Goshtoian posited with a calm demeanor.

"You know I don't — "

"We do," Goshtoian interrupted. "We do. But we have to try. This is a serious situation."

"Pete and I walked up on a few guys on his old crew," McIntosh added. "They were telling us about him. They were frightened, ready to risk court martial. Now I see why."

"You guys face German — "

"Is there no possible way?" Savage interrupted.

"I've been telling you guys. No! There's not." Gast did not deliver the news with pleasure. He understood their angst, but they had jobs to do.

"Homer Haile was willing to sacrifice his career to get away from Fulks," Bud said in a hushed tone. "That tells you everything you need to know."

"Gentlemen, I wasn't supposed to tell you this." Gast looked at his former crew. "Right now, Fulks is in with Major

Harper getting his ass chewed out. This will put a lid on his stupidity."

Several of the men groaned. Words, they believed, were not a deterrent to the rogue pilot.

"He doesn't have any room for screw-ups anymore," Gast added.

"He doesn't have many flights left, either," Holbert reminded his former pilot.

"Look, today's September 26," Gast said as he looked at all the men one-by-one. "If you're not comfortable with him by October 26, we'll bring this up to the major. Fair enough?"

Bud had made his single contribution to the conversation with nothing else to add. As the men agreed, with reluctance, to Gast's compromise, Bud understood nothing would change.

•   •   •

The lieutenant burst into the barracks. The other officers were not present, having left to go into town on passes. The enlisted men either played cards or wrote letters to loved ones. When Fulks entered, his usual swagger accompanied him. Guys on his prior crew had mocked his strut, attributing it to the man's own self-worth. Whatever the reason, Fulks' friends could not deny he carried himself as though his presence would be enough to save the day.

"Hey, fellas," Fulks said, innocence in his voice.

Bud immediately realized the pilot did not want anyone to know he had been chewed out by a major.

"What'cha doin'?"

McIntosh, Stodtmeister, and Lane held up their cards so he could see. No one spoke to him.

Fulks approached Bud, who sat in his usual position, back against the wall as he wrote. "Who are ya writing?"

Bud glared at him for a long three seconds before responding. "My brother."

"Well, tell your brother your pilot said 'Hi!'"

Bud smiled.

Within a few seconds, Fulks stood over Holbert, who also had pencil and paper in hand. Bud could not hear much of the conversation, but then Holbert raised his voice. "You guys hear that? Mrs. Fulks is gonna have a baby."

Several of the men spoke at once, and for a moment, the animosity faded.

"Yeah, back in Ottawa, Kansas," Fulks explained. "My wife's getting ready to have our first child. I'm not gonna make it before he's born, but I plan on seeing him soon."

It was the first time the men saw a human side to Fulks. His antics and attitude had made him less man and more cartoon character up until this moment. As the conversation continued, he grabbed a chair and chatted with the men while they played poker.

Bud continued writing Conrad and tuned out the chit chat.

•　　•　　•

At mail call, the men cheered Bud's receipt of a package; they all knew what that meant. Sure enough, the first item Bud pulled out was a bag of Hulda's homemade oatmeal cookies.

They lasted three minutes. He guarded his cigarettes from prying eyes, then pulled out stationery for writing letters.

"She's unbelievable," Bud laughed. By now, the men knew a number of stories about Hulda and understood Bud had neither asked for the stationery nor possessed enough to write another letter. "How she knows I'll never understand."

As Bud read her letter, he felt relief to learn Hulda had received the watch he sent home — the $21 watch he purchased in Brazil.

The crew's nerves were not calmed and anger was not assuaged, but between the oatmeal cookies and the bit of a breakthrough with Fulks, the Tuesday afternoon in September passed without incident.

Chapter Thirty-Six

In mid-July of 1944, prime minister and military leader Hidecki Tojo, the man nicknamed "The Razor" in his youth, resigned because of his failures while leading the military. The final straw was the defeat at Saipan, considered to be the "gateway to Japan." Twenty-four thousand soldiers were killed and another five thousand committed suicide.

Tojo lacked field experience, yet made the strategic military decisions, frequently with the emperor's involvement. Tojo's ill-advised excursion into India produced the opposite effect he had hoped. Rather than knocking the British out of the war, he took Japan a step closer to defeat.

While the emperor did not like Tojo, he tolerated the vicious leader. The latter man's cruelty extended to military and civilians alike. In China, the Japanese conducted horrific experiments on people, depriving them of anesthesia in order to avoid having the medicine interfere with their heinous, invasive experiments. At Saipan, after the Americans conquered the island, Japanese civilians followed Tojo's orders and plunged off cliffs to their deaths.

Considering all battles, Japanese soldiers were killed in action at a 10:1 ratio under the military leader's tenure. With the war not progressing as planned, Tojo wanted to hide the Saipan defeat from the Japanese people, but the emperor overruled him and demanded the former broadcast his failure. Tojo did so, then resigned.

His legacy continued even after his own military career ended. The military had reached deep into the Japanese past and urged soldiers to summon their samurai spirits. Japanese soldiers attacked, and died, in waves when battles became hopeless. To surrender was to be a coward. Even generals fought to the death or took their own lives rather than be captured.

In September, the Allies were preparing for battle in the Philippines, with a focus on Leyte. General Douglas MacArthur had with great fanfare promised "I shall return." The American military prepared for that return in order to begin the final island-hopping drive to Japan itself.

• • •

A week to the day prior to the *Paper Doll* crew's meeting with Captain Gast, Conrad shipped out in a Liberty ship; he wondered whether his brother helped to build it.

Now assigned to the 69th Field Hospital, Conrad finally belonged to a permanent unit. His voyage would be a long one, and he could not receive mail. In fact, even after he arrived in Leyte it would take time for his mail to catch up with him.

The trip proceeded in more comfort than he had imagined, though when he did arrive at last, he was ready for solid ground.

• • •

On September 27, 1944, the crew of *Paper Doll* prepared to join the many other aircraft and squadrons destined to bomb the rail center and tank factory in Kassel, Germany. The 489th's briefing began at 0315 and take-off would be around 0615. Their path would take them over the Netherlands and into Germany, north of the Ruhr River, as they looped to the south at 22,000 feet, concealing their destination as well as attempting to avoid flak concentrations. Bud knew Kassel lay northeast of Koblenz, their most recent target, and approximately seventy-five miles due east of Dusseldorf.

The men of *Paper Doll* should have felt confident and calm. German fighters had become rarer by the mission, flak intensities had seen a gradual decrease, and the targeting by the Mighty Eighth Air Force and all of the Allies' bombardments proved successful. The strategy worked and the crews could see the results of their success.

They knew they would face anti-aircraft artillery and understood the Messerschmitts and Focke-Wulfs continued to fly sorties, and they could not escape the fact that danger followed every aircraft, every squadron, every man.

Yet the men of *Paper Doll* did not feel the confidence they should have been able to grasp, almost see and touch, as though it were an actual object.

Paper Doll lifted off and flew its pre-determined, unpredictable path toward Kassel.

• • •

Around 0930, the time had come to fulfill the mission.

"Bombardier to pilot, we're gonna have to eat our eggs."

"Pilot to bombardier, negative. Let's drop and run. Drop by radar."

"Radioman to pilot, we haven't used this radar much. I have no way of knowing how close we are to our target." For chatter over the interphone, Holbert's plea was a long one.

Puffs of white smoke began appearing like popcorn all around them. Because of the cloud cover, the Germans could only estimate the bombers' altitude by their sound.

"Co-pilot to crew, anyone else notice the flak is white?"

"Roger that, Savage," Bud answered. "Any idea why?"

"They changed something, Pete. I just don't know what."

"Pilot to radio, you were trained in using the radar, correct?"

"Radio to pilot, affirmative. But a class isn't much and you can't ask it questions. It takes time to learn."

"Pilot to radio, you were trained to use it, and we're going to use it. The lead and his group bugged out. We're the lead of our formation — ain't that right Lane?" Fulks referred to Lane's view of the world behind them.

After a hesitation by Holbert, he responded to his pilot. "Roger." After a longer, tense pause, Holbert broke the silence. "Radio to bombardier, crews up ahead are reporting the clouds are breaking — 5/10th visibility."

"Roger," Goshtoian answered. As a top bombardier, he had learned to despise clouds, the thieves which stole his accuracy.

"Sounds good to me," Fulks responded to Holbert. No one wanted to return to base without dropping their bombs.

"Pilot to bombardier, transferring control."

"Bombardier to pilot, accepting control."

"Opening bomb bay doors. Bombardier to radio, confirm when doors are open.

"Radio. Roger that. Doors open."

The flak continued, but *Paper Doll* remained unscathed.

The plane traveled for several more minutes until the clouds parted somewhat, but not enough for Goshtoian's liking.

"Bombardier to pilot, I see what looks like a factory. Stand by. I'm holding course and speed. Maybe radar won't be needed."

"Roger."

After a half minute of quiet, the announcement came. "Bombs away."

Fulks waited to bank the plane, staying in formation as the Liberators behind him dropped their bombs. Once the command was given, the formation banked hard to port.

Bud had a good view of the ground when clouds did not shroud his view, and he need not struggle to see flashes on the ground signifying anti-aircraft artillery. As *Paper Doll* continued its flight from Kassel, he noticed something and made a call over the interphone. "Waist to crew, the flak stopped — just all of a sudden."

A little chatter ensued. Either the enemy believed the planes were out of range, which was not possible, or, more likely, fighters were inbound.

The crews did not yet know they had missed their targets by twenty miles. Whatever Goshtoian and other bombardiers saw was not a tank factory or the marshalling yards at Kassel. The lead formation had turned in the wrong direction before bugging out, causing a column of bombers many miles long to follow the incorrect route, away from their waiting fighter escort.

As they left the target area, Lane called out, "Fighters! Six o'clock, low. Way behind us."

The men of the 489th Bombardment Group were about to witness a battle which would not be forgotten in history. The rumor that later circulated around Halesworth was the Germans held a grudge against the trailing 445th Bombardment Group. The 445th previously had dropped its entire payload on civilians; whether by accident or design, the Germans did not care. Messerschmitts and Focke-Wulfs, the theory went, remained grounded until the correct tail color was spotted, and now they streamed upward.

Whether this belief was true or not, the men of the 489th would be long gone from Halesworth before the truth was revealed because the U.S. military covered up the "Kassel Debacle."

More likely, the debacle occurred because the lead formation turned the wrong way when departing the target area, thereby turning away from their air cover and leaving them exposed. It took time for the German fighters to scramble, which meant they did not get to the lead bomb groups. With cloud cover making targeting as difficult for the Germans below as for the Americans above, withholding further flak and sending up the fighters likely made the most sense to the defenders.

Approximately 130 Fw 190s and Bf 109s, modified with heavier guns and armor as "bomber destroyers," zoomed in for the kill. The German fighters shot down 25 of the 32 Liberators of the 445th Bomb Group. Including cripples which had to ditch, only two of their bombers returned to base.

For their part, the Liberators shot down 29 enemy fighters.

As they watched the scene unfold behind them, the men of *Paper Doll* knew little of why the event progressed as it did.

In fact, in the confusion of war, some said P-51s were involved in the battle. Others gave differing totals of survivors, but officially, 117 American airmen died, whether immediately at the scene or as the result of crash landing on the way back to their bases.

The battle lasted anywhere from thirty seconds to a handful of minutes, depending on the perceptions of the witnesses.

•　　•　　•

Bud had never witnessed such a massacre. The entire crew took the same approach: quiet contemplation. Little post-battle banter interrupted the deep thoughts.

This was flight number fifteen for the Minnesotan.

As they neared the British coast, less than 10,000 feet above the North Sea and dropping steadily, *Paper Doll* accelerated without warning and climbed.

"Hang on, boys!" Fulks half-shouted.

"Oh, hell! Not again!" Savage cried out in anger.

The interphone screeched with static as voices overlapped one another. Bud grit his teeth and shook his head. His mind was made up: he was going to have a little "talk" with his pilot after this mission, rank be damned. The absurdity of Fulks' behavior had reached an insufferable crescendo. Passing another plane on approach represented a dangerous disregard for the safety of his crew which, besides the mission itself, was a pilot's overriding responsibility.

"Dammit!"

"You're not gonna make it!"

Paper Doll lurched upward, above and to the left of *Special Delivery II*, but pilot Lieutenant Culkin, unaware of *Paper Doll*'s move, slowed but climbed slightly as his aircraft possibly encountered turbulence. With no opportunity for Fulks to react — B-24s were not built for agility — *Paper Doll*'s right wing and *Special Delivery II*'s left wing clipped one another.

Bud watched from his vantage as port-side waist gunner, in the rear half of the bomber; he could see through the opening created for the starboard waist gunner. Bud did not know the details, but he understood enough of what was happening to realize his fate. Once the planes made contact, their trajectories changed, causing them to lurch toward each other.

"NO!" Bud cried, but again the men shouted over one another.

Bud knew.

Bud's mind raced as *Paper Doll* flipped over, causing her left wing to scrape down the fuselage of the other bomber. The wing ripped off *Paper Doll* and became part of the descending debris. Fuel stored in the wings of both B-24s escaped their tanks. As the wings broke apart, the fuel contacted the hot engines.

The thoughts flew by. Mother working hard to keep the family going. Carl in and out of the Puposky area. Innumerable days with Conrad. Along the Missouri River with Chrissy. That first kiss they shared. His sweet sisters, Thelma and Elsie. The laughs with the boys while in training. His nieces and nephews. Strolling the streets of Salt Lake City with Conrad. Sneaking in so he could see the quarantined Conrad. The "hotdog." Chrissy ice skating with him in Williston. Their pledge to wait for each other. His poor mother, with all of her sons out of state — or farther. Puposky and Bemidji, and his many friends. Memories of his father. The pained look on his mother's face in those rough days of 1929.

The explosion ripped *Paper Doll* apart, putting an end to the thoughts racing through Bud's mind.

Special Delivery II exploded, sending metallic debris and body parts in all directions.

The next plane back, flown by Joe Woerner, turned at the first sign of trouble and narrowly avoided becoming part of the unfolding carnage.

At 12:35 p.m., local time, both Liberators, in pieces, crashed into the swampy ground near the River Blyth, a mere seven miles from the base.

Twenty men perished. There were no survivors.

• • •

One of the men who witnessed the collision while on approach was Homer Haile, Fulks' engineer until Haile co-led the revolt against the pilot. He watched from his top-gunner position as *Paper Doll* came down on top of *Special Delivery II*.

Haile knew it could have been him and his crew.

• • •

The explosions rocked the area and were heard and felt by many Brits. A young nurse by the name of Eileen had this particular Wednesday off. When she heard the explosions, she leaped to her feet in fear. She looked out in time to see the mighty planes crashing to the Earth.

Horrified, she feared the worst.

As she ran out the door, she saw her friend Jill arriving on her bicycle. Rather than a genteel visit, the two young ladies sped toward the crash site on their bicycles. Eileen needed to see identification numbers of the planes. She could not wait to hear from her fiancé later in the day to learn all was well, that it was someone else who perished in the swampy ground. She had to know — now.

At the first sign of debris, Eileen jumped off her bicycle and allowed it to fall over undamaged a few feet away from her. At the edge of the debris field, she ran to the first item she saw, stopped, and covered her mouth. Jill did the same upon arriving three seconds behind her. A human foot, covered by a bloody sock, lay on the dry ground. Eileen bent down and touched the foot, turning it over in an attempt to see whether a name was sown on the sock. No luck.

She ventured from the road, knowing she could not get to the far wreckage because of the swamp. The nearer aircraft lay on dry ground. She dodged jagged debris and continued, running through the debris field. She saw a piece of the fuselage still intact. She ran to the other side. Horror raced through her veins and into her heart. Eileen saw the two words she dreaded to see.

Paper Doll.

She could not stomach seeing the mangled body of her fiancé, radio operator Donald Holbert, so she turned and ran. When she slowed, Jill caught up to her and put her arm around her friend as they both sobbed, backs to the carnage.

B-24s continued flying overhead, on approach to the base, yet she did not hear them. She did not feel the rumbling from the engines which vibrated through her entire body. Eileen was only marginally present, in body, but not mind.

•   •   •

After a knock, Hulda opened the door to see Thelma. The mother looked haggard and the daughter noticed immediately.

"What's wrong, Mother?"

Hulda frowned.

"I had a bad dream — four, really."

"Four bad dreams?!" Thelma almost shouted, her surprise evident. "Tell me about it."

"Let's sit at the kitchen table," the mother directed.

As they sat, Hulda began her story. "I wrote all this down. Here, let me go get the piece of paper."

Thelma grabbed her mother's hand as Hulda began to rise.

"Just tell me, Mother. What's wrong?"

Hulda's body succumbed to a small jerk, as though she had just produced a silent hiccup. She knew telling the tale could prove to be a challenge. "A voice called out. Everything was murky at first." Hulda spoke in a hushed tone, as though someone or something might hear her words and recognize the fear. "'Mother!' is what the voice said. And then it repeated. And then it paused and said it again. 'Mother!'"

Thelma leaned forward as though she were being literally sucked into the story.

"It was Bud's voice."

Thelma flinched as horror smothered her face and chest.

384

"Then, I could see his body. It was all torn up and bleeding bad."

Mother! The word and the possible meaning of the dream now haunted both of them.

"The next thing I knew, I was holding a telegram from the Army saying that Bud was dead." She fought back tears and her voice cracked as she uttered the final three words.

Thelma rose and wrapped her arms around her mother, who did not stand. Thelma then returned to her chair as Hulda continued.

"I woke up, just wide awake, trembling and afraid." Hulda took a deep breath. "Thelma, it troubled me to my soul."

Hulda did not realize Halesworth was seven hours ahead of Bemidji's time, and she did not know whether Bud had been scheduled to fly on this day or not.

"I went back to asleep," Hulda continued. "I was already on the emotional edge, but I did fall asleep. And that's when I had the second dream." She paused again, her heart racing, her nerves fraying. "In the second dream, I told you about what my dream was. Then, I woke up again, eventually went back to sleep, and in the third dream I told Elsie about what I dreamed."

Thelma was used to her mother's odd premonitions, but Hulda did not frequently speak of dreams — especially potentially prophetic dreams.

"My fourth dream," Hulda started but was interrupted by the gasp from Thelma at the thought of four nightmares in a row. "Was me telling Mother," referring to Grandma Thompson. "So, when I got up this morning, I wrote a note to myself, what the dreams were about and how I woke up."

Tears flooded Thelma's eyes. To most people, these were mere dreams, albeit frightening ones. With Hulda, the family now had to be concerned whether these were premonitions.

"I don't usually have premonitions in dreams," Hulda stated. "At least that I remember."

Hulda was not yet aware Bud's life came to an end at 5:35 a.m., Bemidji time. She only knew what she dreamed, and she wrote down the dreams on a piece of paper and dated it. After the description of the dreams she wrote of her strained nerves and "a feeling of a terrible dread, it's hard to keep from screaming."

She knew. Bud was dead. In her own inexplicable, peculiar way, Hulda knew. Thelma now harbored the same fear.

•   •   •

On *Impassionada*, bombardier Sam Syracuse was told to look out the window with haste. Already harboring a cold and now sick to his stomach, Syracuse did not do as urged. In retrospect, he felt relieved he did not. A member of his crew saw the reaction of *Special Delivery II,* out of control, slide back into *Paper Doll*. Syracuse felt thankful he missed the sight of two American aircraft exploding in mid-air.

At chow, as most of the men ate in silence after witnessing the collision, Syracuse learned of the Kassel debacle. He had several friends in the 445th, and only his best friend in the ETO survived — several other friends went down with their B-24 Liberators.

   •   •   •

In the accident report, which was later declassified, the Army placed 65% of the blame on Lieutenant Fulks and 35% on Lieutenant Culkin. Many, either because of what they saw or what they knew of Fulks, placed 100% of the blame on Fulks.

   •   •   •

The day after the death notification to the family arrived, in Kansas, Frank Fulks' wife gave birth to a boy.

Chapter Thirty-Seven

Friday, October 13th. Hulda sat alone in her rented house. No one knew, so no one was there to comfort her, and she preferred it that way. She endured brief moments of wondering whether her dreams caused his death, but she shook off the senseless thoughts, remembering she had no control over the situation.

She did her best to keep tears off the paper she clutched with both hands. The Western Union envelope lay on the table next to her. She stared out a window, seeing nothing. Birds, automobiles, people — to her nothing existed outside of her thoughts and emotions. She felt hollow, almost numb, yet the pain crushed her spirit. Her thoughts crashed like a ship into rocks on a shore. Over and over thoughts were born, flashed through her mind, then destroyed on the sharp rocks of her aching spirit. Yet those same thoughts could not be grasped, could not mature, and so she felt as though her brain was about to break down.

She did not play favorites yet maintained a different relationship with each of her children. Not as serious as Carl, not as shy as Conrad, Bud was simultaneously reserved but open. Like most of the family, he was principled, stubborn, and fierce, yet he held his temper better than some in the family and he made friends easily.

Hulda's mind drifted away from Bud the man to Bud the warrior. She wondered whether his bomber had been shot down or he sustained a wound from that word she had learned from young men who had returned from Europe: flak.

She also pondered whether he passed quickly and painlessly. Tears welled up — again — as she wondered whether he may have suffered through a long, agonizing death.

She cried; she talked to God; she trembled; she cried some more.

The one thing she could not do was think about the future: a memorial service; bringing his body back to the States; continuing with life.

In time, she would contact Reverend Stolee, her friend and the first pastor of Our Redeemer's Lutheran Church in Puposky. Reverend Stolee and his family had moved to Hibbing, and while Hulda liked the new pastor, she never fully adjusted to him and missed Reverend Stolee's sermons and his entire family.

Now, she felt the duty to contact her daughters and to allow them to notify the extended family. But first, she had to continue shedding tears. Her Eugene was gone and she struggled to process that fact.

•   •   •

In the top right corner of the letter, Conrad penned: "Somewhere at sea." While undated, the envelope bore the postmark of October 26 — a full month since Bud's death.

Will try to answer your letters now if I can. I can't find any place to write on this tub so I'll just have to do the best I can.

I hope everyone up there is getting along O.K. Sure wish I could get some mail. I'm still feeling fine but this ship

*is driving me nuts. It's the same thing day after day. All
we can see is water. Some scenery!*

Conrad launched into an explanation of daily life on one
of the ships his brother built, although he had no way of knowing
whether Carl actually built the ship on which he found himself.

*We have movies every night and there is a pretty good
band with us so we even have music once in a while. The
ship's library is on the other end of a long line of men so
I've never had the pleasure of seeing what it looks like.
The chow line is by far the most provoking of all. We get
up in the morning, stand in line until the whole U.S. Army
eats breakfast — then we go in and eat what is left. When
we come dashing out of the mess hall we find the end of
the line again with a little hope that we will get dinner.
I spent five days on K.P. right off the bat and I'm sure
glad it's over. That galley is really   hot. I guess that
gives you a pretty good idea of life on a ship. It's
tiresome as the devil and I don't like it.*

When Hulda, Thelma, and Elsie read the letter, they felt
pained from the knowledge Conrad remained unaware of his
brother's fate. Unable to receive mail, Conrad's ignorance of the
tragedy became starker.

*Is there anything interesting going on around home? I'm
looking forward to getting some letters from you so don't
stop writing. Greet the girls and ask them to write, too.*

As always, he referred to his sisters as "the girls." To Hulda and "the girls," Conrad's complaining always possessed a comical element. Even though they each cried when they read the letter — largely because Conrad remained unaware of the dreadful news — they also laughed at his innocent, comical, and frustrated observations.

For now, all laughter came mixed with tears.

Chapter Thirty-Eight

General Douglas MacArthur promised the Philippine people he would return, so when he fulfilled that promise, fulfillment had to be grand. On October 20th, the man who came across as larger than life strutted through ocean water reaching his knees until he arrived onto Philippine soil as cameras whirred.

Advanced forces had secured the area for the general, but an overwhelming majority of the soldiers about to fight in Leyte remained on their ships for hours. In Conrad's case, he did not disembark until after 11:00 p.m., local time.

• • •

"Doctor! Over here!" Conrad shouted.

"Doctor! Over here!" another medic shouted.

A Marine corporal entered the large tent, which lacked walls, and grabbed the first person he saw, a brown-haired nurse who had been sweet, innocent, and happy one month prior. Now, she saw gore which would haunt her the rest of her life.

From the air, the tent city of over three dozen olive drab canvas tents, which sported the occasional red cross on a field of white, filled a large opening at the edge of the jungle. Though ten miles from the battlefront, it always amazed the doctors, medics, and nurses how often gunfire and explosions could be heard.

"Miss! Excuse me, Miss!" The corporal grabbed her as he reached her. "Is this an Army hospital?"

Baffled by the question, the nurse looked at the corporal with bewildered brown eyes. "Yes. Of course." She lifted her hand toward the noisy and frenetic attempts at mending American soldiers.

"My men are carrying my sergeant in. He's bad off!" The Marine's voice conveyed his concern for his superior. He looked over his shoulder and interrupted the nurse as she was about to speak. "There they are!"

Two Marines carried in the sergeant, whose left leg ended just below the knee.

"Can you help?" Again, he grabbed her shoulders.

"Yes, yes. We can help." Her soft voice did little to soothe the worried enlisted man. Under different circumstances, the men, who had rarely seen women during the war, would have laid on the charm to gain her attention.

Conrad saw the Marines, then looked at another man who needed attention; an Army private who had been shot clean through near his left shoulder. Two field "aid men," as medics were called by Army personnel, from the Battalion Aid Station had dropped off three soldiers, with this man in the worst condition. The lone doctor at the battalion station had treated the men the best he could, but felt they needed the advanced services available at the field hospital.

"Nurse." Conrad ordered. "Keep pressure on both sides here." Conrad demonstrated what he meant, pressing bandages on both the entrance and exit wounds at the same time. "The doctor signaled he'll be here in a minute."

Conrad made his way to the Marines. He had gotten a quick glance at the sergeant's condition when he entered.

"Let me help you, Sarah," Conrad said to the nurse. He grabbed a canvas stretcher, which included two rounded wooden poles to provide both support and handles for the patient to be carried by two-to-four people. He saw most of the blood of the prior soldier who required the stretcher had been cleaned off, though it remained stained. He brought it over and set it on an empty bed. With all the gentleness of a basketball player practicing his dunk, the Marines dropped their leader onto the canvas.

"Sorry!" The corporal looked horrified at their ham-handedness. "Sorry!"

"This one needs immediate surgery!" Sarah shouted in the direction of two doctors.

As Conrad and Sarah worked to slow the bleeding, they discovered a blood-soaked belt wrapped around the leg. They had not noticed the tail of the belt which had, before he reached the destination of the board, managed to stay covered by the sergeant's body.

Sarah reached to see whether she could feel the belt's tightness around the man's limb.

"Don't touch that belt," Conrad ordered.

"Oh, don't worry," Sarah answered. "I'm not. If that had come off during the trip here, he'd be a goner."

A doctor examined the patient for all of three seconds before giving his verdict. "Nurse, get a couple of orderlies to carry him in." He then disappeared behind a curtain to prepare for surgery.

While Conrad washed his hands, he heard, "Aid man! Aid man!" He and several other medics looked up from their tasks. Conrad dried his freshly washed, now blood-free hands.

"Excuse me," a soldier with dark curly hair entered the tent near Conrad. "I got separated from my company and I was wondering if you could help me out?"

"Sure," Conrad offered. "What do ya need?"

"I just got a nasty little scratch." The soldier pulled his bloodied sleeve up to his elbow to reveal a cut on his forearm. "It keeps bleeding. I can't make it stop, and I don't want it infected."

"Come on over here." Conrad led him to a cache of bandages and medicines. "Does it hurt?"

"Nah. It's just irritating, and you know how everything gets infected in these jungles."

"So I'm learning." Conrad wiped off blood and applied Mercurochrome. "What's your name, soldier?"

"Buttress. Walter."

"Where are you from, Walter?"

"California," the private responded. "I was helping bring in a wounded man, and at the Battalion Aid Station they directed us here. I didn't know the other boys, so they took off when they were ready."

Conrad put a bandage on Buttress' arm as he spoke. "Have your company's aid man change the bandage a couple of times a day so you don't get infected."

"Sure thing."

"Go find your company," Conrad patted the young man on the shoulder.

"Oh, that'll be easy," he responded. "Just follow the sounds of gunfire and grenades."

With that, Conrad's patient exited the tent and found a ride back to the battle.

Before Conrad could return to helping his assigned patients, an officer approached him. "Peterson, you'll be back on normal duty tomorrow," which meant surgical duty.

Conrad nodded and smiled. "Yes, sir." After the officer walked outside of ear shot, Conrad added, "More lovely gore, but away from this craziness."

Upon arrival at the area of the tent where, at least on this day, he supervised the nurses and their assistants, he approached one of his patients. "Private Giaboni. How are you doing?" The thin soldier, with dark brown hair and matching eyes, lay on his back with the look of a half-crazed man pursued by killers.

"The scraping sounds are so loud!" He attempted not to shout. "My sarge thinks I'm trying to get out of combat and the battalion hospital said the same thing." His inconsistent contortions and jerks of his body came in waves rather than in rhythmic timing.

"The doc told me he'll be here in a couple minutes," Conrad attempted to console the man as he slipped toward the edge of sanity.

Private Giaboni did not care about such details. "You've got to stop this racket! It's so loud!" He thrashed as he bellowed, though through the cacophony of screams, shouts, and other expressions of excruciating pain, the outburst barely caught anyone's attention.

The doctor, a distinguished looking man with splashes of gray seemingly painted above his ears, arrived faster than expected and engaged the private in conversation as Conrad stood back. The doctor had been a civilian physician with no military experience, but volunteering for the Army had become a much more harrowing experience than he assumed it would be.

After the brief conversation, the patient sat up and the doctor bent over to put his otoscope into the man's right ear. He only needed moments to diagnose Private Giaboni's descent into madness. He stepped back and sighed as he looked at Conrad.

"We're going to have to flush his ear canals," the physician said in a slow cadence as he shook his head with an equally slow motion. "The noises are maggots having supper in his external auditory canal, maybe on both sides — I haven't looked. We've got to get them out of there." He looked at the patient. "You're gonna be fine, son."

Despite all the bloody sights and sounds, the missing limbs and doctoral excavations to pull out bullets and shrapnel, dealing with trench foot, leeches, and gangrene, and sundry other maladies he had already experienced, something about maggots inside a man's ear canal turned Conrad's stomach. Although throughout history doctors had used maggots to eat away dead tissue, somehow the Army private managed to get the nasty thought of flies' eggs stuck in his mind.

As he walked with a queasy expression toward the supply station deeper into the tent, he mumbled to himself, "Now the war can end. I've seen everything." He had been on Leyte for less than a month.

Chapter Thirty-Nine

Exhausted, head down, shoulders lowered, his boots soaked with moisture through his socks to his feet, Conrad traipsed to the barracks ready to fall into bed in his current condition.

"Private! Make sure you shower and get those feet dry. We don't need you getting trench foot."

"Yes, sir." Conrad neither looked up nor recognized the voice. "Too late for that," he mumbled.

The Sun dropped below the horizon as Conrad made his way out of the tent city. The brilliant oranges and pinks served as an exclamation point to the beauty of southeast Asia. He never noticed.

He knew that he should take the order-in-passing seriously — whoever delivered it. He showered, then allowed his feet to dry. He grimaced at the tingling pain which traveled through his feet from ankles to toes. He saw the number of blisters and realized there were more today than yesterday.

As he prepared to fall into his bunk, he saw his mail. The only explanation was one of his friends had grabbed it for him.

It was mid-November and Conrad had yet to receive mail; the military had a difficult time catching up with many of the men. Multiple letters from his mother and sisters provided the majority of the small stack. Struck by an odd thought, he flipped through each envelope — no letters from Bud. *He's gotta be awfully busy, too*, Conrad thought when he spread them out on his bed.

As he placed the envelopes in chronological order, he noticed a gap. For a brief time, no one had written to him. *Maybe they waited because I couldn't write back.* A letter from Reverend Evans of Our Redeemer's Lutheran Church in Puposky jumped out at him. Not only was this Reverend Evans' first letter to him, it seemed to fill the gap in time.

All he wanted to do was sleep, but the adrenaline rush from the sight of all the letters from home ensured he would not fall asleep for at least an hour. He read two of his mother's letters, then one each from his sisters — all written in mid-September.

That Carl had not written was of no surprise, but the lack of a letter from Bud struck him as odd. He knew they had both encountered periods when they were so busy they only wrote their mother, but now no news from Bud ate at him.

Conrad took the stack of letters and prepared to stash them away with his other belongings when the letter from Reverend Evans again came to mind. He barely knew the minister, having grown up with Reverend Stolee, whose family remained friends with the Petersons even after the former moved to Hibbing. The family did not mind Reverend Evans, he just was not Reverend Stolee.

He began reading the letter but within seconds dropped it onto the floor.

•   •   •

Hulda sat in the middle of the second row, with her daughters and their husbands on either side of her. Carl sat next to Ray. The ladies of the Sande family — Eileen, Donna, and Ethelyn — sang "Friends of Jesus in Their Parting."

Reverend Stolee delivered the eulogy. Stolee knew Bud well, including leading him to Christ. The combination of a tiny town and Bud's involvement with the church ensured the young man was known well in the area.

Reverend Evans had been gracious enough to allow the church's former leader to eulogize Puposky's second fallen son, and Hulda would have it no other way. First Sonny Martin and now Bud. For little Puposky, war was more hellacious than they could imagine.

After a bugler by the name of Bender played Taps, adding to the tears already shed, Mendelssohn's "Rest in the Lord" filled the small sanctuary as Patsy Mahar gracefully played the church organ.

Many of the locals had called him "Morris" when Bud was a boy because of another boy named Eugene. Now, many of the same locals returned to their home church to remember the life of the young man who died as Staff Sergeant Eugene Morris Peterson.

•   •   •

The family gathered at Elsie's house to talk. The get-together felt uncomfortable — not only because of the loss of their brother and son, but because the youngest sibling remained in harm's way. As the memorial service bulletin put it, "Pvt. Conrad Peterson, in Medical Corps somewhere in the Pacific." "Somewhere in the Pacific" felt like an apt description. The unspoken fear could be summed up as: "Could Conrad be next?"

Glassy-eyed and solemn, Carl tuned out the chatter as he sat in a living room chair. The children were told to play in another room and the infant Delbert lay asleep on his aunt and uncle's bed. As the sisters talked about the sweet memorial service, Hulda and Carl had little to say to anyone. Ray and Jake joined their wives in the conversation.

"I'm gonna try again," Carl announced to no one in particular.

Thelma heard his words but failed to understand the meaning. "Try what again?"

"I'm gonna join the Army." His words lacked humor or emotion.

"Why?!" Hulda did not take the pronouncement in stride. "What are you gonna achieve? What are you gonna gain?" She sat on one end of a couch and looked with concern and disdain at her son.

Carl turned his head to look at his mother. "I'm going to honor Bud."

On the forefront of everyone's minds was what they had just endured with Bud and what could happen to Conrad. Injecting Carl into the mix would not help the family — at least in the view of everyone in the room except Carl.

Hulda chose not to fight. Each member of the family felt a hole in his or her heart where Bud had resided until now. She decided now was not the time for arguing — any time would be better than now.

Carl did speak throughout the evening, but not again of his desire to make the Nazis pay for starting the war which threatened the free world — and for killing his brother.

• • •

Hulda and Carl sat alone; they had remained the least talkative after the service. Carl stood to depart.

"Mother, Elsie is taking me to the train station tomorrow." He paused for acknowledgement but received none. "After we save more money we'll come back here some time, after the baby gets a little older."

He took a step to leave the room when Hulda rose and stepped into his path. Without a word, she put the side of her head onto Carl's chest, put her arms around him, and squeezed. After several long seconds, she let go and stepped back.

"I want his body sent home so we can bury him with Father," she said in a weak voice, referring to her late husband. "He can rest next to William." She paused. "Or he can rest in the church cemetery — I don't care. I just want him home."

Carl dropped his head and controlled his response. "Mother, let the Army bury him there."

"Why? He belongs in Puposky."

"I know, Mother. He does. But you don't want that."

"Yes, I do."

"Mother, listen." To his surprise, Hulda awaited his response. "Do you know what happens to a man in a crash? They crashed into the ground. Do you know what happens to a body in something like that?" He paused to judge her reaction, then decided he could continue. "You don't want to know what a man looks like after his plane crashes."

Hulda put her hand to her mouth. "Don't say that!"

"I'm sorry, Mother, but let the Army take care of this."

"I want him home!"

"You want him alive, but that's not going to happen, either." He again tried to speak with more care and concern; he

402

felt it, but speaking in such a manner was not always his strong suit. "It's not just that. Don't forget, there were nine other men in his plane and ten in the other. How do you know whose parts are who?"

Despite the semi-gentle way in which he spoke, the words did not go over well. "What are you doing, Carl? That's awful!"

Carl raised his voice. "I'm sorry! But his body isn't the Bud we knew. He was mangled up! We have to accept that and let the Army take care of it. Knowing them, they'll send us body parts of other people and throw some rocks in to make the casket heavier."

Hulda transitioned from the presence of tears in her eyes to weeping. After dropping her head to hide her tears, she lifted it to face her eldest son. "I'll let the Army handle it." Without a pause, she raised her voice to express the firm commitment to her wishes. "But if they move him, I want that move to be home!"

Carl stepped forward and put his arms around her. After a brief embrace he retreated a step. "You tell the Army that. They'll bring him home if you want."

Without another word, Carl embraced her again and left the room.

•   •   •

Upon his return to California and without telling anyone, Carl visited the Army recruiter's office in Richmond. He stated his intent and one of the recruiters took his information, then directed him to the physician, who had a line of only two men awaiting his services. The halcyon days of December 1941 and the early days of 1942 were only a memory for the U.S. military, but young men coming of age continued to enlist in a weak trickle in these latter months of the war.

When Carl's turn saw him escorted to the doctor, he had one advantage over the Army: the Richmond recruiting office did not have access to his records of rejection in Bemidji.

Within minutes, hopes were dashed.

"Young man," the fifty-something doctor said with a stern expression. "Your knees are in bad shape."

"How can you tell?" Carl asked, acting surprised.

"I watched you walk in. I just observed the range of motion in your lower legs. I can hear ligaments popping as they get stretched like a rubber band against bones. Your knee caps don't move properly; they're like the knees of a man thirty years older. And I'm a doctor." He looked Carl in the eye. "Does that answer your question, young man?"

Carl's stiffened. He clenched his fists. He forced his teeth together. He relaxed just enough to say, in a quiet voice, "I want to kill some Nazi sons of bitches!"

The doctor did not look up, but flipped through the little information on Carl in his possession. He looked up and again looked Carl in the eye. "Mr. Peterson, you're twenty-nine, you've got a wife and two kids. You should go home and keep building ships for our country."

Too emotionally spent to fight, Carl's locked jaw and narrowed eyes hid his anger as effectively as a beacon attached to a surfaced German U-Boat helped it conceal its position.

The doctor nodded as he repeated, "Go home. Your country needs you in a different way than fighting."

Carl did not wish to get away from his family; in fact, he would move the family back to Bemidji during his absence. He did wish to finish a job — an opportunity which was robbed from his brother. At the moment, the man who did not reveal his emotions had them on full display.

Chapter Forty

"Dear Mother," the letter began.

I just received the letter from Rev. Evans breaking the news about Bud. I can't begin to tell you how terrible it makes me feel, but I'm sure you understand.

Conrad continued with words to console his mother, yet they also, at least to a small degree, consoled him, as well.

Mother, it's hard to understand why such things have to happen but God is with us and Bud is in His hands now and nothing can harm him.

After referencing Carl and Reverend Stolee's presence, he added:

I only wish I could have been there because it's so hard for me to say what I want to in a letter.

He finished with, "Your loving son, Conrad."

On the other side of the world, Conrad missed the catharsis which accompanies expressions of grief and commiserating with loved ones. On the other hand, his commitment to Uncle Sam kept him busy, and he was not afforded the time to think about the loss; Conrad could not grieve in the same way he would have had he served stateside.

•   •   •

Rain fell every day. Respites, even sunshine, occurred daily, as well. Hot, humid, wet. The Philippines left a lot to be desired from Conrad's point of view, though he did appreciate how hard Filipinos worked.

"Package" was all the young Filipino man said with a broken accent as he entered the large tent. The unusual aspect, at least to an outside observer, was the location of the package: on top of his head.

"Thank you, Dio," Conrad said as he watched Diasdado, with one calm motion, remove the large cardboard box from his head and set it on top of a similar box on a table. They could not place supplies on the ground with all the mud and water which slowly ate away the feet of everyone who set foot on Filipino jungle ground. "You can carry more on your head than I can in my arms," Conrad marveled. "Good night!"

"We going to get you a Christmas present," Dio's thick accent made him difficult to understand, but Conrad had adapted and he could understand the young man if his voice was not drowned out by yells and screams throughout his tent and adjoining hospitals-without-walls.

"Christmas present? Really?" Conrad asked. "Can you make it a roasted chicken, please?"

"Roasted chicken?"

"Yes, roasted chicken. I'm sick of eating this stale Army food."

"I don't know," Dio responded.

Conrad smiled and, in good nature, chased the fifteen-year-old out.

"Enema!" a doctor called out.

Conrad closed his eyes and considered various ways to get out of the task, including walking out of the tent. In a sign of his surrender, with slumping shoulders and hanging head, he ambled over to two other medics and the doctor who called out the need.

"Sorry, guys," the doctor knew his request was not a popular one. "But it needs to be done."

With a hurried pace, a Chinese nurse's aide named Tom dodged a nurse and a Filipino orderly as he approached the group. "I do it. I do enema!"

The other two medics exchanged smiles.

"Are you sure you want to do this, Tom?" The doctor smiled in amusement at the nurse's aide's enthusiasm.

With a fat smile, the small man provided an exuberant response. "Yes. Yes, please. I am happy to do enemas."

"Bed Fourteen-D. I'll be right there," the doctor ordered. As Tom bounced away, the doctor looked at his fellow countrymen. "Thank God for Tom. I didn't want one of our nurses to have to do it. Those ladies do enough around here." The doctor winked, then departed, off to ensure Tom found the correct patient.

Conrad's blue eyes bulged as he stared toward Bed Fourteen-D.

With big smiles of their own, the two medics looked at Conrad.

"What's the matter, Peterson?" asked one of the medics. "Ain't you ever seen a man who likes men?"

Conrad's brow furrowed and his expression changed from shock to bewilderment. "What?"

"You've never seen a guy who prefers boys over girls?"

408

With a slow shake of his head, Conrad answered. "Nope."

The other medic laughed. "Just remember Tom the next time you have someone who needs an enema."

The two medics went their separate ways within the tent. Conrad stood frozen and stared from over twenty yards away as he watched the doctor depart from Tom, leaving the young Chinese man to perform his task.

Conrad turned and hustled back to the patients in his assigned area.

•   •   •

In his barracks, Conrad took off his bloody socks, holding his display of pain to grimaces and barely audible moans. With splotches of skin missing below his ankles, he stuck his feet into a previously commandeered bucket. Unfortunately, the warm water did not provide immediate relief for the pain.

"Seems kinda backwards, doesn't it?" a medic and friend asked.

Conrad opened his eyes and looked at the man.

"We get this from standing in that jungle mud all day, then they tell us to soak our feet for five minutes every night."

Conrad wanted to laugh, but the pain only allowed a nod and a grimace. "My problem is, I can't ever get my boots dry." His sullen expression underscored the seriousness of the problem. Due to the humidity, the insides of his boots were damp every morning. Conrad often wondered whether they would dry in a week.

"I saw you elevating your feet last night," the soldier added. "Does it work?"

"I don't know. Maybe." Conrad shook his head again. "Doc Fey told me to take two aspirin every night.

"Doc Fey? I thought he's a dentist?"

"He is," Conrad answered. "I'm on the verge of losing three teeth and he's trying to help me out." He pondered his situation before adding, "I'd get some new boots but it'd just happen all over again."

Conrad battled through the pain and constant discomfort but had heard enough stories from the front-line men to understand he was living large compared to the many hundreds of thousands of others. The first difference was obvious: the combat soldiers lugged around their gear and M-1s in the muddy, other-worldly, intense jungles. If a Japanese soldier did not get you, a bizarre snake, spider, venomous caterpillar, crocodile, or — worst of all — mosquito would find you. Second, if any of the aforementioned inflicted a wound, infection or gangrene could finish you off.

The medics were protected under the Geneva Convention, but Japan was not a signatory. In fact, they regarded medics as legitimate and tactical targets. If they shot the man who could help a soldier continue his fight, the wounded soldier would be less likely to fight on. In many units, commanding officers ordered their aid men to wear plain helmets to present a less obvious target.

Additionally, Conrad did not have to worry about assault orders, operations orders, annex orders, or any other sort of order and instruction which was sent by General MacArthur and his upper brass. Unlike the armed fighters, Conrad did not have to

410

be told to move here or there unless the medical leaders needed to ensure full coverage for all wounded. Conrad's day was not dependent on daily orders; rather, on how well — or not — those orders were planned and executed. The general and his staff did not experience the results of a poorly planned or executed mission, but Conrad and his corps of life-givers knew full well when the plans went awry.

The screams of those shot, run through by bayonets, or clutching a body part no longer attached — thanks to a Japanese Type 97 fragmentation grenade or the newer Type 99 — lasted for but moments, yet those screams echoed for a lifetime.

As he completed the nightly task on behalf of his feet, Conrad counted his blessings. Despite being unaware of the immediate world surrounding him as he slept, he preferred nighttime slumber. The day shift suited him; the Japanese could be spotted by the camp guards. At night, Conrad felt on edge. The brave young man remained as tense as expected for a twenty-year-old whose first trip away from home culminated in the daily stench of blood and death. On the night shift, his nerves troubled him, but during the day, he forgot about the risks, at least to a reasonable degree.

•   •   •

Bare feet propped up by extra pillows, a sheet covering him from knees to waist, Conrad tried to slip into unconsciousness, but between the pain in his feet and the ache in his heart, sleep proved a challenge every night. He felt the hole which had been created on the other side of the world. It mattered little to him that he was not the only member of the

411

military to lose a brother. Such a cold rationalization did not enter Conrad's mind as he drifted off. There was only one Bud, and now there was none, except in memories.

. . .

Propitious timing marked the birth of Carl's second son. Even though the Minnesota family could not see and hold him, the knowledge of his entry into the world uplifted the family, even more so because the little one carried the name of his brave uncle.

On November 12, six weeks and four days after Bud was killed, his namesake started his life in Alameda County, California, oblivious to war, death, and destruction. By giving the baby boy the exact name as his brother, Carl displayed his love for Bud. Carl almost never showed pain or excitement; so, for him, naming his son after his deceased brother was indeed a deep display of emotions — it just did not appear that way to those not part of the family.

Proud of his son and of the opportunity to honor Bud, Carl sent a telegram from Berkeley, California, dated November 12, to his mother at her rental house at 710 America Avenue.

Dear Mother Eugene Morris arrived 130 PM Sunday weighs nearly 9 lbs. Everything under control. Ann doing nicely Love Carl.

Chapter Forty-One

Two days before Carl's son was born, the 489th Bomb Group went on its final mission, to the Frankfurt suburb of Hanau, 115 miles south of Kassel. The squadrons dropped their bombs and returned to Halesworth for the final time.

The men were given furlough in the States, then reported for duty to greet their new airplanes: Boeing B-29 Superfortresses. The war in the Pacific ended before they could leave the U.S.

·   ·   ·

It took three seconds for Hulda to understand the true meaning of the telegram, aided by the words "weighs nearly 9 lbs." But those words felt like a kick in the chest after the excitement, the confused elation, over "Eugene Morris arrived 130 PM Sunday." The excruciating pain and dark emptiness could not be overcome by the exciting news Carl had just announced: the birth of another grandchild.

Hulda was elated and jubilant, but also wounded. That three-second moment of time, which pumped up her heart, which caused her brain to overload what other areas of her brain knew to be true, felt like someone had scraped at her soul with a pick axe.

For his part, Carl had sent the typical birth announcement: "'So and so' arrived safely" and is now a member of the family. The baby's weight and, sometimes, length served to give loved-ones additional information, although to save words, and thus money, he left out frivolities.

Three seconds. An unfortunate wording. The written words cut deep. To the grieving mother, the wording did not feel like an accident.

· · ·

As leader of the Army Air Force Band, Glenn Miller received orders to go to newly-liberated Paris. However, when he boarded a UC-64A Norseman, his flight was grounded for inclement weather. Miller, the pilot, and another passenger all agreed that, despite the storm, they should go. Miller was anxious to get to the French capital, and the pilot was anxious to prove his worth so he could become a fighter pilot.

Somewhere over the English Channel, the single-engine Norseman disappeared. The great composer and entertainer Alton Glenn Miller was lost without a trace. Neither his body nor the aircraft were ever found.

· · ·

On February 15, 1945, the Army awarded Conrad two Bronze Stars for his work at Leyte. The man who did not want to be an Army "aid man" now had medals on his chest.

At the end of March, the 69th Field Hospital began the arduous task of packing up and moving out; the Army, Navy, and Marines had completed a wildly effective trouncing of the Japanese. The war was headed toward its conclusion.

American forces invading Okinawa expected heavy fighting from the moment the landing operation began. Instead, the Americans marched onto the island as though they were on a Boy Scouts field trip.

Seventy miles long and eight miles wide, Okinawa was a bigger mystery than the military brass cared to admit. A three-month bombing campaign appeared to have had success, but the military maps were inadequate. After four days of walking, the troops reached objectives expected to take two weeks of hard fighting.

The Marines went north, the Army south. What ensued from the largest Pacific Theater amphibious landing proved astounding — and astoundingly brutal. When the armada of ships eight miles wide finished unloading 500,000 men, only 100,000 were expected to survive the first two weeks without injury.

The Easter Day landing became a non-event and Operation Iceberg was underway. However, five days later, on April 6, the Divine Wind blew in, just as at Leyte. Young men and boys — some brainwashed into believing their duty lay in dying for the emperor, others chosen because they were deemed not patriotic enough and thus were ordered to sacrifice their lives — drank *sake* from a ceremonial cup, climbed aboard their Zeroes, Vals, and Judys, and died as kamikaze pilots, with the goal of taking as many Americans with them as possible.

Out at sea, 350 Japanese launched their kamikaze attacks, sinking three ships, including two destroyers, and damaging fifteen more. Conrad watched one of the planes strike a ship, which one he could not be sure, and stood in amazement. He had heard about such attacks but this was the first, and only, time he actually saw one happen.

But on land, the Americans could not find the Imperial Japanese Army.

On April 12, Franklin Delano Roosevelt passed away in Warm Springs, Georgia, with his mistress, two cousins and dog, Fala, present. The new president, a little-known politician from Independence, Missouri, became the commander-in-chief, leaving Americans wondering about the depth of the new man.

Conrad wrote home to tell his family he thought he would like the island. Rather than a mud pit, the island was more of a giant rock. The weather, he wrote, was similar to Bemidji in October.

And then they found the Japanese Imperial Army.

It did not take long for the Americans to realize the Japanese were not fighting to win, rather fighting to deter attack on the Japanese homeland.

On May 8, Victory in Europe was declared. The men in the Pacific viewed the news with relief and envy, with an extra measure of hope added in.

Okinawa became synonymous with brutality. The close-in fighting ensured the stench of death hovered over the battlefield. American and Japanese bodies — or pieces of — lay side-by-side as one side took a strategic hill only to lose it again. Some of the troops found themselves under attack for four straight weeks. At Hacksaw Ridge, Desmond Doss entered the history books by saving seventy men.

Not only were Japanese soldiers trained to never surrender, if a captured soldier was offered to the Japanese government, the government refused to take the man with the logic he was a coward for not fighting to the death. This mentality meant brutal fighting as the Americans attempted to convince enemy soldiers to surrender their caves and tunnels.

Kamikaze attacks were killing an average of thirty sailors a day. On the carrier *USS Bunker Hill (CV 17)*, 600 men were killed or injured. On the hospital ship *USS Comfort (AH 6)*, the kamikaze airplane traveled through three decks and exploded in the surgery bay, killing doctors, nurses, and patients.

Throughout the entire Okinawa campaign, 1,900 kamikaze attacks sank 26 ships and damaged another 164 — the greatest concentration of naval losses since Pearl Harbor.

Back on land, in one day, Sugar Loaf Hill changed hands eleven times between the Imperial Japanese Army and the U.S. Marines. At that hill alone, 50,000 Japanese soldiers were killed in two months.

After sending a message to Japanese General Mitsuru Ushijima that was met with derision, General Simon Bolivar Buckner, Jr., visited the front line. The son of Civil War General Simon Bolivar Buckner received advice to remove his "three star" helmet and wear a plain one, which he did. A military photographer captured the general in a photograph as he inspected the area. Minutes later, an artillery shell landed next to him and killed him.

On June 21, with his back to the sea, General Ushijima obeyed orders and lost with "honor." He plunged a sword through his spine in an act of *hara-kiri*. The Battle of Okinawa became the only battle of the war in which both top commanders were killed.

On June 22, the American flag was raised on the island, leaving only mop-up firefights. American casualties were 12,520 deaths and 36,000 wounded. Fourteen thousand fighting men encountered a malady they called the "thousand-yard stare," or what was better known at the time as "battle fatigue." The Americans counted over 100,000 Japanese bodies, although there were innumerable dead in their tunnels and caves. Additionally, out of an approximate population of 300,000 Okinawans, 100,000 civilians lost their lives. They were neither for nor against either country.

Even though 4,000 Japanese soldiers surrendered, the message was understood: American forces did not want to invade Japan. If the enemy fought that hard, and refused to surrender, at Okinawa, imagine how they would fight on their home soil.

Conrad never wrote or spoke much at all about his experiences on Okinawa.

·   ·   ·

"Dear Mom." Her children's use of the more formal "Mother" was replaced in Bud's final letter home, dated September 19, 1944 — eight days before his death. Hulda held the letter, written on onion-skin paper, as she re-read it, wishing to feel closer to him. The letter, read with vigor when it originally arrived months prior, served as the last interaction from her son.

Well, it's the same old story, I am just as slow as ever to write. It's a cloudy and damp day, just the kind for sleeping. Seems that I made use of it too. Just got up and in a few minutes I can eat dinner.

Bud did not have a lazy bone in his body, but in the Army he had learned to sleep whenever possible for as long as possible.

I feel mean that I should be asking for something every time I write but I appreciate all you do. This time I'd like to have you try and find some 616 film. It's rather a foolish request but try any way.
I'd also like a king size bottle of Vaseline hair oil. I can't get good hair oil over here. And you know what miserable hair I have.

Hulda had not purchased the film and felt a twinge of guilt. Saddened and empty, she continued reading. After commenting on the difficulties of obtaining cigarettes and sweets, he turned to family.

It sure don't seem possible that JoAnne is starting school this fall. I'd like to have seen Judy that day she got lost. She is some kid.

Bud always loved playing with his nieces, and he had been looking forward to seeing his nephews when he returned from Europe.

I haven't heard from Connie for some time but have hopes that I get one today.

Bud did not know his brother had been preparing to ship out, setting sail from the Hawaiian archipelago.

Must sign off as there is no more to write, have to go eat
any way as I'm starving.

All my love
Bud

As mothers are wont to do, Hulda had saved every letter and photo, down to the photo of Miami Beach Bud took while in his early Army days.

She could not bring herself to re-read every letter, but after reading his final communication to her, she felt no desire to continue torturing herself. She felt so close to him, yet she could only see or hear him when she closed her eyes. She had lost her husband; now, fifteen years later, a son. Her heart felt like it had a hole in it large enough to fly a B-24 through.

•　　•　　•

The bombs dropped — Little Boy, then Fat Man — and still the Japanese government did not surrender. Prime Minister Suzuki Kantaro and Emperor Hirohito determined they wanted to surrender, but militant resistance rose within the Japanese military structure. On August 15, six days after the second bomb was dropped, a coup was beaten back and Japan announced its surrender.

Surrender led to the cancelation of the November invasion of the Japanese islands. Many in the U.S. military and government believed an invasion of the militaristic nation would have cost one million American and two million Japanese lives.

The next Herculean feat for the United States military was the wholesale shut down and pack out of the war machine. The tremendous logistical undertaking of moving man and machine back to the States took many months; some men did not arrive home until 1946.

On the voyages home, medical crews received the best rooms and treatment. Going into battle for the first time, Soldiers and Marines thought they were the most important elements of a fighting unit, but once the shooting began, they quickly learned the men and women of the medical teams were the crucial cog in the military machine. After the mud, muck, cold, and heat, and the blood, guts, and screams of wounded men, Conrad and his peers welcomed the special treatment on the journey home.

• • •

The families of the *Paper Doll* crew had developed an intermittent rapport in the summer of 1944. They organized care packages and displayed some degree of coordination with their overseas mailings.

Julian Sund, brother of navigator Lieutenant Gilman Sund, exchanged information about the crash with Hulda and other family members. A Sergeant Callahan of the 489th Bomb Group had written Hulda, who in turn wrote other crew family members, thus informing everyone of the peculiar and sad way the men perished.

Sund's widow, Ann, remained in Boise when she was not spending time with Sund's Wisconsin family. She suffered through the agonizing hope the news was mistaken and the crew had indeed survived.

   •   •   •

While on Okinawa, Conrad had learned of the death of a friend from Puposky. Private First Class Russell Grande, an infantryman who had earned a Bronze Star, was killed on November 28, 1944, in the Philippines. He was buried at an American cemetery in Manilla. Though his family moved multiple times, Grande lived in Puposky for a number of years.

After he returned home, Conrad learned of the death of another boyhood friend. Fireman First Class Clifford Bernard Pearson lost his life when *USS LST 577* took a torpedo from a Japanese submarine and quickly sank. Pearson was one of 100 men who were reported as "missing" and subsequently listed as "Killed in Action."

From little Puposky, population 288, four men lost their lives in the war: Sonny Martin, Russel Grande, Cliff Pearson, and Eugene Morris "Bud" Peterson. The pain of war raced through the shrinking town, through Our Redeemer's Lutheran Church, across the farms, and through the hearts of every area resident.

   •   •   •

Even after she married, Chrissy Anderson stayed in touch with Hulda, until the tides of time eventually washed away the link between the two women who never met.

   •   •   •

For the Petersons, words could not convey the relief felt when Conrad arrived safely in Bemidji. For Conrad, it was his first opportunity to grieve with family members, so Bud's passing remained a sharp, painful subject. Of course, the pain would fade but never depart. Just as it had with William, the hole in the collective heart of the Peterson clan caused by Bud's death became another defining element of the family's identity.

Chapter Forty-Two

The baby blue Ford Granada rolled onward, toward the magnificent setting desert Sun. The few stops and vast emptiness along the way made the drive feel like they were plodding across a foreign planet.

As they approached Reno, Nevada, Carl felt spent. Feelings were not to be discussed — they were private; they were his own. This moment was no different than any other. Throughout the day's drive, Carl regaled his wife with stories she either had forgotten or never known. At other times, Carl ceased speaking and allowed his mind to swim in the sea of memories.

Hours prior, after their gas station incident in Salt Lake City, they had crossed the border from Utah to Nevada, unaware of how close they were to an important location in Bud's life — Wendover Field.

When Carl made his first trip to California, riding the trains, he left his wife behind with one small child. Now, in 1976, their two sons and two daughters were adults, with their own families, living in the San Francisco Bay area and the Kansas City area.

Hulda had passed away eight years prior. Conrad had married and his wife, Margaret, gave him two daughters. And Bud — Bud never received the opportunity to become the man he was destined to be. Four-hundred-fifteen-thousand Americans, including Carl's brother, never came home from the war.

His thoughts traveled to Hulda, specifically the misunderstanding of the birth announcement — so minor yet so painful to her. Of course, he had not intended for it to cause harm; the announcement was standard. On the other hand, his relationship with his mother had proceeded as expected: they were two people so much alike that incidents of butting heads were not surprising.

Bud had received the Air Medal for bravery and the Bronze Oak Leaf Cluster — both of which were awarded after serving on a requisite number of missions — and, posthumously, he received the Purple Heart. Like Conrad, Bud was decorated for his service, which added fondness to the memories of their service to the country.

Carl turned the Ford into the parking lot of a small motel on the outskirts of Reno. Tired and hungry, the time had come for the couple to get out of the car again, stretch their legs, and acquire food and rest. Tomorrow they would be back home, in Clear Lake, California.

After the Ford came to a stop, he shut off the ignition and the couple exited, where they rejoined on the small sidewalk in front of the motel. As they walked, Anne reached up and, with gentle pressure, touched his shoulder. "Carl." It was the only word she spoke.

With a grimace, fighting back emotions, but on the edge of a smile, Carl turned to his wife of thirty-seven years. "Well, life keeps going." His smile grew. He thought of the setbacks and the treasured moments, the tragedies and successes. He understood the memories which surfaced due to the acquisition of a lone, autographed dollar bill was just a snippet of what made the Peterson clan who they were.

"Maybe over dinner," Carl said as the couple neared the motel door. "I'll tell you a few stories you've never heard about my father. You know how interesting he was." He held the door open for his bride and they disappeared into the small motel's lobby.

Afterword

The powerful, emotional impact on the Peterson clan caused by the loss of Bud, as would be expected, lasted for years. Bud possessed an affable personality closer to that of his sister, Elsie. The Petersons lost an effusive, energetic family member when Bud was killed. That same shock, sadness, and soul-wrenching pain was repeated throughout our nation over four-hundred-thousand times with other families.

As has been said by others, Time does not heal all wounds, you just learn to live with the pain better.

Eugene Morris "Bud" Peterson is buried in Cambridge American Cemetery and Memorial, outside Cambridge, England.

Hulda lived to become a great-grandmother. While adored by her family, she epitomized the tough, strong-willed Petersons of which she was the matriarch. I never met her; I was two years old when she passed away.

By piecing together Hulda's life, I realized she was a different person during the timeframe which encompasses this story. In her younger days, she was an impish, fun-loving prankster who made people laugh. She returned to that delightful personality over time as callouses covered her emotional wounds. She not only endured the loss of her son Bud, but that of a dear friend, my other paternal great-grandmother, Gertrude (Strand) Graham. Friends were losing sons overseas, as well, adding to the gloom and pain.

I talked to several people who knew Hulda, including Wendell Knutson and Hulda's nephew, Bob Gustafson — Hap and Violet's sixth child. Everyone, family and otherwise, knew of her premonitions, whether or not they witnessed them. Additionally, people regarded her highly.

True to form, in early 1968, she wrote a card to her pregnant granddaughter Valrae, Thelma and Ray's eldest daughter. In the note, she wrote that Val would give birth to a boy, but Hulda would not live to see the baby. Wesley Ward Caple was born three weeks late, on March 26, 1968. Hulda Josephine Peterson passed away on March 2, 1968 — the date Wesley was due to be born. Hulda had slipped in one last premonition before going to meet her Savior.

When Carl built a house for his family in the early 1950s, in El Sobrante, California, he did everything: framing, drywall, electrical, plumbing, roofing — even surveying the property. A great amount of his knowledge came from Hap's teaching.

Carl lived out his life with Anne until passing away November 28, 1984. My grandfather was a man of few words and lacked patience around children, which meant I did not really get to know him until I matured. While I was around him a number of times through the years, including the 1976 visit from which they were returning home, depicted at the beginning of the novel, I did not have meaningful conversations with him until a 1983 family visit to my grandparents' Clear Lake, California, home and his trip east to attend my high school graduation in May of 1984. On Halloween of 1984, from my college dorm, I called and spoke with my grandparents — the occasion was Anne's 67th birthday.

Typical of Carl, he rarely spoke and chose to listen throughout my conversation with my grandmother. Then, late in the call, when he learned that I had given up on baseball, he chided me with the words, "Don't ever give up. If it's your dream, then work harder." I knew I wasn't a good enough ballplayer to be successful, but I think back to that phone call from time to time and apply those words to my writing projects — this is my fourth published novel.

The man who was, both mentally and physically, perhaps the toughest man I've ever known, passed away less than a month later. His eldest daughter, Carla, awakened in the middle of the night and insisted that her husband, Wayne Frazier, drive her to Clear Lake from Clayton — no time to use the phone, she said. On what sounded like a wild whim, they raced to Clear Lake and arrived as the EMTs were about to load Carl into the ambulance. He would never return home. Carl August Peterson had 10 grandchildren and four great-grandchildren when he died.

All four of Carl and Anne's children survive: Carla Ann (1940); James William (1943; my father); Eugene Morris (1944); and Sandy Jean (1950). My delightful grandmother, Anna Marie Peterson, passed away in 1999.

Conrad overcame his odd but comical fear of young women and married Margaret. They settled in the Atlanta area, where he worked for the U.S. Postal Service until retirement. His daughter Carol Kay (1960-2004) passed away as an adult, and his daughter Cheryl Lynn (1961) is the only surviving member of the family.

Uncle Connie told me stories of being in the Philippines and Okinawa, though he did not speak much of the latter, from which I was able to gain a clearer picture of his military service. A kind, soft-spoken man, he kept himself under control no matter the circumstances. Where his brothers would have reacted with swift firmness — or ferocity — Conrad would quietly shake his head and walk away.

When my father was ten years old, Conrad gave him a model airplane — a Korean-War-era jet — which Conrad had taken great care and effort to assemble. The moment he received the gift, my dad went into the backyard, attached two strings to the plane, poured lighter fluid on it, lit it, and began spinning his body, flying the plane in circles as it burned. Conrad watched for a moment, then shook his head and walked away.

And that epitomizes Uncle Conrad... and my father epitomizes most of the rest of the Peterson clan.

Two years before his death, Conrad wanted to see Puposky and Bemidji one last time, so his daughter Cheryl, my dad, and a family friend accompanied him to northern Minnesota. Our family reunion included relatives who reside in Norway, and I met relatives whom I had not known previously or knew they even existed. The family presented Uncle Connie with a "Quilt of Valor" for his military service which my wife, Mindy, made. We all cried some, laughed plenty, and celebrated the last of the five siblings of William and Hulda. Conrad Gilmore Peterson passed away on November 7, 2017, at age 93. Few people in life are as likeable as Conrad.

While this book focused on the three brothers, it is certainly worth mentioning my great-aunts, Thelma and Elsie. Both were intelligent; Elsie had a sharp, humorous wit and florid writing style. She possessed a playfulness — a trait which she shared with other family members, including her mother — yet reached a level of vivacity which set her apart from her siblings. I was a little kid when around her, so I never knew her well, but reading her letters to her brothers gave me a strong sense of her wit.

With Jake, Elsie had four children: Joanne Margaret (1938-1994); Judith Arlene (1941); Dennis William (1943); and Joel Dennis (1947). Dennis was the infant who died ten hours after birth. Elsie Mercedes Buzick lived from 1918 to 2001.

Thelma was good-natured, and I remember her as a loveable lady who wanted everyone around her to be happy. Through her letters and what I learned through other letters and investigation, she was a woman worn down by life, with numerous health problems; but, as with her sister, I only spent a limited time with her in my childhood. Her eldest daughter, Valrae Annette (1938), was the eldest of her generation in the family. She was followed by Beverly Ann (1939); Delbert Arlyn (1944-2010); Marlys Erlyn (1945); and Douglas Morris (1952-2009). Thelma Alvina Beckstrand lived from 1913 to 2002.

The family fathered by William Peterson was a typical, "average, everyday" American family, with successes, failures, joy, pain, and love. They had admirable traits and strengths, and they wore their shortcomings and emotions "on their sleeves." On the one hand, the extended Peterson family is no different than millions of other families throughout the American centuries. Yet, that same family is part of the fabric that binds together the American experience: immigrants from Norway, Sweden, and Denmark, who worked the soil, sweated and strained to build homes, families, and lives. They ground their fingers to the bone to reach beyond mere existence to obtain comfort and happiness.

The main characters of this true story are deceased, but their progenies live on, creating new stories — some equally as difficult to believe. But whatever is accomplished by this family, they owe it, in part, to the lives and opportunities Hulda created through her faith, sheer force of will, and incessant hard work, for it was Hulda Peterson who had to endure in order to nurture her five offspring through difficult circumstances, against the odds. She taught all of the Petersons how to live, including those of us who never knew her personally. In a way, this book was her story.

Acknowledgments

Almost nothing intimidates me but writing this novel did just that; I began working on this project over 20 years ago. I had to be accurate given that I decreed this a true story. I also had the concern that, if I did not execute this story properly, the general, non-family audience would not find the story entertaining.

And I had to do a ton of research. For a fiction novel, research consists of making sure I name part of a boat correctly or describe a '54 Ford adequately. This was like David McCullough researching Truman. Well, not quite, but you get the idea.

Marlys Hanson, daughter of Thelma, made this book possible when she gave me a box full of letters — a true treasure for me — while I was in Minnesota for the family reunion referenced in the Afterword. After reading and taking notes on over 300 letters — between Hulda, Bud, and Conrad, with a few letters from Carl, Thelma, Elsie, and others — I learned a plethora of information about the family. When she was in school, Marlys wrote a short story about Hulda, to which I also referred. If I wrote for ten pages about the importance of Marlys' contribution to this book, that would still not suffice.

Val Wolf, Thelma's eldest daughter, provided enriching information about Hulda which allowed me to paint her with depth and character. Having information such as what Hulda liked to bake or grow in her garden meant I did not have to fictionalize minor details about her, and she provided additional information about the man who showed interest in Hulda after William's death.

Michael Peterson, my first-cousin and the eldest son of the Eugene Morris Peterson born in 1944, has completed a lot of research into the Peterson, Gustafson, Christensen, and Strand "family trees." I was able to tap into some of his prior research for birthdates and other information. My Uncle Eugene also provided information about his father, Carl, which I appreciated.

Dan Knaus edited my prior novel and this one. His military background helped immensely, and any mistakes in the text of the novel are mine. I appreciated Dan's input and expertise. He also made a tremendous contribution to getting the in-flight conversations true-to-life.

I was able to track down Tami Auchter online in hopes of gaining a little information about her first-cousin-once-removed, Richard Auchter, who was from Puposky and served in WWII. What I got instead was a gold mine. She put me in touch with her godfather, a lifelong Puposky resident who remembered from his childhood both of my paternal great-grandmothers, Hulda and Gertrude. Wendell Knutson's knowledge of Puposky helped me beyond description. It was not until perhaps our third phone conversation we discovered one of his good friends many years ago was my great-uncle, Leroy Graham (Anne's half-brother). Like my family, Wendell's family also populates the tiny cemetery at Our Redeemer's Lutheran Church in Puposky.

Cara Edwards, the niece of Sonny Martin, helped me with information about the Martin family. It was obvious from family letters that the Petersons (and perhaps Gustafsons) were close to the Martins, but without Cara, I would have known very little about their family.

My third-cousin, Melissa Swor, whom I did not previously know, gave me information about extended family and directed me to Bob Gustafson, the sixth child of Hap and Violet. That led to Bob becoming an important source about his father. If not for Bob, I would not have been able to provide depth about Uncle Hap. It was a pleasure speaking with Melissa and Bob.

Duke Sumonia, who passed away in 2015, provided my father and me with information about the *Paper Doll* crew, and he utilized an army (no pun intended) of veterans who proved invaluable. He faithfully and repeatedly contacted his sources in order to answer our many questions. Mr. Sumonia was the second step in the chain of events which culminated in the publication of this book. My parents' former neighbor, Hubert Chartrand (1926-2001), a former Army mapmaker and WWII vet, put my father in touch with Mr. Sumonia, who put him in touch with Charles Freudenthal of the 489th, which led to contact with Captain Robert Gast and others. Freudenthal wrote a book about and edited a bi-monthly newsletter for the 489th, which retold war stories and kept the men in touch with each other. Those newsletters were incredibly helpful to me.

Cheryl Peterson's southern charm makes her a delight to speak with and she possesses a unique perspective of her father, Conrad. After the letters, the best documents I had to help the story along were Bud's flight records, which Cheryl sent to me. The flight records informed me of not only when Bud went on missions, but that two of his flights were not on *Paper Doll*. When a soldier does not come home from war, there is no way of knowing what happened unless he kept a diary, which Bud did not. Their letters were censored — illuminating information could not be written in letters; thus, Bud's flight records were invaluable.

Dick and Darlene Pearson kindly invited me into their home and told me about Dick's brother, Clifford Pearson, who lost his life on LST 577 when it was hit by a Japanese submarine's torpedo. As with everyone else in Puposky, the Pearsons knew my family well.

Steve Nagle was my beer man, knowing which beers were popular in various regions of the country. He found several people on the internet for me and provided newspaper front pages. For example, when Bud and Conrad walked around Salt Lake City and encountered a newspaper, thanks to Steve, I knew what that front page looked like.

Melinda Patrick designed my cover art (for all four of my novels, actually) and helped me get this into print. She designed, and now updates, my website and makes me look pert near smart. I can never praise and thank her enough for all the ways she has helped me.

My father, Jim Peterson, son of Carl, more than anyone is the reason why this book made it into print. He requested, cajoled, pushed, and drove me crazy until I said "yes, I will write the story." Then he wanted to know when — every time I spoke to him over the phone or in person. For years. Finally, I told him it would become my fourth novel and he left me alone.

My father did a lot of the initial research, learning who the people were on the Short Snorter, gathering information about the crash, etc. He spoke to Captain Robert Gast (as did I) and gained insight into the crash and where *Paper Doll* traveled before England. My father wrote a brief history of Bud's time in the 489th, to which I repeatedly referred to ensure I had my

436

timeline straight. He had a lot of information and helped answer my questions countless times. He was also an important source for me — though not the only one — about my grandfather Carl.

People tell me I should write a book about my father, but if you think people had trouble believing some of the things in this story, give it up when it comes to some of the crazy things that happened to him (hint: most were his fault).

My wife, Mindy, always has to deal with a husband who sequesters himself to write. She looked up a lot of information for me throughout my research and writing and is always willing to help. When I say "a lot of information," that does not do justice to how much she helped with this book.

To everyone listed above, I thank you from the bottom of my heart. To members of the extended Peterson and Gustafson families, this book is for you.

William Peterson, 1914; Hulda in the background holding Thelma.

Hulda Gustafson, age 14, less than four years before she married William Peterson.

Carl Peterson, age 19, at a Civilian Conservation Corps camp; he wrote on the back of the photo, "Just sunning myself at Noon."

Eugene "Bud" Peterson, in Bemidji while on leave, 1943.

Conrad Peterson, August 1944, in Hawaii not long before shipping out to Leyte.

Carl Peterson and Anne Christensen on their wedding day, May 1939.

Chrissy Anderson, photo likely taken after Bud was killed.

Officers with the cardboard cutout of the "paper doll," L-R, bombardier Andy Goshtoian, pilot Robert Gast, navigator Gilman Sund, and co-pilot Robert Savage.

L-R, Front: Gilman Sund, Frank Fulks, Andy Goshtoian, Robert Savage, Robert Clendenning;
L-R, Back: Donald Holbert, Eugene "Bud" Peterson, Fred Stodtmeister, Lige McIntosh. (not pictured, Alfred Lane)

Appendix A
The Unbelievable Can Be True

I realize this is not a "normal" novel: it is not fiction; it purports stories that are unbelievable, yet they are indeed true; and it contains appendices and photographs.

I normally write fiction, so this is a story which I initially resisted but had to write; it was too intriguing. The family events which unfolded should not be lost when my father's generation passes. The trick was to weave together disparate family stories into one compelling tale. Had I written this story in documentary/historical book form, the appeal would have been limited to the Peterson and Gustafson descendants (and to some degree, Christensen and Strand). Writing the story as a novel broadened the appeal.

Before I decided that I would indeed write the book, I determined it must be a true story, not "based on a true story." To do otherwise would devalue the legitimacy of Hulda's premonitions and the episode which started the chain of events 45 years ago, which culminated in the publication of this book: the discovery of the silver certificate (dollar bill) with Bud's name on it, in his handwriting.

As I started this project, I knew there would be interesting aspects: my grandfather Carl's story; the story behind *Paper Doll* and the life of a great-uncle I never knew; three brothers coming of age during the Great Depression, with two going off to war and one badly wanting to do so; the mother, worried sick, with two sons overseas. This was a family, and like most people of their time, a family which did not travel or live in the manner so many people travel and live today. Thelma was

447

born the year after the Titanic sank and Carl was born before the U.S. entered World War I; it was a different time.

Lots and lots of research was involved, including reading letters between family members and interviewing various people. At times, it was fun, such as when I learned from her letter to Bud that Chrissy, to quote her, "... what if I hadn't blurted out about me envying the girl that finally got you ...?" Or when I was reading reports in the letters about my newborn father. Other times, it was sad, such as Chrissy expressing her increasing fear about Bud's safety, while the contemporary reader knows what was about to happen. Still other times, it was painful, such as reading the letters when Conrad and Hulda were trying to be strong for each other or when Aunt Elsie lost her baby (that was a *really* sad letter).

The letters were invaluable; I learned about many stories — many of which I used — such as Bud's little adventure in Miami, passing through a lady's house during war games. I also learned of their attitudes and opinions.

Then there was the little matter of my great-grandmother Hulda's premonitions. Yes, she really had them — a lot of them. Routinely. Appendix B is the word-for-word description she herself wrote the morning after the dreams. Thanks to Thelma's daughter, Marlys, I have that piece of paper.

As I referenced in the story, her sons marveled at how she knew things, from when in the Army they would be almost out of stationery and she would send a package of writing material (referenced in a letter) to when they were about to have a visitor at their residence. Conrad told me the story about his mother suddenly rising out of her chair in her Bemidji rental, opening the front door, hearing the train whistle, then announcing that her mother, Grandma Thompson, was on that train. He did not tell me the year, so I squeezed it into this story.

I found it quite interesting she told Bud he would probably be going to North Dakota. No one possessed this knowledge, and why would she say it? That's just how things happened with her around.

Conrad told me the train/pot of coffee story with a chuckle, understanding this was simply standard procedure for his mother.

Conrad told me a story which I did not use, mainly because I did not have any place to fit it in, and I had already used the train/coffee story. Conrad was driving with Hulda as his passenger. They were lost in the Red Lake area — Upper or Lower, I do not know. Hulda announced, "Turn here!" multiple times. She was lost, too, yet she gave directions. After driving the roads in the night, she declared to Conrad, "Go down that driveway" — pointing to a long driveway of a country house. He dutifully followed orders. Hulda then got out of the car, knocked on the door, and the man who answered was an old friend of hers. They had not seen each other in years, and Hulda had no way of knowing the man lived there — besides, they were lost. That was my great-grandmother. The lost woman directed her driver to a friend.

Conrad told me of the incident with the Chinese orderly named Tom, and I had to include that story — couldn't resist. He also told me of treating men with trench foot while he himself suffered from the same malady. I was fascinated when he told me about the Kamikaze attack — one plane is all he mentioned — which occurred with him on the shore at Okinawa.

It is important to highlight the story of Donald Holbert's fiancé. Eileen's brother wrote a brief submission for a 489th Bomb Group newsletter and detailed exactly as I describe it, down to the severed foot, although in reality he accompanied the young ladies. Unfortunately, my copy of that particular newsletter was incomplete and did not include attribution, so I do not know the name of the brother who submitted the story (thus I left him out) or Eileen's last name. Jill was the actual name of her friend, as well.

Some of the stories, including the Silver Certificate "Short Snorter" episode, sound too wild to be true, but welcome to my family. By the way, I considered using "Short Snorter" in the title of this book, but uh, yeah. You can see why I didn't. People looking for cocaine stories might buy it.

The "Short Snorter" episode, when my grandmother, Anne, was given the dollar bill as change for a purchase, by itself is too wildly, mathematically unlikely to be true. But it did happen. My father, Jim Peterson, has the dollar bill, given to him by his parents. My grandparents told him about what had happened, then brought it to him on their next trip to Missouri.

Actually, the toughest story for me to believe was neither the discovery of the short snorter nor the premonitions; I *know* they are true and I knew about them going into this project. It was the Army not getting mad at Bud for going into the Miami lady's house that blew my mind.

The unlikely, wildly almost-impossible events which took place in my family was another reason why this story was intimidating to write. The story is true, but I understand as a rational, reasonable person, it is difficult to believe. I'm just used to "the unbelievable." I don't know how all the other branches

450

of Petersons around the world turned out, but my branch is interesting, to say the least.

This odd ability to foresee — or at least get a feel for — future events has touched multiple people in the Peterson clan. Carla — Carl and Anne's first child — as a young girl calmly explained in detail to her brother, Jim, that a stopped car at a nearby stoplight was going to turn right (no right turn on red in those days; and the car could have gone straight), pull to the curb in front of them, stop, back up, then collide with the car which was parked nearby. So, as the sister and brother sat on a bus bench, the car did exactly as Carla predicted. When Jim asked her how she knew it would happen, she simply replied, "I don't know. I just said it."

Conrad's daughter Carol, who is now deceased, possessed an odd propensity which I share. I call it a "watered-down" version of Hulda's premonitions; my wife calls it "doing a Brian." Carol did and I still say things which happen seconds later or at the exact moment. They are unpredictable but minor in scope, yet odd, nevertheless. They are coincidences yet occur far too frequently to be labeled with such a cavalier classification. I think most people do these types of things, but with me, it's almost regular, several times a week, sometimes multiple times a day.

For example, I will wake up with a person on my mind — someone with whom I have not communicated in a long time, sometimes years — then later in the day I will get an email from that person or see someone with the same name (different person) on television. In a vacuum, as a single incident, it's nothing more than a comical coincidence, yet I (and Carol, years ago) do it over and over and over.

The best example to which I refer happened while I was in the middle of writing this book. I saw something happen which I had never before seen: a car in the fast lane of an interstate darted at a sharp angle from the fast lane, crossed four lanes and a gore point, then completed a hasty exit from the roadway, up the exit ramp. Weeks passed until my wife was with me as I drove the same stretch of roadway — I only drive through this particular area three or four times a month, at most. As I neared the location, I pointed toward the windshield and described the crazy driver from weeks before. As I did, a car seemed to follow my finger and completed the same — exactly the same — maneuver at the same off-ramp as I described it — at the exact moment I described it, as though I were providing play-by-play and guiding the reckless driver. I had never seen it happen ever, but then it happened for a second time at the precise moment I uttered the description.

I understand "doing a Brian" is nothing in scope compared to Hulda, but it is a bit odd.

So, yes, the dream of Bud calling out to her really happened, as well as the subsequent three dreams of her telling her family members. Because of the time difference between Bemidji and Great Britain, it does not appear Bud's plane crash and her dreams were simultaneous. I cannot prove that, but it does appear to be quite unlikely she would have gone back to bed and had three more dreams, waking up each time, after he was killed, given that he was killed at 5:35 a.m., Central Time (Minnesota was years away from adopting Daylight Savings Time, but Great Britain had already adopted it). Given the timing, the odds, and what I know of her, I'm going with Hulda's dreams coming first. The timing doesn't make sense, otherwise.

452

I do not know who Hulda told first about her series of four dreams and whether she told anyone the same day; however, I wanted the dreams to be in the story, and I did not want the dreams to be revealed first or the (non-family) reader would know what is coming. Given that, in her dreams, the first person she tells is Thelma, it made the most sense to write it that way. For all I know, Hulda could have told her daughters days later. Since it does not matter (in terms of understanding what the family experienced), I let the reader know of the dreams after the air collision took place.

The odd events of the Peterson family are more than mere lore. The proof is in the dollar bill we possess and the contemporary description Hulda wrote of her dreams: she told family members about her dreams many days before the family knew Bud had been killed.

I don't know how to explain it so all I can do is try. It took me an entire novel to explain just a few members of my family.

Appendix B
Hulda's Four Dreams

The following is word-for-word what Hulda wrote on a single sheet of paper the morning of September 27, 1944. Only spelling has been corrected; punctuation errors remain. I did add a word, which is in parentheses. Her letters were not this poorly written, so I have to believe she was an emotional wreck when she wrote this.

This is the 27th day of Sept. 1944 And on this date I had a dream so real, that I can not get it (out) of my mind, I am still so upset but can't help put it on paper.

In my dream I saw Bud all torn and bleeding, but first I heard his voice calling me from far away later I dreamed I was reading a wire telling me he had been killed in action.

I awoke and for some time lay thinking of my dream. I slept again dreaming I told my dream to Thelma. again I awoke and again dreamed I told it over to Elsie it happened again a third time, in telling it to my mother

I awoke this morning so upset and nervous, and a feeling of a terrible dread, it's hard to keep from screaming.

_____ *Hulda*

454

At the bottom of the page, she added the following, 16 days later:

Friday 13, Oct 1944
Tonight, my dream was explained a wire came telling me. Bud was killed in action on the 27th of Sept.

Appendix C
Names on the Short Snorter (as written on the silver certificate)

Short Snorter E.M. Peterson
F.O. Andy Goshtoian
C.O. Joe Parker
Sgt. W.H. Stodtmeister
Sgt. A.G. Lane
Sgt. L. McIntosh
Sgt. W.E. Lowther
Sgt. Thomas F. O'Brien

As referenced in the novel, it was dated 4-30-44 in Bud's handwriting, followed by:

Fortaleza, Brazil

All names were signatures except Bud's, which was printed.

Appendix D
The Men of *Paper Doll* and *Special Delivery II*
at the Time of the Crash

Paper Doll
Lt. Frank Fulks, Pilot
Lt. Robert Savage, Co-Pilot
Lt. Robert Clendinning, Navigator
Lt. Gilbert L. Sund, Navigator
Lt. Andrew Goshtoian, Bombardier
S/Sgt. Donald Holbert, Radio Operator
S/Sgt. Eugene Peterson, Gunner
S/Sgt. Lige McIntosh, Gunner
T/Sgt. Fred Stodtmeister, Gunner
Sgt. Alfred Lane, Gunner

Special Delivery II
Lt. Lawrence P. Culkin, Pilot
Lt. John F. Tankersley, Co-Pilot
Lt. Robert Ellis, Navigator
Lt. Chester Poole, Bombardier
S/Sgt. Vernon Coxon, Gunner
Sgt. Sidney Ableson, Radio Operator
Sgt. Frank Bender, Gunner
Sgt. Robert McClain, Gunner
Sgt. Ralph Winter, Gunner
Pvt. James Grimes,
Gunner

Tidbits for the Family

As an author and the eldest son of the eldest son, I felt a responsibility to ensure this story was published. With that duty came the desire to write the story as accurately as possible. While I cannot go through the entire novel and point out here what actually happened versus facts expressed in a different setting (i.e., information from a letter which I turned into a dinner conversation), I can tell you I did not invent anything about our family members' character, history, or important incidents. The only aspects of this novel which are not known to be true are minor conversations (i.e., about the desire — or not — to meet Glenn Miller, or that Donald Holbert said he'd wait to get himself a girlfriend after returning from the war). In fictionalized dialogue, I stuck with what Bud (and frankly, most of the rest of the family) was like; i.e., meeting someone famous was not high on his list. It's "creative non-fiction" because the story had to be carried somehow or this would be a documentary — a history book; no one but family and maybe five historians would read that.

I was careful with the portrayal of Frank Fulks. I'm sure if his family were to read this they would be unhappy, but I spoke with men of the 489th Bomb Group who knew Fulks and knew of his behavior, and I stand with confidence that my portrayal of him was accurate. I spoke with John Lamar, who transferred from *Special Delivery II* in time to stay alive, at length about his and Homer Haile's opinions about the cocky pilot. Haile, whom I did not meet (he passed away before I attended a reunion), was quite outspoken in his opinions of Fulks. One interesting item is that Fulks' entire crew opposed

458

flying with him; that is remarkable, considering at least three were officers. I took their accounts seriously, with multiple people telling me the same thing about the crash and Fulks.

I do not know exactly what Fulks did to infuriate the crew of *Paper Doll*, but according to Captain Gast, the entire crew came to him just before their crash, enraged. Given his habits, I used the pre-crash incident as a foreshadowing of the actual crash. The odds are pretty good that I am right: Fulks did *something*, the *Paper Doll* crew begged to get rid of him, and then they were killed. I used the accident report, which included witness statements, in my description, then added information provided in my interviews with the men of the 489th.

Four-Eighty-Ninth veteran Charles Freudenthal told me to trust the military report, which assessed 65% blame to Fulks and 35% to Culkin, but everyone else said "no; the report is wrong," and then would explain why. Mickey Baskin told me the crash was a frequent topic until the 489th left England two months later.

I believe the reason why some of the firsthand reports which referenced Culkin crowding Fulks or moving toward him was the result of not seeing the entire set of events. *Special Delivery II* did indeed move, out of control, into *Paper Doll*, but from other descriptions it appears at least a couple of witnesses did not notice the crash until the second contact was about to occur. Their eyes were drawn to the unusual movement but did not witness the incident until after contact by *Paper Doll* caused Culkin to lose control of *Special Delivery II*. In other words, at least a couple of the official witnesses saw the accident after the string of events began.

The conversation between Fulks and Ground Crew Armorer Neville Dortch, about scraping an "X" on the field, came from Charles Freudenthal's "A History of The 489th Bomb Group," in which he quotes Dortch. I relayed the conversation as reported. This conversation confirms the attitude Fulks had, as conveyed to me by some of the men of the 489th.

A word about details: I could spell out how much research I did, but it would sound like I was patting myself on the back (or crying!), but that's not my intent. Just so you know how I came up with specific information, here is an example. Bud wrote in a letter that he walked from Bemidji to Puposky to check on Anne and Carla in -20F weather. (I verified it was really that cold. Yikes!) I knew within a narrow date-range when that walk occurred, looked up the weather in Bemidji for the possible dates, and narrowed it down to two days: either January 4th or 6th, 1943. Both days experienced similar conditions and the snow depths were the same, so I went with the Monday over the Wednesday — the day was immaterial to the story, but I did not want to use January 3rd or 5th, when it was 15 degrees "warmer" (oh boy!). Unless someone chose to dig through the records to prove me wrong, no one would know the difference if I had used the 3rd or 5th — but I would know. I did not wish to make things up, and I was flat-out amazed that Bud took that trip, on foot the entire way; most people wouldn't have gone out in those conditions while in a car.

When I referenced what was in newspapers, it was because, thanks to someone I know and subsequently thank in the Acknowledgements, I saw a digital copy of what the newspaper front page looked like for the date in question.

I do not know that Bud visited the Bemidji Pioneer and the Army recruiter on the same day, but I do know, because of his telling of the stories in letters, those events happened within a brief period. Bud was calm, rather quiet, and fairly patient — unless you made him mad.

Something that really helped me was when the letter writers referenced what was going on around them, such as Uncle Connie listening to an FDR fireside chat. I was able to find that speech based on the date, then intercut Conrad's words with FDR's. It's legit; he wrote his letter while listening to FDR.

Here are a few other important matters for the family:

- The man interested in a relationship with Hulda a year after William's death was not portrayed because I knew almost nothing about him, other than he was interested in her before she married William.
- A man proposed marriage to Hulda while the boys were overseas, but I did not know who he was and thus left the episode out of the story. Bud thought it was funny the man proposed, so I knew it was not a serious relationship — or perhaps even a relationship at all.
- Because I knew nothing (except the man's name) about the family in the Gaylord, Minnesota, area which employed Hulda, I changed their names. The man's real name was Dalton Plantz. The only things I could gather from letters was that Hulda was a nanny for two little blonde girls, and Plantz had a lot of money and lived in a fantastic house; no other names were changed in the novel. Plantz also offered Bud a job not long before he entered the Army; Bud declined the offer because he knew the Army would soon call him to duty.

- Bud was not necessarily friends with every member of the 489th Bomb Group I reference, but because I met and spoke with them, learning so much, I found a way to include them in this book. I needed more characters, so why not use the men who were actually there? For example, Mickey Baskin, whom I found to be a delightful man, only knew who Uncle Bud was and had met him — he did not know him well. With the exception of Sulo Landela, who was Bud's Army friend in Miami Beach, I did not know the names of Bud's Army friends outside of *Paper Doll*. It did appear all the men of the 846th, to which Bud belonged, and 847th squadrons would have known each other well.
- I never found out why Bud hated or left the Navy. Sixteen days is even less than my dad's naval career (7 weeks; they learned he was a sleepwalker). Bud's "Certificate of Discharge" states he left the Great Lakes Naval Training Station by recommendation of a Navy medical board. He was officially discharged on September 18, 1942; two years and nine days prior to his death. Because Bud had knee problems, referenced in the novel, I suspect it's why he was discharged. I know that his friend in North Dakota — Stanley — was a factor in entering the Navy. When I applied for Bud's Naval records, I was told it would take a while due to the pandemic. After over a year, I still have not received the information. It was from the Navy discharge papers I possess that I learned Bud was not six-feet tall like his brothers, rather 5'8¾" and weighed 150 pounds (but remember, that's before he gained weight eating Army food). His height surprised me. From what I gather from the Army veterans with whom I spoke, he likely would not have fit into the B-24's ball turret had he been six-feet tall.

462

- When Uncle Connie told me the train whistle story, he did not tell me when it happened, and I did not think to ask. I decided to include it in the story, even though it may have happened after the events described in this novel. I wanted something that captured Hulda's odd ability — an ability which everyone who knew her knew she possessed. Val witnessed a similar event, in which Hulda put a cake in the oven because she foresaw someone coming to visit. Sure enough, they had "unexpected" company not long later. Val also told me Hulda put an egg in her coffee grounds, apparently a "Swedish thing."

- Much of the dialogue was based on letters. An example is the dinner incident with Ray and Bud. I know from one of Bud's letters that the conversation took place — almost certainly in greater detail than I describe — but I limited it to what I knew. As previously referenced, I did not wish to "create" the personality traits of our family members, so I was portraying my Uncle Ray accurately.

- While Hulda's relationships with her mother and eldest son were similar, she maintained frequent and positive contact with Carl and his family. In later years, Hulda did speak about her mildly strained relationship with Carl, as did Carl.

- It was clear, including from Carl himself, that his life may have been entirely different if not for Uncle Hap. I was not able to peg exactly how long he lived with Hap and his family, but it appears to have been close to three years. Of course, when I finally got to know my grandfather when I became an older teenager, I had no idea I would one day write a book about him, so I lost opportunities to learn more. Please do not lose opportunities with your older loved ones! Our family should know these stories.

- The incident in the street when Carl knocks out a difficult individual is a true story but set out of time. Carl really did get out of the car, knock an annoying man unconscious, and then climb back into the car and announce, "Well, I tried to tell him." However, in reality, Anne was with him and it was in the 1950s. The man was angry because my father had beat up, with cause, the man's son. Carl told the man he was tired after a long day of work, the man persisted, and my grandfather proceeded to exit the car, silence the annoying man with one punch, leave him unconscious on the sidewalk, and drive away. I moved that story into this novel because I wanted to capture how Carl didn't take any crap from anyone.
- As most of you know, Carl's wife was "Anna;" however, he called her "Ann." I used the spelling of "Anne" because that is how she signed her letters when I was a kid.
- I don't recall where I first found the Knut Lier-Hansen quote, but I thought it was a great fit for this story. Besides, the guy was Norwegian; I had to use it.
- People really did use the word "dude" back then. ("You're looking quite the dude," as in "looking good.") I was surprised. They didn't use it in the same over-the-top, declarative manner people used it a few decades later, but its use is accurate.
- Had Bud survived, I am confident he would have married Chrissy. They discussed marriage on multiple occasions and decided to wait until after the war. They did not get engaged; although, in one of his pre-war letters to his mother, Bud joked he was about to get married. That shook Hulda up a bit and he later apologized. With her vivacious personality and fiery nature, Chrissy would have fit in with the Petersons just fine. She remained in touch with Hulda for a number of years, even after she

married and had children. Chrissy, whose first name was Minnie (which I left out of the story to avoid confusion — so many people with multiple names!), met her future husband in Andy's Bakery and they married just a few weeks shy of three years after Bud's death. Before I found information about Chrissy's life after Bud, I knew of Andy's Bakery from her letters. She again suffered through the death of the man she loved — her husband of over 40 years — and she passed away in 2016. I did not read her letters until after she had passed, but I would not have contacted her just as certainly as I will not contact her children. Who wants to hear stories about who your mother or grandmother loved before dad or grandpa?

- One of my favorite lines in all the letters I read was Chrissy's: "Why is there always a bus or train to take you away from me?" To not use that would have been literary malpractice.

- One thing I would have never guessed about Uncle Connie, based on knowing him personally, was his biting sense of humor. His observations were frequently amusing. Uncle Connie was an intelligent man, but his sharp, terse wit was something I never witnessed when around him. Maybe others who knew him better were familiar with his pointed observations.

- Like the rest of the family, Bud was intelligent — the Army thought enough of him to make him a squad leader early on — but his humor and observations were a bit more guarded than his younger brother's. For example, the letter in which he described cutting through the lady's house during urban warfare games was amusing, but his point was to tell what happened, not to discuss the humor of the situation. I got the feeling he knew incidents were amusing, but he left that for the reader to put together. I thought the incident in which he walked into the lady's house was the most illustrative incident of what the Peterson family was like: audacious; brave; and determined to win. Runner-up stories would be when he paid angry visits to the Army recruiter and newspaper. He was not happy with either entity, that is for sure.

- I also thought it was illustrative when Bud was determined to visit Conrad when the latter was quarantined for scarlet fever. The little matter of rules applying to us like they apply to everyone else... Well, he didn't think the rule should apply to him.

- Bud and Conrad hated Texas. Hated it. They would just reach a point where they thought it wasn't that bad and then experience another flash flood or heat wave or sandstorm. I've maintained friendships with a lot of Texans over the years, and they might assume the shots at their state were my humorous poking at them, but Bud and Conrad frequently complained about the state and were thrilled when they left it. Additionally, it was amusing to read their letters as they dealt with people from other areas of the country — something new for them.

- When you converse or correspond with someone, you do not repeat what the other party already knows. For example, Chrissy referenced numerous people Bud knew, but I was unaware of their identities. Because Bud knew the people, no reason existed for Chrissy to provide details about them. Because of this, some information could not be gleaned from letters; i.e., "Thank you for the gift, Bud." What was the gift? Such information was lost because the letters were only meant to be read by the recipient. This concept applied to all letters and letter-writers.

- Bud and Chrissy spent more time together than referenced in the book, but the story was not just about them, so I conflated several of their visits (a minimum of four) into two. I "watched" Chrissy grow up, from an immature, gossiping 18-year-old, into a mature young woman. I was amazed how her letters changed over time, in depth and maturity.

- I kinda hated referring to Uncle Connie as "lazy." He was a heck of a man and I'm proud to have known him. But he was lazy when he was young and it was funny. His little incident of falling asleep in the laundry was from one of his letters. Bud marveled in multiple letters over how little Conrad spoke and how much time he spent in thought. In his younger years, Uncle Connie was a hard worker when he wanted to be, but he was lazy to the point of being hilarious. He grew out of it, of course.

- I learned from my cousin, Michael Peterson, and the booklet he put together, that Uncle Hap spent an extended time in the hospital while in Europe. When I spoke with Bob Gustafson, Hap's sixth child, he informed me Hap never talked about World War I, so Bob possessed no additional information about Hap's experience. Bob did tell me about Hap's personality, education, and abilities, which are reflected in the novel, including his ability to calculate in his head the number of board-feet needed for a particular job.

- When pilot Will Plate told me he flew in every position during training and was scared to death in the ball turret position, I was amused because there were no indications in Bud's letters that he feared or hated it. (He began training in the position before his letters were censored.) I can see him accepting it like it was no big deal, so naturally I had to work in Plate's information. Bud did inform the family he was assigned to the ball turret position, even circling the position on a photo of a B-24. He gave no indication he was fazed by it.

- Cheryl Peterson — Conrad's daughter — told me about the maggots in a soldier's ear; Conrad had shared the story with her.
- I did my utmost to make this story accurate. If you see your uncle or grandfather portrayed as imperfect, please know that such imperfections were not displayed lightly and I took great care to ensure they were not exaggerated. If you were happy with this novel, feel free to let me know. If you didn't like it, tell my dad. He made me write it.

Special Thanks to the Men of the 489th Bomb Group

On October 22, 2008, my parents and I joined the reunion of the 489th Bombardment Group. Held in Dallas, I met men who were at Halesworth Airfield, flew the same model of plane as my great-uncle, and in some cases, knew him.

Speaking to those heroes was an honor I will never forget. They were mentally sharp, humorous, sentimental, and opinionated. They were exactly what I needed when piecing together Bud's story. Even though I only spent a few hours with them, I felt like I knew them. I'm not a very emotional person, yet I still cannot describe the attachment and fondness I felt toward these men.

The information they provided helped me understand Bud's life once he left the States. They supplied the kind of depth a non-fiction story needs. They provided a surprising level of knowledge about *Paper Doll's* crash and I took copious notes.

Unfortunately, even though a couple of men knew him, no one remembered the name of the man Bud accidentally killed while cleaning one of *Paper Doll's* guns, which we first learned about from Captain Gast. This is why the man's name was not referenced — I did not want to invent one. Marlin Gehrke informed me of the man's military role.

The men also told me of Colonel Napier's propensity to suspend men from flying for the sake of their own mental health. Colonel Napier was ahead of the curve on this subject; mental health was not a concern to military leaders of the time (ask General Patton about that).

The following men I met includes squadron, job responsibility, and city in which they grew up or in which they were born:

- Jim Gilliland, 845th, Navigator, Dallas;
- Joe Modrich, 844th, Radio Operator, Detroit;
- Will Plate, 847th, pilot of *Plate's Date*, from Bennet, Iowa, moved to Crane, Texas; he was an amazing man — even his obituary was amazing;
- Mickey Baskin, 844th, Radio Operator on the *Lynda Lee*, Brooklyn, New York;
- R.B. Tolson, 846th, Tail Gunner, College Station, Texas;
- Charles Freudethal, served in Headquarters and flew with different crews on nine missions;
- Marlin Gehrke, 846th, Radio Operator; shot down, captured by the Germans and held for 10 months, "liberated" by the Russians, had to escape them, then returned to the 489th and flew one more mission (I think I would have gone home before that last mission);
- John Lamar, 845th and 847th, Dallas; flew on *Special Delivery*, then *Special Delivery II*, but was transferred before the *Paper Doll* crash. He probably knew more people involved in the collision than anyone I met;
- Sam Syracuse, bombardier on *Impassionada*, which he wanted me to point out was spelled wrong in Charles Freudenthal's book about the 489th Bomb Group, so here ya go, sir; the spelling is now corrected. He said that he made up the word and told his crew it meant "passionate woman." I later discovered Walmart.com has a poster of his plane for sale.

These men told me about events they endured and challenges they encountered. Some told me about their planes and weapons, others told me about some of the men in their squadrons, while others told me sundry information which provided me a better understanding of their duties and military lives.

As is common, men who go to war do not often speak of their experiences, and family members have to pry information out of them; it's like pulling teeth. During their service to our country, they see blood and guts and gore no one should have to see. They see their best friends die in front of them — or in their arms. As I listened to their stories, I got the feeling they were telling me things they did not speak about except on rare occasions — except, perhaps, with their families.

Interestingly, they were all humble about their service and did not see themselves as heroes. Even men who appeared to possess healthy egos belittled the danger and the risks they took and only spoke of the men who did not come home as the heroes. They are, now *were*, great men who refused to acknowledge it.

Will Plate prematurely thanked me for writing this book: "Thank you for what you're doing. We won't be around much longer." Sadly, 13 years later, we have lost all of the men listed above. The thought of one of these brave, selfless men thanking me for anything more than holding a door open for them is not comprehensible to me. My generation and later owe them everything, including our very lives.

I only spent a few hours with these mentally tough, brave, and heroic men, but the gentlemen of the 489th Bomb Group were unforgettable. May Heaven have airplanes — just because they'd want that — and may the wind be always at their back.

God rest their souls.

Sources Other Than Family

Television shows:
An Ocean Apart—Pacific Life
Battlefront—Okinawa
Battle of Okinawa in Color
Bombing the Reich
Evolution of Evil
MacArthur vs. Yamashita
Planet Earth—South Pacific
Red Sun Rampant
Secrets of World War II—Okinawa
The 8th Air Force
The Pacific War in Color
Tojo: Japan's Razor of Fear
World War II—Witness to War

Publications:
North Country History (edited by
Hilda R. Rachuy)

489th Bomb Group Newsletters (from June 2003 to
March 2012)

Podcasts:
Hardcore History, by Dan Carlin

Services:
Richard's Tree Service, Yuba City, CA
(to get the trees right around Camp Beale)

Websites:

398th Bomb Group Memorial Association
445th Bombardment Group
489th Bomb Group Museum
8thAirForce.com
Air Force Historical Research Agency
af.mil (US Air Force)
Ag.NDSU.edu
AirplanesofthePast.com
AmericanAirMuseum.com
Ames History Museum
Apple Maps
Archives.gov (The National Archives)
Arlington National Cemetery Website
ArmyAirCorpsMuseum.org
AtlasObscura.com
Aviation-History.com
B24bestweb.com
Babel.HathiTrust.org
BehindtheName.com
Bemidji Pioneer
BESS Utility Solutions
Billboard Top 100
Biography.com
Blog.EpicMilitaria.com
Blythburgh.net
Britannica.com
c2.staticflickr.com
Careers in Healthcare
Daily Mail (U.K.)

Websites continued

database-memoire.eu (France)

daverothacker.com

Defense Media Network

Dignity Memorial

DuckDuckGo

eBay

Eidness Funeral and Cremation Services

Environmental and Energy Study Institute

Express.co.uk

FamilyRelatives.com

FBC Radio

FederalPay.org

FindaGrave.com (an awesome website)

FlugzeugInfo.net

FortWiki.com

FreePages.rootsweb.com

gearthhacks.com

Genius.com

GermanWarMachine.com

GlobalSecurity.org

Guns.Fandom.com

Gun-Tests.com

Halesworth.net

HalesworthAirFieldMuseum.co.uk

Healthfully.com

Healthline.com

Heddels.com

HeritageCenter.com

History.com

Websites continued

HistoryandHeadlines.com
Historynet.com
HistoryofWar.org
History.ND.gov
HonorStates.org
Idaho Statesman
ImTribune.com
Inert-ord.net
i.pinimg.com
IsraBox
Issuu.com
JewishVirtualLibrary.org
JoeBaugher.com
Kaiser Permanente
KansasCity.com
KasselMission.org
Kensmen.com (43rd Bomb Group, 5th Army Air Force)
Legacy.com
Library of Congress
LilAudrey.Weebly.com
Live in the Philippines
Macrotrends.net
MayoClinic.org
MedalsofAmerica.com
Merriam-Webster.com
MightyEighth.org
Military.com
MilitaryFactory.com
MilitaryIndexes.com

Websites continued

MilitaryWikia.org

Minnesota War Deaths

MysteryofUtahHistory.blogspot.com

MyZone.HomesoftheRich.netdna-cdn.com

National Museum, United States Air Force

NationalWW2Museum.org

National Park Service

National Weather Service

NDstudies.gov

Obituariesus.com

Ohio.HometownLocator.com

Online Etymology Dictionary

Pacific Wrecks

Pier39.com

Plane-crazy.k-hosting.co.uk

Preceden.com

PsychologyToday.com

Population.us

Railway Wonders of the World

Rosie the Riveter Trust

SalutetoFreedom.org

SelfGutenberg.org

SFGate.com

ShipBuildingHistory.com

Stockton Field Museum

Surnames.BehindTheName.com

ScottyLive.com (The Mighty Eighth Daily Calendar)

Smithsonian National Air and Space Museum

Sports-Reference.com

Websites continued

Surnames.BehindtheName.com
Swamp Fire Site
Tax-Brackets.org
The Arrowhead Club
The Aviation History Online Museum
The Diary of 2nd Lt. Charles J. Mellis, Jr.—Co-pilot, 603rd Squadron
The Diary of Samuel N. Syracuse—Bombardier, 489th BG, 847th Squadron
The Eighth Air Force Historical Society
The Kassel Mission Historical Society
The National Interest
The Spruce Eats (in case you want the Swedish Egg Coffee recipe; by Kari Diehl)
The United States Navy Memorial
ThoughtCo.com
TimeandDate.com
Totally History
Traces of War
Trains.RockyCrater.org
TreesForMe.com
TwinBeech.com
U-S-history.com
UWGoldstarHonorRoll.org (University of Wisconsin)
Vintag.es
WallysWar.wordpress.com
WebMD
WillistonHerald.com
WiseGeek.com

477

WorldWarPhotos.info
WWIISoldier.com
xmacis.rcc-acis.org (an excellent weather history site; thanks, Joe Lauria)
YouTube.com

Note: I made a special point not to use Wikipedia. I use the site occasionally in my personal life, but I chose not to for this project.

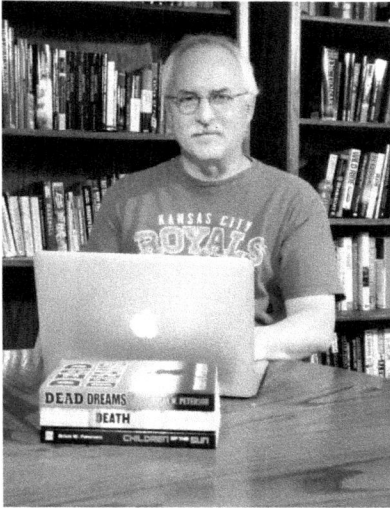

About the Author

Brian W. Peterson is a sci-fi and thriller author who changed genres for this novel in order to write the fascinating family story which is *Paper Doll*.

When you finish this novel, Brian would like for you to do three things: 1) tell your friends and family about this book; 2) follow him on Facebook or Twitter, and/or email him to sign up for his blog so you can learn when his next novel will come out; and 3) learn about your family history; learn their stories, their challenges, and their successes. Every time an elder loved one dies, you lose another part of your family's history.

Thank you for reading about one of Brian's family stories.

Website	: WrittenByBWP.com
Twitter	: @WrittenByBWP
Facebook	: Facebook.com/WrittenByBWP
Email	: WrittenByBWP@gmail.com

Milton Keynes UK
Ingram Content Group UK Ltd.
UKHW021142280924
448786UK00022B/582

9 781733 789356